Flowers on a KARGIL CLIFF

India's first war correspondent in the line of fire in Kashmir & Kargil

Flowers on a KARGIL CLIFF

India's first war correspondent in the line of fire in Kashmir & Kargil

VIKRAM JIT SINGH

Title: Flowers on a Kargil Cliff
Author: Vikram Jit Singh

ISBN: 978-81-979897-9-7

Published by:
JGS Enterprises Pvt Ltd
Imprint: The Browser | Fauji Days

Publisher's Address:
SCO 14-15, FF, Sector 8-C, Chandigarh 160 009

Website: thebrowser.org
Email: service@thebrowser.in

Publishers & Booksellers
Oral History and Military Publishing

Contents

Kargil War

Kashmir

Beyond the Kargil Horizon

❧

In Gratitude and Dedication to

The unsung soldier.

The stoic and heroic war widows and children who display a lifetime's courage and grace in facing the loss of their soldier gone in a flash, in a blaze of glory or otherwise.

The jawans, young officers, and those up the chain of command who held the fort in Kashmir and demolished the enemy's impregnable citadel in the eternal snows of Kargil.

Late Lieutenant General Krishan Pal, Lieutenant General JBS Yadava (retired), Lieutenant General Mohinder Puri (retired), Major General RK Shivrain (retired), Major General Raj Mehta (retired), Brigadier Sudhir Uppal (retired), Brigadier MPS Bajwa (retired), Colonel Jasbir Singh (retired), and Colonel VS Bhalothia (retired) who unhesitatingly granted me leave to accompany frontline troops at the point of contact in battle.

My esteemed journalist colleagues—Khursheed Wani, Tariq Bhat, Nazir Masoodi, Mir Ehsan, Mufti Islah, Muzamil Jaleel, Tahir Mohiuddin, Ahmed Ali Fayyaz, Masarat Islam Suharwardhy, and Surinder S Oberoi—who generously shared with me their expertise of the ground in Kashmir.

My dear friend, Saqib Mehboob Janjua, from Pakistan, who generously shared his perspective and a wealth of information on the Kargil War.

That nameless Srinagar *autorickshaw wallah* who drove me 21 km during a winter night to the Safapora battle zone when everyone else had baulked, and all those peasants, villagers, and simple, unassuming Kashmiri folk who guided me when I was lost in the hinterland and provided me shelter in critical moments.

My wife, Hemani, to whom I sent alpine flowers whose fragrance was tinged with the odour of cordite. She is the inspiration.

My children, Adhiraj and Amrit, whose unwavering belief in me has kept me going. For them, I strive to be a father they can be proud of.

My two sets of parents, one natural and the other whom Hemani brought into my life. Their love and belief in me and the values they have given me set me on the path to this book.

Publisher's note:

The author has donated his royalties and earnings from this book to educating children extremely stigmatised by the social circumstances of their birth and whose fathers will never claim them.

Foreword

India Needs War Correspondents

'There are no atheists in the foxhole.'
—Ernie Pyle, War Correspondent

'It may be that the war has changed me, along with the rest. It is hard for anyone to analyze himself. I know that I find more and more that I wish to be alone, and yet contradictorily, I believe I have a new patience with humanity that I've never had before.'
—Ernie Pyle in *Here is Your War*

'A journalist's job is to be an outsider.'
—Anna Wintour, Hong Kong (Danish Siddiqui Foundation)

We have many categories of journalists in the international reportage spectrum. Journalists who report on war in its various iterations: internal, proxy, external, near abroad, and far abroad. Some analyse war for think tanks or print media, and some analyse war in TV studios or on OTT platforms, in seminars, and in town hall mode. Some study, research, and teach war and warfighting in an educational environment. We now have an emerging trickle of military veterans reporting on war as a second career on TV and social media platforms. We also have media agencies, private and public, who also report on war. We've, of course, always had those who write about war in books, columns, periodicals, or blogs. We've another class of people who comment, if not report, on war. These are diplomats, bureaucrats, often veteran military officers across uniforms, and other influencers who, in retirement or when authorised by the Government, offer their opinions on war. Not the least, we've had a rare bunch of bravehearts who've actually entered the war zone to report on it. In the West, in international hot spots where war often erupts, the discipline of reportage by war correspondents actually entering the war zone has, over the decades, become well established. It is a respected practice there. Coverage of war by such men and women forms the historicity of war reportage in the West and a few other regions across the conflict continuum...a compromise for journalists 'whose primary job is to be an outsider'.

A recent, somewhat ambivalent (cringe-worthy) variant of war reportage is 'embedded journalism', the practice of placing journalists within and under the control of one side's military during an armed conflict, as reported by Encyclopaedia Britannica. It writes that such embedded reporters and photographers are attached to a specific military unit and permitted to accompany troops into combat zones. Embedded journalism was introduced by the US Department of Defence during the Iraq War (2003–2011) as a strategic response to criticism about the low level of access granted to reporters during the Persian Gulf War (1990–1991) and the early years of the Afghanistan War (which began in 2001). Savage US military criticism of what was perceived as slanted/biased war reportage of the disastrous-for-USA Vietnam War led to declining public support for continuing the same. It led the USA in January 2003 to 'offer journalists the opportunity to join US troops after undergoing boot camp-style training and accepting a series of ground rules' on the eve of the later Gulf War.

During the invasion of Iraq, Encyclopaedia Britannica reports that approximately 600 embedded journalists were permitted to join American forces. Since their protection also became the responsibility of the unit they were embedded in, one presumes that the embedded reportage was less critical of the military handling of the Gulf Wars.

India really hasn't had a system/process/regimen or established process of war correspondents reporting on war by being physically present inside it with correspondents actually witnessing its arabesque nuances of life and death; its hardships, command challenges, uncertainties, hardships, denial; its guts, grit, injury, death; its opaqueness; its motivational as well as its grey zones and, of course, witnessing the camaraderie of men under fire...of men sworn to be buddies till death or grievous injury do them apart.

Let me be candid and state that when I was deployed as a CO to help our Police forces combat insurgency in Punjab in 1991–1993 when it was in flames, I saw no correspondent accompanying us in our operational mode. What was covered in the media was post-action coverage or Government reportage in print and video formats. My repeat tenures in Jammu & Kashmir (seven in all in the period 1971–2006 in varying ranks and assignments) saw no war correspondent coverage in the face of flying bullets or IEDs blasted on muddy hinterland tracks or on blistered, rutted once-tar macadamised roads but for one maverick reporter, Vikram Jit Singh, who in his spanking new 1998 model dark green Maruti 800 car became a ubiquitous fixture on proxy war coverage duty as that complex war unfolded in the Kashmir Valley. But more on him later.

My experiences of warfighting and proxy war covered the Shakargarh Bulge, both inside it post the 1971 War and its adjoining areas of Samba, Jammu, and Akhnoor extending to the Chhamb area; a major part of Doda District and extending up to Pangi, Lahaul, Spiti valleys, the Kashmir Valley end to end;

its adjoining Poonch and Rajouri areas; the areas of Udhampur, Bhadarwah, Bani-Machedi, Kathua, and Mamun. This is a fair amount of area affected by real as well as proxy war. What was available by way of media coverage was, to my mind, post-event/ post-encounter coverage. I was posted in the Military Operations Directorate at Army HQ in 2003 when the much-publicised counter-terror operation, *Operation Sarp Vinash*, unfolded in the Hilkaka part of Poonch-Surankot and nestled in the pale of the Pir Panjals. I was unaware then, as I am now, if there were war correspondents that entered those desolate forested mountains with, or independent of, the Army to witness Special Forces-led troops neutralise the large numbers of terrorists, as claimed. Months later, I was to be posted back to the Valley to command a Division, with my inquiry on 'hype versus reality' remaining where it was – unanswered in cognisable terms.

I am not certain if there is any major change today – decades after my service career ended with my superannuation in May 2006. War correspondents that enter war to report war as it unfolds in its proxy or other iterations remains a rare discipline.

Looking back to 1947, we started off well in that we had a pedigreed war reportage precedent. The first war journalist who deserves coverage and our respect is GK Reddy, who escaped from 'Azad Kashmir' to cover the tribal invasion of India in October 1947. Bobby Ghosh started his journalism in India and is now *Time* magazine's world editor. He has done stints of hardcore war reportage in his variegated career. Najmul Hasan was a Delhi-based *Reuters* journalist covering the Iran-Iraq War when he was killed in August 1983 in a landmine explosion. Danish Siddiqui stands out as a war correspondent in the classic Western mould. He was a Pulitzer Prize-winning photojournalist who was killed in 2021, covering a clash between Afghan and Taliban forces near the Pakistan-Afghanistan border. His second Pulitzer prize was awarded to him posthumously when working as an embedded journalist with the Afghan Special Forces. He was one of our best when measured against the metrics of seeing war up front, face-to-face, with the possibility of death or injury very real. In his case, evidence suggests mutilation and more, but covering war is, at best, a very risky venture with sudden death close at hand always and every time.

We have seen several Indian reporters in the recent past covering the ongoing Russo-Ukrainian War and the Israeli-Hamas War. Despite careful study, I have not found instances of our reporters accompanying the protagonists into actual combat where the life and limb of the reporters were as vulnerable as those of soldiers actually fighting the war. The coverage we've seen has been somewhat close but, perhaps, not close enough to qualify as war correspondent coverage in the sense one gets to see pretty much often on foreign Western media channels and in print reportage. One would want to recall *Operation Pawan* closely too. One realises that much bravery and courage was at play in interviewing LTTE Supremo Prabhakaran, more so by a lady journalist, Anita Pratap, in his remote jungle hideout. Was that, however, close enough as to be caught, say, in a fusillade of LTTE automatic fire? One does not know, not having come across such accounts of bravery or boldness in any war our forces have engaged in, at least during my almost 39 years of a military career. Yes, the *Operation Pawan* coverage does cover grisly photographs of the LTTE carnage involving Indian soldiers in the Jaffna University area, which choked viewers, but was this the stuff of live war coverage or a photo opportunity permitted by LTTE consequent to the execution of the dastardly carnage? One would seek education on this count.

While in service, I was given the task of creating a war museum for its subsequent inauguration by the then President of India, Dr APJ Abdul Kalam. I thus had free access to archives in Delhi containing huge albums of pictures taken by Government agencies since independence. I had extensively read about our war coverage since 1947, both official and by private authors. While the coverage has been interesting, most of it is illustrated by stock coverage and not quite what one might expect from a war correspondent's coverage.

One is aware that in 1971, we had strict media access to the war zone in place, unlike the Pakistanis. They had permitted free coverage once the holocaust in East Pakistan began; this, to a few foreign journalists. This coverage was graphic and numbed the world when the text and supporting pictures and videos were released...the turf of classic war correspondent coverage. As we neared the epicentre of the war in what is now Bangladesh, a group of these war correspondents covered our race to Dhaka in its closing stages. That coverage would remain a war correspondent watershed even if the coverage was foreign and not Indian. The coverage was objective and bold despite exchanges of intense firing with cornered Pakistani troops.

The Kargil War 1999 had its road-accessible areas which the media could and did access with permission, or sometimes by circumventing military restrictions on media coverage. This coverage was in the areas stretching from Zoji La-Mushkoh-Drass to Kargil. The war also had its remote areas – the Batalik Sector extending up to the Saltoro Ridge – areas where access to war areas was counted in days after debouching from the road head. So, we have elaborate TV and later print accounts in articles and research papers or books initiated by correspondents who reported on the war. The question of whether they were war correspondents who accompanied the soldiers into battle remains. The 'drawing room war', as it was touted, brought us close to war but not inside the war. This is my belief, and I'd be glad to be challenged and proved wrong. Be that as it may, this was the state of our media coverage in areas where road access was mere hours away...close but not close enough.

So, was the insanely remote Batalik Sector any different? Its achievements, voids, heroes, and non-heroes suffered from invisibility as media coverage was itself a void in the main...with most correspondents reporting on the Kargil War where road access and benefits of civilisation were hours, not days away... giving this remote and daunting Batalik Sector the go-by. The story hereafter takes a turn, a twist, but let that happen a bit later.

Keeping the lay reader's interest in mind, it is fair to put war reporting in its historical context and, thereafter, explain what war correspondents do and how before informing readers about greats across genders who reported on war as it played out. This information sharing will prepare the template against which Vikram Jit Singh, as a war correspondent who dared to be different, can be measured.

History

Herodotus covered the fifth century BCE Greco-Persian Wars, as did Thucydides shortly thereafter, covering the war between Sparta and Athens in ways we could term a war correspondent's reportage. However, our first modern war correspondent would be the Dutch painter, Willem van de Velde. In 1653, he observed a naval battle between the Dutch and the English, of which he made many sketches, which he added to a war report. War correspondent Henry Crabb Robinson covered Napoleon's campaigns in Spain and Germany for *The Times* of London with correspondent William Hicks, describing the Battle of Trafalgar (1805) and correspondent William Howard Russell, covering the Crimean War, also for *The Times*. Technological advancements such as the telegraph and faster printing facilitated near real-time publication of reports.

World War I was characterised by rigid censorship. During World War II, the British War Office authorised limited 'eyewitness' coverage to Journalist Alex Clifford, who became the first 'eye-witness' joining the British Army in France in September 1939; his reports were subject to censorship. Elsewhere, strict censorship was the norm. It was during the Vietnam War that technological advancements allowed war correspondents to be equipped with video cameras, allowing investigative journalism to come into its own. As many as 400 reporters covered the war in Vietnam, of which 68 were killed. Many in the US Governance, however, blamed the media for the American defeat, claiming that media coverage shattered US troop morale and destroyed public support for the war in the homeland USA.

The Gulf War found war coverage severely inhibited for war correspondents. They were divided into 'pools' with very few allowed live fighting access. Critics claimed that the allied coverage was 'jingoistic' and overly favourable to the American forces, in harsh contrast to the criticism and muckraking that had characterised coverage of Vietnam. These trends extended to the later Afghanistan and Iraq wars, where the pool model was replaced by embedded journalism.

The Ukraine War coverage, as judged by much-respected journalists, is the most savage seen over the last 30 years and overshadows the savagery of the far smaller Gaza War. At least 17 journalists and media workers have been killed in Ukraine since Russia's full-scale invasion began. One of them was French journalist Arman Soldin. A Russian missile took his life on 9 May 2023, while he was reporting from the front lines. French President Emmanuel Macron praised Soldin, saying that 'Arman Soldin embodied a passion to convey the truth, tell stories and gather testimonies, with a sense of duty to inform.' If it is of any reassurance, it may be noted that war correspondents are protected by the Geneva Conventions of 1949 and their additional protocols.

What Do War Reporters Do, and How?

The first witness to evolving history: that's how stark and compelling war reportage is all about or can be. A war correspondent is, simply put, a journalist who covers stories first-hand from a war zone. This is journalism's most important and impactful form. Such journalists try to get close to where combat is unfolding to provide written accounts, photos, or videography, all at huge cost to personal safety and sometimes even to their professional interests. Today's war reportage uses mediums such as digital news, personal diaries, and traditional journalism to provide for sharing personal experiences, and insights into the realities of war. Doing so may involve ethical as well as moral challenges and dilemmas concerning personal safety as well as problems arising from the fallouts of the war reportage they are doing, ranging from success in all its shades to abject failure and all that is in between. Objectivity in reportage also becomes an issue depending on the mode in which the war reportage is being executed. One has to understand that the linkages that come into play are social, cultural, technological, as well as military in terms of understanding the dynamics of the action being covered and why conducting it becomes germane. Not the least, the reporter, whether free to do his own thing, controlled through various means or censored, or even when used as a propaganda tool, serves a critical function which is primary and stark: to inform.

In the prescient words of AA Stenin, a Russian photojournalist who died covering the war zone in Ukraine in 2014, 'journalists are the eyes of the citizens and the world'. From yet another perspective, war correspondents 'audit war and warfighting'. A book by that name has, since its 1986 publication, been considered 'the most thorough and sustained assault so far' on wartime orthodoxy. Audits, as audited agencies wryly confess, are not quite liked though they might be feared for the power and clout they wield through the disclosures they make or imply.

A war reporter's work starts with finalising where he should be for his coverage and getting there. He also needs to keep himself alive, as quite often, he is responsible for his own safety. One way to ensure survival is to be environmentally aware and updated. Twice Pulitzer Prize and George Polk award-winning American-Lebanese war correspondent Anthony Shadid of *Washington Post* and later *New York Time*s is a good example. He covered the war in Syria and Iraq. One night in Baghdad he was to make a prophetic comment: 'The more I know about Iraq, the less I understand it.' I think the best reporters strive to maintain such humility and openness. Shadid was to later die covering the war in Iraq. These seem basic but are, in fact, the essence of successful war reportage. As we witness the war in Gaza, several reporters and cameramen have paid the ultimate price for their courage in being where it matters—on a fast-changing and unpredictable front line. Many more are still there risking everything to tell the truth. Readers are fascinated by the minutiae of war because it's only this that brings home the horror of what is actually happening. When you, as a war reporter, are there, readers sitting in the safety of their homes get an intimate view of the bravery or desperation, death or injury that you are witnessing. This makes true war reportage indispensable when it happens.

The terminology 'war correspondent' said in English seems apt. Though unarmed, they remain at the heart of the action and participate fully in the experience of combat. Mandated to report war, war correspondents accept the ambiguity of their perspective. They recount war first and foremost, describe it and position themselves as witnesses and as narrators. Reporters experience war on a day-to-day basis, in direct contact with combatants and civilians, perpetrators and victims. Far from being simply columnists, they are authors, conveying knowledge, emotions, feelings and stories, both real and sometimes embellished, about war and its many fallouts and effects—white, grey and black.

The 1917 statement by US Senator Hiram Johnson that the first casualty of war is the truth is a harsh reality that soldiers and war reporters must live with. This impacts media coverage of war and causes complexities in Army-media relationships. The borderline behind propaganda and objective coverage of war, thus, remains blurred between embedded journalists, independent war reporters, and special war correspondents, the common thread being that such coverage does provide a fresh perspective on war with its truth element being a matter of speculation or belief, depending on the war reporter, his/her standing with the military, and the level of objectivity demanded, conceded, or achieved. Some might call 'truth' as the very essence of war reportage.

Let's examine why the military and media covering war are naturally antagonistic towards each other. Warfare is about secrecy, whereas journalism is about publicity and exposure...extreme positions these; both seemingly irreconcilable. This is what has always led to the usually strained relations between the media and the military. Media wants to tell in war and the military inhibits telling. This is what is clinically described as 'intense love-hate mutuality and dependency'.

An equally serious issue is the 'fog of war'. Although Von Clausewitz, in his classic treatise *On War,* has discussed it at length, it has always shadowed war for millennia. He describes the nature of war as very complex and ever-changing. Luck, chance, the power of personality in war, weather, terrain, demography, morale or its lack, all create unique and often unpredictable circumstances that cause 'friction' between these complex conditionalities. There is also friction within these elements and between them. Hence, war is conducted in a churn, a medium of friction including within the mind of the commander, his troops, as well as between the commander and his commander, the commander and the enemy and, not the least, between the commander and the media as an outside agency whose functional parameters are opposed to what the military seeks.

It is in such an environment that the war correspondent must chart his path and manage his own friction, his safety, and his ideological friction within his system and with the military. He must overcome or, at least, manage this conundrum to put the jigsaw puzzle of often confusing reports and actions he sees or hears about to make a credible, reader-appealing story: a tough task by any standard and certainly those of stringent journalistic norms. Discussions on the complexities of war reportage do not, of course, imply that the complexities are eased somewhat. An example from the Falklands War between Britain and Argentina is indicative, and I quote the British correspondent Max Hastings who, during the Falklands conflict, famously remarked, 'When one's nation is at war, reporting becomes an extension of the war effort. Objectivity only comes back into fashion when the black-out comes down'. Not infrequently, journalists and photographers return from war with the confession that they ceased to be mere observers and became participants.

Some of the World's Best War Correspondents

There is no dearth of war correspondents in the West; this to the extent that even choosing their best is a major undertaking. Despite subjectivity playing its part, this writer's list would start with Robert Capa, the Hungarian-American photojournalist considered by some as controversial yet the greatest of his genre. He covered the Spanish Civil War, the Second Sino-Japanese War, World War II across Europe, the 1948 Arab-Israeli War, and the First Indochina War. His friends and colleagues included Nobel Prize winner Ernest Hemingway, Irwin Shaw, and John Steinbeck. Capa accompanied then-journalist and author Ernest

Hemingway to photograph the Spanish War, which Hemingway would later describe in his novel, *For Whom the Bell Tolls* (1940). Capa was famed for saying, 'If your photographs aren't good enough, you're not close enough.' He was killed when he stepped on a landmine in Vietnam.

John Steinbeck is known for his books such as *The Grapes of Wrath, Of Mice and Men, Cannery Row,* and *East of Eden.* He worked for the *New York Herald Tribune* and the Office of Strategic Services (an agency of the US Joint Chiefs of Staff) during the Second World War. Covering Vietnam, he produced quality war correspondent copy. Margaret Bourke-White and her legacy live on today with her groundbreaking experiences and wonderful photography. She was the first known female war correspondent and the first to be allowed to work in combat zones during the Second World War. She spent time in North Africa, Italy and Germany with the nickname 'Maggie the Indestructible' because of the combat operations she survived. She was the last to photograph Mahatma Gandhi before he was assassinated. Walter Cronkite is known as the 'Father of Modern Journalism' and anchored the *CBS Evening News* for decades. His work as a reporter in World War II involved covering North Africa and Germany, *Operation Market Garden,* and the Battle of the Bulge. He reported on the Vietnam War during the Tet Offensive in 1968.

However, the war correspondent that stands out for this writer is American war correspondent Ernie Pyle. He became a national folk hero by reporting on the average soldier in World War II from England, North Africa, Italy, France, Saipan, and Okinawa. He covered the war from a unique human interest perspective that got him the Pulitzer, among a barrage of other awards. He was killed by enemy fire at Okinawa in 1945. His perspective was to get 'the worm's eye view' with his 'everyman' approach to reporting in syndicated columns across a swathe of newspapers. Present-day war correspondents, World War II veterans, and historians still recognise Pyle's World War II dispatches as 'the standard to which every other war correspondent should strive to emulate.' *Life* magazine, thus, described Pyle and his work: 'He occupies a place in American journalistic letters which no other correspondent of this war has achieved. His smooth, friendly prose succeeded in bridging a gap between soldier and civilian where written words usually fail.'

David Chrisinger stumbled upon Pyle's legacy of war reportage in Okinawa in 2016 while he was researching his own grandfather's battle experiences of the Second World War. Chrisinger went on to write a book on Pyle, suggesting that research showed that your story will stay with people longer if you appeal to their sensory imagination and Pyle was amazingly good at being selective. 'He found a way to do a lot more showing than telling...Where people felt like they were there and had experienced it for themselves,' Chrisinger said. 'Pyle could make his readers see what he saw and hear it and feel it and smell it. And that's an incredible skill set to have. It's so powerful, and the power remains, even in reading those pieces today. What he was trying to address was this belief among his reporters that all the best stories get scooped up, and that unless you're first on the beat, you're just not going to get it....So, Ernie Pyle was good at finding the story even when he wasn't there for the story and I think that's something all (war) journalists can take a lesson from,' Chrisinger ended.

War Correspondent Vikram Jit Singh and I

My association with him started almost as soon as I took over command of a Rashtriya Rifles (RR) Sector in South Kashmir. With my hands-on experience gained in counter-insurgency mode in Punjab and thereafter extensively in Doda and adjoining remote areas, which were then a terrorism melting pot, I was quietly sure of what needed to be done to keep my areas under firm control and the *awaam* neutral if not tacitly friendly. Vikram was known to my six COs: a mix of RR, regular, and paramilitary units, as well as to the police and the administration, the *intezamia*. He had the reputation of being a persistent newshound with his own intelligence means and environmental awareness, which I never tapped into, being part of my ethics. The GOC was battle-hardened in counter-insurgency, having had repeat tenures in such areas and would be present for big encounters. Vikram Jit was known to him and had secured permission to personally track encounters in a conflict zone where clashes, both planned and incidental, occurred routinely.

Everyone takes a 'settling-down time' in a war zone or should. It was during these opening few months that I did my quiet checks with my command hierarchy and occasionally with my GOC and his key staff. I concluded that Vikram Jit, if accompanying single or joint unit operations in my command or out-of-area operations, would involve himself in responsible and objective war reportage.

Several such operations followed where, strictly on time, his ubiquitous green Maruti car would be parked, with him ready for his involvement as a free, uncensored war reporter, nowhere near the American example of embedded reportage. He was young, fit and wiry, self-contained where he needed to be, and graciously accepted the security help we provided by way of body protection, food, and shelter. His physical protection was also ensured since he was unarmed. This was the military ethic followed to keep the journalist free and unfettered for objective reportage.

Without exception, I was present on each such occasion, yet never interfering with the CO's command authority or control of his flock. This was repeated day and night, climbing up steep hills or traversing terrain undulations, including during the exchange of fire. Vikram Jit was found alert and ready to face the outcome by way of dead and injured personnel...and the clear possibility of injury to himself.

One is wilfully avoiding specific reference to operations. Suffice it to say that the trust either way with him/us wasn't ever belied. This is how things panned out in those hyper-active two years or so when the RR Sector did its job quietly but effectively. We never ever made a media issue of our successes or sought suppression of our occasional setbacks. This kept the media-military-police relationship healthy, forward-looking, and objective.

My reference to Ernie Pyle was with clear intent. I saw Ernie Pyle in Vikram Jit. I am comparing him with the best war correspondent I've heard of because I saw the same traits in this war correspondent; the only journalist in my service career that richly deserved this rare honour. Death in proxy or limited war is the same. The wounds are as grievous, death as sudden and as shocking. I saw him in encounter after encounter entering and departing with grit, guts, and a soldierly demeanour. I do not recall too much of his reportage from those Kashmir days because, frankly, there was 'no time to stand or stare'. South Kashmir was intense with terror and its corresponding anti-terror activity, and, at times, you exited one encounter to enter another. What is germane is that a quiet and determined young man of courage was there where the bullets were flying, and he was unafraid, keen to be where the action or the snafu was...non-interfering, watchful for reality, success, or sometimes the truth's other side, warts and all. In the war zone, we have 'buddy pairs' who protect each other's backs. For Vikram Jit, his buddy was his self-faith, his drive, his conviction, and his endless hunger to be 'among the boys'. I recall a Best Wishes letter I wrote to him when he got married in November 1999. I addressed him as Dear Vikram Ernie Pyle...The opening salutation had said all that needed to be said to a young man who was a war correspondent...a man about to be bound by sacred matrimony. He connected. He was quick on the uptake and erudite.

Both before and during the Kargil War, I had much to do as a RR Sector Commander. I was part of the War Game Control Staff in April 1999 when HQ 15 Corps had war-gamed Kargil. I had visited the Zoji La-Batalik stretch by serial helicopter flights in preparation for the war game. Batalik was forbidding, gaunt, and several thousand feet higher than Mashkoh-Drass-Kargil. That information remained with me as I learned post-war how Vikram Jit had been the only war correspondent who climbed those gaunt Batalik peaks and navigated its daunting cliffs. He courageously lived with the troops there and was shot at and shelled as we transited from surprise to victory at alpine heights that remain unsurpassed in modern warfighting. That, however, is Vikram Jit's story to tell. This foreword is just the trailer.

I wish his readers enough.

Major General Raj Mehta, AVSM, VSM (retired)
3 September 2024.

(Raj Mehta is an author, editor, and freelancer who is also a motivational speaker. His interests include ecology, environment, treating women as 'equal but different'; encouraging children to 'reach for the sky' and museum-making, of which the Punjab State War Museum & Memorial and the Madras Regimental Centre Museum are often-visited niche museums)

CHAPTER 1

Staring at a Dog's Death

At 15,700 feet, I was clinging on for dear life. Like a lizard's belly, I had pressed my body tight into the cliff. There was no safety rope around my waist to secure my passage along the cliff wall, which was nearly perpendicular in stretches. My hands and feet had the barest of holds, and pressing against the wall was the only safeguard against the force of gravity that would send me plummeting thousands of feet into the Gragario Nullah.

As the Kargil War raged, the Pakistan Army's bunkers on the Kukarthang Ridge flanking us to our west were intermittently firing mortar shells, MMGs, UMGs, and RPGs[1] at the Indian soldiers and myself, a war correspondent. We were exposed like game animals as we manoeuvred on the cliff leading from Point 4812 on the southern extremity of the Khalubar Ridge in the Batalik LoC Sector.[2] The ledge running along the cliff face was fine enough for a Himalayan Ibex's passage, but the wild tenants of the high altitudes

1. Medium Machine Guns, Universal Machine Guns, and Rocket-Propelled Grenades

2. Line of Control Sector

had been evicted by the warring armies since the fateful advent of May 1999. The ledge was so narrow that it did not have enough space for me to place my Army-issue Hunter shoes side by side. My upper body was twisted as I clung to the cliff face and my right knee was doddering over the chasm in the other direction. At some points, this errant, doddering knee was helpfully pressed in by the havildar assigned to chaperone my passage in the war zone.

The evening of 7 July was fading fast. Under a canopy of dusky orange hues emanating from a LoC sunset, I was left staring at the massive rock face and virtually kissing it. In some stretches, the walls of the Khalubar cliff were so smooth that they lacked clefts for the fingers to grasp and secure a mentally comforting, if somewhat facile grip.

My heart was jumping and thumping at my throat. I was aware that the slightest external manifestation of jangling nerves, like a severe shudder or a momentary loss of nerve as I slid torturously along the Kargil cliff, would dislodge my fragile hold in a millisecond and send me hurtling to a dog's death. If I slipped, there was nothing to arrest my plunge save the treacherous cushion of thin air. My scream would echo between the mountains before ebbing into an unheard crash of bones and flesh. My body would be the last one to be retrieved by the Army. If the Pakistanis won, they would leave it to be ravaged by wild animals. To add to my discomfiture, tales of the perilous navigation of heights that I had heard from warring soldiers earlier were playing on my mind—tales of comrades plunging off the heights and not a bone left intact on the recovery of the forlorn remains. There were no gallantry awards for deaths from a fall. My final silence would prevail among forgotten rocks, the smattering of my blood would serve as the inscription for an anonymous end. A bullet or shell splinter seemed an infinitely better choice for me to court death's messenger flying invisibly alongside me on the cliff. At least, I would secure a membership to the world's most elite club—an honourable name tablet at a war memorial commemorating those who laid down their lives for the nation by taking a bullet square on their chests.

This was a war over the Kargil heights, a conflict that Pakistan had ignited in its pursuit of a ridge too far. A fight that even the Indian Army was learning on the job, as there was no orientation prior to this war for offensive operations in the high-to-super-high altitudes to evict an entrenched enemy from one ridge line after another. The Army had not even prepared a contingency plan to offset an eventuality such as the Kargil invasion. At the outset of the war, the Pakistani intrusions, which strung across a swathe of snowbound frontiers from Mashkoh to South Siachen Glacier, had been described from an air surveillance sortie as 'an outbreak of chickenpox'. It was no less than a daylight rape of the LoC's sanctity by the Pakistan Army. It had exploited to the hilt the strategic neglect of Ladakh by the Indian Army's higher command ever since 1991 when the 28 Infantry Division had been moved out of Kargil to the Kupwara LoC in Kashmir. This neglect was compounded when the reserve formation for Kargil-Ladakh (70 Infantry Brigade) was subsequently shifted to the Kashmir Valley to hunt terrorists in 1997.

I was then a war correspondent for *The Indian Express* stationed at Srinagar since October 1997 and experiencing first-hand the risks soldiers were taking routinely to dislodge a wily and audacious invader. The odyssey of life and death that evening had been the outcome of my determined pursuit of reporting the Army's operations live from the points where the bullets crisscrossed. Prior to Kargil, I had done so similarly in Kashmir by reporting anti-terrorist operations from villages, forests, and mountains in the line of fire in the company of the honourable riflemen and sepoys. My experience of accompanying troops during night operations, ambushes, and cordon and search operations in Kashmir for terrorists had stood me in good stead when the Kargil War broke out. I spent the night of 7/8 July under enemy fire on the Khalubar Ridge with the assault troops of the 12 Jammu and Kashmir Light Infantry (12 JAK LI). I was the only media person granted this kind of war reportage access. It enabled me to file war reports for *The Indian Express* under the unique dateline: Point 4812 (i.e., a summit at a height of 4812 metres or approximately 15,700 feet). The formidable contingent of national and international media was, otherwise, strictly confined to the valleys of Drass, Kargil, Mashkoh, and the Indus thousands of feet below the towering ridgelines along whose spurs and spines the Pakistani bunkers were situated. The distance could be gauged from the fact that it took our soldiers and war porters several hours, and sometimes, even days, of climbing and marching from road heads in the valleys (under continuous artillery and small arms fire emanating from the enemy bunkers on the top), to reach the ridgelines.

For the next two hours, I proceeded by placing one boot ahead and then cautiously bringing the laggard boot over it so as not to lose my balance on the cliff. At some points, I was reduced to inching forward on all fours. The so-called track along the cliff, narrow enough to begin with, had taken no time to peter out to the width of a Hunter shoe. My life was literally on a razor's edge that evening. Here and there, tiny mops of flowers peered out cautiously from clefts in the cliff and from under massive slabs of rocks. They bloomed on the knife's edge of these gaunt mountains in that brief interlude of June to August when the snows melted, and the soil temperature lifted above 5.5 degrees centigrade. Save the bubbling brook tumbling from the snows and wary, resilient blooms in the precarious niches, there were no birds, bees, and animals left on the warring heights to represent nature. There were no eagles that dared these war-torn cliffs. I picked some flowers from the cliff's clefts for my fiancée, Hemani, in Chandigarh. But as the passage got exceedingly perilous along the cliff's sheer and smooth walls, thoughts of flowers vanished from my mind, and all that my clammy hands sought was a reassuring lodgement on the cliff face.

Karan Singh, the Signals Havildar and a trusted subordinate of the 12 JAK LI's Commanding Officer (CO), Colonel VS Bhalothia, Sena Medal (Gallantry), was assigned to my safety. He would vigilantly press in my wobbly right knee when he found it gawking over the chasm. He was virtually walking backwards along the cliff with a heavy radio set and antenna strapped to his back as he kept an eagle eye on my tortoise-like passage. I did not have the best of heads for heights. Looking back over the shoulder or sideways and down into the smirking chasm made me dizzy and dulled my reflexes. I had faced nothing like this cliff passage even in my reportage of operations from Kashmir since November 1997. But repeated exposures to Kashmir battles had inculcated in me the one principle soldiers abide by when stepping into the proverbial valley of death: that fear is going to shadow you, so calm yourself, control your fears and never show them in an unexpected situation, and press on. So, in that dusk cast in unforgettable orange-golden hues, I steadied my breath and once again repeated the mantra that had seen me through other Army frontline operations in Kashmir and Kargil: 'If I die, so be it. When I started out, I fully knew the consequences of going so far out with the Army. One day, my luck may run out. But the prospect of death will not deter me from my being a war correspondent in the truest sense of the profession.'

Bhalothia was ahead of me on the cliff face.

At one point, I tried to make light of the grim situation and quipped in dark humour to the seasoned CO: 'Please take down my personal will by memorising it. Relay it to my family after my death. I think there is a very slender chance that I will survive this cliff face and Pakistani firing.'

Bhalothia grinned gently at my predicament and assured me that I would live to tell the tale. He was inwardly pleased and satisfied that at least one representative of the media had got to know firsthand the kind of risks the Army routinely took to evict the enemy from those heights of madness where not beasts but men were warring.

As the Pakistani Artillery OPs[3] directed ground-burst shells of 81mm mortars onto our cliff, we would take shelter amid rocks, move forward for a few minutes, and then again duck into whatever cleft we could find.

Karan rendered some consoling artillery-evasion expert advice to me with a straight face: 'Protect your head, Sir. If that goes, nothing of you will remain, and we can do nothing for you. If your legs go, we can always amputate them and find you artificial legs from the prosthetic centres later. There is one such good prosthetic centre in your Chandigarh.'

Despite Karan's best efforts to nurse my laboured passage across the cliff, our progress had stalled that evening.

'Sir, let us move a bit faster. Firing is on, and darkness is going to start setting in soon. We can be killed here,' was his hushed, urgent counsel. On realising that his suggestion would not work beyond a point, Karan resorted to an emergency measure. 'Let me carry you on my back, Sir. I will remove my radio set's antenna and lift you on top of the set in a fireman's lift,' he offered gallantly.

Aghast, I refused. The radio set on his back was an ANPRC 25 weighing 18 kg. 'With my weight across your shoulders in addition to your radio set, the slightest imbalance from me or the slightest slip of your foot, and both of us will tumble down. Even the process of mounting me on your shoulders while precariously balanced on this cliff is fraught with risk. If either of us makes the slightest of errors and disturbs the balance while I mount your shoulders, I could tumble and take you down with me,' I replied.

My decision proved correct.

3. Observations Posts

Years later, Karan admitted: 'Sir, you were right in over-ruling me that evening. We could have both died.'

After we safely traversed the nerve-wracking passage across the cliff to the tent location of the 12 JAK LI's Adjutant on the Khalubar ridge where I was to spend the night, Karan blandly consoled me: 'Sir, we got through because the Pakistan OPs did not have good coordination with their mortar detachment.'

Karan was particularly accomplished at handling the battalion's guests. Just before the Kargil War, Karan had been deputed by Bhalothia to ensure the safe dismount from a helicopter of Defence Minister George Fernandes during his tour of the Northern Siachen Glacier. Fernandes had famously, on the spot, decided upon a slew of welfare measures for soldiers deployed in the world's highest battlefield. Fernandes had been deeply moved by the plight of the soldiers. He had likened them to '*kaale bhooth*' (black ghosts) in the white ice caves as their faces had been darkened by prolonged exposure to the high-altitude sun, snow glare, and thin, rarefied air. Fernandes had taken a revolutionary decision to send a top bureaucrat of the Defence Ministry's Finance department and get him to stay at the 12 JAK LI's forward posts so that he could experience the difficulties first-hand and speedily clear the bureaucratic hold-up on the sanction of snow scooters.

I felt it was an honour for a war correspondent to venture into the warring heights of the Batalik Sector with Karan and his valiant battalion. The 12 JAK LI had been the first unit inducted into the Batalik Sector when the war commenced, and its troops had won India the bloody battles for Point 5203 and 4812. The remoteness of the battlefields from the road heads in Batalik had ensured that no media person, except Shiv Kunal Verma and I, had got to the Ganasok valley while only I had made it to the top of the Khalubar Ridge.

❧

My foray as a war correspondent to Batalik had been authorised by HQ (Headquarters) 15 Corps in Srinagar. The assignment authorised by 15 Corps should have seen me safe and sound in Srinagar by the late evening of 7 July and far away from that eerie cliff. In fact, I had not even gone through the three-stage acclimatisation programme before climbing either the Tololing Nullah or the Khalubar Ridge. A three-stage acclimatisation is mandatory for troops before they are sent into the high altitudes.

The plan that the Army had sanctioned for my foray to Point 4812 was a limited one for the day, and which would have kept me well away from the cliff and the night stay on the Khalubar Ridge in the thick of battle. I received an early morning call on the landline in my paying guest accommodation at Rajbagh, Srinagar, on 7 July. It was Brigadier (General Staff) Arun K Chopra from HQ 15 Corps. The 15 Corps Commander, Lieutenant General Krishan Pal, UYSM, had immense confidence in my abilities to go into battle with frontline troops. 'Vikram can do it,' was his quip whenever my request for battle reportage would come up before his subordinate staff tasked with media clearances. Brigadier Chopra asked me that morning if I wanted to venture into the high-altitude battle zone again for a unique and challenging war reportage assignment. I told him that I was forever ready for Army operations. He told me that the Corps Commander wanted me to fly down to the Ganasok valley TAC HQ[4] of 70 Infantry Brigade in the Batalik Sector and then climb for four hours to Point 4812 to witness the honourable burials of unclaimed bodies of Pakistani soldiers. I was to return to Srinagar the same evening by the Army helicopter deputed for my assignment. My eyewitness account as an independent journalist was to lend credibility to the claim made by the Ministry of External Affairs before the global community that the Indian Army had accorded respect and undertaken the due religious rites

4. Tactical Headquarters

while burying dead Pakistani soldiers on the heights in Kargil. The clearance for my foray into the battle zone was an exceptional one because the Army was otherwise extremely strict and vigilant in confining the media contingent to the inhabited valleys thousands of feet below the bunker battles raging on the towering ridges. Leave aside getting to the ridges for an eyewitness reportage of battles, very rarely would media persons even be allowed to enter the battalion/brigade/divisional HQs in the valleys. For a period of time during the war, Army personnel were forbidden from any interaction with the media, though the order was subsequently revoked.

I was also tasked to collect other stories of ordeal and triumph from the Batalik heights, a sector under-reported in the war as compared to Drass and Mashkoh, where NH-1A[5] had lent easy access to TV crews. Though a much harder war zone by way of terrain, height, and extended supply lines, the Batalik battles could only be accessed by a two-day march under fire, with mule packs and manpacks from the nearest road heads, such as Dah, in the Indus Valley, or by Army helicopters flying along the intruded ridgelines that emanated from the watershed on the LoC. Naturally, the televised war beamed into living rooms from battles such as Tiger Hill in Drass completely skipped the valourous deeds and bloodshed by the Batalik soldiers, the civilian truck drivers transporting war supplies under shelling, the Ladakhi porters, and war-load native donkeys and Army regulation mules. The Batalik war effort was an unsung one of fighting fearful odds without instant media gratification and breaking news on TV. It was a hard war fought in the shadows of the limelight.

That morning, I was flown from Srinagar by an Army Aviation Cheetah helicopter to Ganasok in the thick of the war zone. From

5. National Highway 1 Alpha

there, I climbed to Point 4812 on the Khalubar Ridge. The ridge runs north and upwards from Point 4812 as a knife-thin feature to Area Bunkers, Khalubar South, Khalubar, Khalubar North, and Point 5287, and then curves to the watershed on the LoC. The climb to Point 4812 was precipitous and razor-sharp and required my going on all fours to negotiate some stretches. Upon reaching the top at 1.30 p.m., I witnessed the solemn burial ceremony during the afternoon and spoke to the soldiers in battle. The Army was so strict that I was allowed to only use a camera issued by them, and that, too, when we reached the site of the burial ceremony. It was taken away from me immediately after the ceremony was over. It was a standard camera loaded with a film. Besides the photographs I took of the burial ceremony, I photographed the cave bunker of the Pakistani post commander of Point 4812, Captain Qamar, who seemed very fond of toiletries and had kept a Lux soap and perfume for personal hygiene in there. The commander had an adjoining niche in the mountain cave where his batman was bunkered.

Assessing the bunker from a military point of view, the 70 Infantry Brigade's Brigade Major M Indrabalan noted that it was very well sited with respect to the fire from the Indian Army and was the size of a car. The two bunks inside had a natural overhead of a thick rock. The cave entrance was well concealed by a *sanger*[6] just outside, which would have been manned by the Pakistani soldiers. According to Indrabalan, the Pakistani officer's bunker was so well-sited that it could only be spotted when one was within 30 yards of it. There were 44 Pakistani bunkers at the Point 4812 Complex and there was one that served as a kitchen and another as a ration store. Among the recoveries of documents from Point 4812 were sanctions of leave by the Pakistani post commander, indicating that the intruding troops had been occupying these heights for a considerable period of time.

---

6. a bunker of piled rocks

The Indian Tricolour and Regimental Standard of the JAK LI Regiment had just arrived at Point 4812. In my presence, despite enemy shelling, all the troops and officers at Point 4812 hoisted the flags on the exposed top despite the enemy shelling. With robust and resounding cries of *Bharat Mata ki Jai* that thundered in the chasms of the Batalik mountains, the Tricolour and the Regimental Standard were hoisted by the troops of 12 JAK LI. Indrabalan and I were there to photograph that joyous moment and those images were reproduced later in a number of volumes published on the Kargil War. To be photographed was a sheer novelty for the unsung troops of Batalik unlike some of the battalions of the Drass-Mashkoh battles who were lucky enough not only to get regular media exposure during the War but took back home albums and video clips.

Having been a state rifle-shooting champion in my school and college days, the soldiers offered me a captured Pakistani G3 rifle to fire. I took shots with the Pakistani rifle at rocks less than 30 yards away. The hard-nosed projectiles took slivers off the rocks. I wondered what those bullets would have done to our soldiers' flesh and bone at those close yardages when they had charged the Pakistani bunkers at night.

After my sanctioned assignment to witness the burials was over that afternoon, it was time for me to commence my climb down to Ganasok, where the Cheetah helicopter of the Army was waiting to fly me to Srinagar. Brigadier RM Malhotra, who was then the Brigadier (Artillery) at HQ 15 Corps, Srinagar, had accompanied me on the flight to Ganasok from Srinagar. Army regulations required a senior officer to accompany a civilian when flying in the AAC[7] choppers. He was waiting at Ganasok for my

7. Army Aviation Corps

return from Point 4812 so that we could both fly back. Had I gone down to Ganasok as scheduled from Point 4812 in the late afternoon, after witnessing the burial ceremony, the odyssey along the Khalubar cliff and my night stay in the high-altitude battle zone would never have materialised. It had turned out to be a unique war reportage foray for a Kargil media person.

The spirits of the soldiers and officers of 12 JAK LI fell on hearing of my scheduled departure. But orders from higher headquarters were orders, and they had to be obeyed, especially as it involved the presence of a journalist in a highly sensitive war zone. The 12 JAK LI soldiers had not been interviewed since the battalion's induction into the war zone in the second week of May 1999. The battalion had suffered 24 killed in action and 39 wounded during the course of their victories over Points 5203 and 4812 in the Kargil War. I, too, was disappointed as the limited time spent on those heights had left me dissatisfied as it was insufficient to fully grasp the scope of the Batalik conflicts. I realised it was the chance of a lifetime for a war correspondent: a night with the soldiers on the battlefield. A brainwave struck us. I asked Bhalothia to radio to the Brigade HQ at Ganasok and the 3 Infantry Division HQ at Kargil that it was too late for the journalist to climb down to Ganasok as it was hazardous due to Pakistani firing and that the journalist was very tired. Bhalothia seized upon the idea and got onto the radio set in right earnest to ensure that I would stay back with the troops after the burial ceremony.

'Sir, there is firing from left and right onto us. The journalist cannot make the journey down to Ganasok in these conditions before nightfall. We cannot risk a civilian's life. I seek your permission to retain him here for the night, and I will send him down tomorrow to Ganasok with the Brigade Major,' Bhalothia spoke on the radio set to GOC,[8] 3 Infantry Division, Major General VS Budhwar.

Hell broke loose at that message. The senior officers at HQ, 3 Infantry Division, were faced with the prospect of a journalist staying on the battlefield at night by having grossly exceeded the sanction of 15 Corps HQs. But the seasoned and battle-hardened Bhalothia weathered the storm over the radio set. He deftly put to good use the rapport he enjoyed with Budhwar, who was initially upset. Budhwar personally got onto the radio set, questioning the CO on the journalist's alleged 'inability' to keep to the evening departure schedule from Ganasok! But Budhwar had to relent as time was slipping away with each argument and counterargument over the radio. Truth is, we were bargaining from an advantage, from a strategic position of 'towering heights'! Finally, the resistance from the brass hats at the higher HQs ended. I would stay back for the night with soldiers and come down to Ganasok only the next afternoon. Down below, Brigadier Malhotra, who was cooling his heels at Ganasok with his patience fraying, finally got the nod to board the waiting helicopter. He flew to Srinagar alone without the journalist he was officially tasked to escort back to Corps HQ.

Up on the heights, I commenced a perilous passage along the cliff as we were to stay the night on the Khalubar Ridge at the tent location of the battalion's Adjutant, Major Vikas Mehta. The troops were simply elated at my presence. They had never imagined a journalist would venture that far and even stay the night with them to hear their battle narratives. They had heard of the battles of other battalions, especially from the Drass-Mashkoh Sector, where the media had concentrated due to the ease of access afforded by the NH-1A. I made it safely to the tent location after the perilous passage across the cliff. We were to spend the night here amid the towering crags and heavy crossfire of artillery. Here,

8. General Officer Commanding

the soldiers would narrate their unheard stories of the Batalik battles to me, which I would pen later for my newspaper under the unique battlefield dateline, Point 4812.

Bhalothia put things into perspective for me. 'We, that is, the troops fighting under 70 Infantry Brigade in the Batalik Sector, were an orphaned lot. We were the last priority of the higher command. The entire focus of the media was on Drass and Mashkoh, whereas we, in Batalik, were left to fend for ourselves, though our battles were no less tough or bloodier than the publicised battles of Tololing, Tiger Hill, and Batra Top. My battalion suffered heavy casualties, including that of Captain Amol Kalia (Vir Chakra), during the battle in June 1999 for Point 5203. I had to evacuate 13 of our bodies from Point 5203, but the Colonel (General Staff), Colonel Avtar Singh, at HQ 3 Infantry Division, ordered that donkeys be used to lug the bodies to the road heads as helilifts of the bodies would cost too much time and resources. This would have disgraced my valourous men who had laid down their lives. The bodies would have been slung unevenly on the donkeys with limbs dangling awkwardly. My senior officers had said that the Kargil invasion was a national shame, and now that our troops had given up their lives to redeem the nation's honour, their bodies were being subjected to such dishonour. I protested vigorously to the 70 Infantry Brigade Commander, Brigadier Devinder Singh, but he asked me to speak directly to the GOC, Major General Budhwar. I warned the GOC that I would withdraw a company of my battalion's troops that I was preparing for the forthcoming assault of Point 4812 and assign eight combat soldiers to each one of the 13 stretcher parties required to carry the bodies down to the road head. I would not allow my men's bodies to be carried on donkeys under any circumstances. How could I betray the faith the men had in their CO? For the men, the CO was a God-like figure who could never do anything that was not for the welfare of the jawans. On my firm insistence, the GOC relented and ordered in the fitness of things that helicopters be deployed to airlift the bodies of my men from the battlefield to Leh.'

A similar incident had occurred earlier in May 1999 when the 1/11 Gurkha Rifles extricated a patrol of the 16 Grenadiers from the Yaldor area of Batalik. The Grenadiers had come under heavy enemy fire, lost four soldiers, and were pinned down. The bodies of the four dead soldiers could not be evacuated as the enemy had them covered by fire from the ridgelines. The Gurkhas finally managed to outmanoeuvre the enemy and retrieve the bodies of the four Grenadiers. However, there was much disquiet in the soldier ranks when HQ 3 Infantry Division ordered that the four bodies be taken out of the battle zone to the road head at Dah on donkeys.

The odyssey along the Khalubar cliff has fuelled my nightmares ever since. At home in Chandigarh, as the years pass, I still wake up shivering, my spine tingling as distorted visuals of that Khalubar dusk visit my sleep. In one of those dreams, I find myself at the end of a cliff ledge where I cannot go forward or retrace my steps. The soil is loose and peppered with slippery pebbles. I can see soldiers much below me. I scream for their help in my dream, but no one is listening, and no one looks up to my precarious position. Before I plunge, I wake up with a start, sweating profusely, and shudders wrack my body. My wife knows the familiar symptoms and she calms me down.

In my waking hours, I am sometimes left wondering as to how I managed to survive the journey along the Khalubar cliff with one leg dragging in the proverbial grave. I still can't believe I am alive to tell the tale of an adventure I had invited upon myself. Was it destiny, was it sheer luck, or was it pluck? The only thing that I am certain of is that I am glad I went for it.

⚜

(My odyssey to Point 4812 is recorded in the War Diary of 70 Infantry Brigade)

CHAPTER 2

HEER Shells Arched like Red Shooting Stars

The austere Batalik mountains acquired the rusty shades of the setting sun in the twilight. The colours faded as the night set in; star by star, they stole out from cosmic crevices over us. From my vantage point at 15,700 feet, it seemed as if the sky had literally turned into a milky bed of stars—a spectacle, not affordable from the plains of the Punjab from where my ancestry hailed. The night sky, as viewed from these high altitudes, was a stage being set for a grand spectacle of war. No media person had ever got a seat at that vantage point to witness the performance and long reach of the vaunted Bofors howitzers.

Fired in trios, the HEER[1] shells of the Bofors came up like red shooting stars from gun pits on the Indus River far behind the ridgelines, arched in the sky, and then travelled silently across, searing at the infinite whiteness of the cosmos. The shells dipped towards the Kukarthang Ridge, disappeared, and fell across the

1. High Explosive Extended Range

LoC. Huge red and silver flashes of fire lit up the sky with the attendant, crashing roars of 43 kg of TNT[2] as Pakistan Army positions were targeted in what is known as harassing fire. The blood redness of the HEERs flying across the whitish-black night sky was due to the burner on the shells, which reduces air drag and enables an extended range for the howitzer. What I had witnessed that night from the tent of CO, 12 JAK LI, Colonel VS Bhalothia, was a fraction of the 23,500 HEER shells fired during the Kargil War across all the battle zones.

The HEER firing evoked a poetic description of the night's celestial amphitheatre. But what would the Pakistani soldiers be thinking as the red orbs advanced menacingly down on them? The beauty of this nocturnal cosmos must have appeared instead as a murderous canvas for the targeted enemy soldiers. Certainly, poetic verses would be reserved for the epitaphs on their graves back home if this was the last night they ever saw before the red orbs of death exploded on them, flinging limbs and flesh high into the cold night air.

It was the night of 7/8 July 1999, and I was in the pug tent of the CO, and we were sharing the tight space with Major M Indrabalan, the Brigade Major of the 70 Infantry Brigade. The soldiers offered us water and biscuits as refreshments that early night in the tent. As we relaxed, Bhalothia was preparing for a long night ahead. He was to coordinate over the radio set a ground assault by troops of other infantry battalions on enemy-held heights close to the LoC. Bhalothia's task was to coordinate the infantry assault with the artillery's battery commanders situated far back on the Indus River. The artillery guns would lend vital fire support for the attack. The soldiers of the 12 JAK LI outside Bhalothia's tent were eager to narrate to me the close-quarter battle they had fought while clearing Pakistani bunkers a few days

2. trinitrotoluene

earlier at Point 4812. As the artillery fire from both sides warmed up and screaming shells whizzed over and around us, the soldiers spoke one by one. They were fervently hoping and dreaming that I would write their stories, and the articles in the newspaper would be seen and read by their near and dear ones back home who would feel immense pride at their achievements etched in blood and guts on the Kargil rocks. Their story was a poignant one as the battalion had a component of Muslim troops, and they had been pitted against the Pakistanis, who had tried to weaken their resolve by the invocation of rabble-rousing communal rhetoric. But our Muslim troops had not wavered, and Bhalothia spoke highly of their steadfast commitment to the nation's cause. After the war, the Chief of the Army Staff, General VP Malik, invited Bhalothia to respond to a questionnaire to ascertain the battle performance and inclinations of the Muslim troops that had served under him during the Kargil War. Bhalothia had responded to the questionnaire from Army HQ, Delhi, by stating that no doubt needed to be entertained about their battle performance as he was witness to them passing the test under fire with flying colours.

The soldiers stood one by one at the entrance of the tent and narrated their battle accounts. I was in the small tent sandwiched between Bhalothia and Indrabalan. Bhalothia had enjoyed the luxury of a bath just once in those two months, fighting with the troops at the front on the ridgelines. Indrabalan was somewhat more fortunate as his location at the Brigade TAC HQ, Ganasok, was along the nullah brimming with snowmelt tributaries.

The sounds of the eager voices of the soldiers narrating their battles served to distract the three of us in the tent from the raging battles that night on the eastern flank of Batalik.

The memories of the Point 4812 battle were fresh in the soldiers' minds. During the final hour in front of the enemy bunkers at the beginning of July 1999, a war of words had punctuated the crackle of machine guns and the explosions of hand grenades. Havildar Karan Singh, relieved of his burden of escorting me to safety across the cliff earlier that evening, now wound back to narrate the events that had transpired before my arrival: 'Sir, we took three days to climb to 15,000 feet. During the day, we hid behind small rocks as the Pakistanis on top could see our approach. We defecated at night only. So tired were we when we got to the Pakistani bunkers at Point 4812 that I could not even speak into my radio set.'

He told me that when they got to within 3–5 yards of the bunkers, they were greeted by filthy abuses and the sobriquet of *kafir*. The charged-up Indian Muslim troops, sensing blood, gave a befitting reply.

Havildar Mohammad Younis recounted how he bellowed through the night as our troops crouched behind rocks bang in front of the enemy bunkers: 'We are Muslims. You are also Muslim. If you have drunk your mother's milk, then leave your bunkers and come out and fight.'

'But,' he said, 'there was still some fight left in the troops of Pakistan's 5 NLI.[3] One of the Pakistanis shouted back at me after rattling off a series of abuses that sought to cast aspersions on the parentage of our soldiers.'

'Another NLI soldier shouted back at me, "Do not dare to come up to these bunkers, or you will be taken alive. Then you will know what fate your soldiers suffer." Yet another NLI voice cut through the air amidst the clamour of machine guns and exploding grenades: "You *kafirs*, we will scoop your heart out and will cut off your ears and noses." It was a threat of mutilating bodies and was aimed at demoralising the Indian troops to weaken their resolve to make the final charge.'

3. Northern Light Infantry

But all this, the soldiers told me, had the effect of further charging up the JAK LI troops, who had gone through enormous difficulties charging up the mountains and surviving on meagre rations to close in on the enemy. Pent-up feelings were now given vent.

'We were determined not to leave the enemy,' said Subedar Mohammad Rashid. 'We shouted back at the intruders, "We will finish you and not let you go back alive," as we rallied our assault party in the face of the enemy's withering fire.'

Younis piped in again, leveraging his position at the tent's opening. According to Younis, the enemy was demoralised by the fear that the native troops of Jammu and Kashmir could easily scale the most formidable rock faces.

'I expended the entire vocabulary of *gaalis* (abuses) that I had acquired over a lifetime. What rattled the enemy was our threat to fight, not to kill them, but to capture them alive,' said Younis, who hailed from Jammu.

'Even as this exchange of hot words was going on, cries of *hai-hai* could be heard from the retreating enemy. These were cries of their wounded soldiers fleeing towards the Khalubar Top. The enemy was totally confused by our three-pronged assault and were frequently trying to re-group under the rallying war cries of Allahu Akbar,' recalled Naik Baldev Singh.

When the 12 JAK LI soldiers took over the 44 Pakistani bunkers on Point 4812 the next morning, they came across a gory sight.

'There was blood all over in the bunkers. It took a few days to clean up the place and collect the scattered bodies of the Pakistanis. They had mostly suffered gunshot wounds and not the dismemberment of artillery shelling,' recalled Bhalothia.

The enemy literally showed a clean pair of heels in the face of the ferocity of the 12 JAK LI's assault. As evidence of the enemy's disorganised retreat, the 12 JAK LI soldiers displayed the numerous pairs of boots the enemy had left behind at Point 4812.

'They did not even wear their shoes, so hasty was the retreat!' quipped Havildar Surjeet Singh.

The enemy now lay dead at their feet. Little did they know that in just a few days, the abuses on their lips would cease and instead metamorphose into the recital of religious verses. Our soldiers would put aside their feelings of animosity for the enemy who had killed their beloved comrades and wounded many. Instead, our soldiers would treat them just as fellow soldiers who had obeyed orders and laid down their lives for their country. Unfortunately, their army had disowned their bodies and even refused India's offer to hand them over so that they could be returned to their grieving families and accorded a military funeral. The Pakistan Army was still pretending its soldiers had never violated the LoC in the Kargil War. It was left to our soldiers to put the orphaned adversaries to eternal rest in makeshift battlefield graves. It was an extraordinary display of grace under fire.

There were many stories to be told that night. I listened and made notes. Soon, it was time for more battle, and the soldiers shuffled to their gun placements outside the tent. Bhalothia was the coordinating officer for 5 PARA's[4] infantry assaults on Point 4100, flanking the enemy's nerve centre at Muntho Dhalo. He was also coordinating the fire of the Bofors HEER shells across the LoC to curb Pakistani *harkat* (harassing fire). His radio set crackled incessantly like cicadas chirping on a monsoon night in our pup tent. The Yaldor Nullah was whistling with 105 mm shells of the Indian Army's field guns as they softened the 'Area Spring' and Point 4100. The Pakistani Artillery's response was more measured because it was riddled with uncertainty and had, in comparison, fewer guns to target the Batalik Sector. I estimated a few hundred

4. 5 Parachute Regiment

Pakistani shells and RPGs whistled by our tent location and burst to our left and right on Khalubar that night.

'Pakistanis are virtually firing blind as their key Artillery OPs have been over-run. They are firing into areas where they speculated our assaulting troops would come from,' explained Bhalothia as he turned his face sideways to me while hunching over the radio set.

Seen from Bhalothia's battlefield command centre on the heights that night, the Bofors HEER shells that left a red trail behind them were a magnificent spectacle. For the intruders holding onto Point 4100, which formed the strategic gateway to Muntho Dhalo, the HEER shells arching towards them must have been a murderous sight. For many seconds, the shells were visible in their long journey in the night skies to deliver death and damnation on the earth sleeping below. But as soon as the shells entered the last 1,000 m of descent to the target, they turned invisible till those crashing roars of TNT shredded the intruders and sent shudders across the ridges. The fall of Point 4100 that night was a decisive battle in the Batalik Sector. The enemy's nerve centre of Muntho Dhalo—comprising the supply and administrative camp—lay exposed. A rattled enemy's spine broke that night, and they literally vacated the strongly held ridge of Kukarthang-Tharu.

Through that night till dawn, the firing sounds outside the tent were interspersed with the crackle of the radio set coming to life in the tent. As I jotted notes, Bhalothia explained to me the exchanges on his radio set in the context of the battle underway.

Bhalothia's radio set blurted as Brigadier Devinder Singh, Commander, 70 Infantry Brigade, detailed the operation from his location below at Ganasok. At 7 p.m., the order came: 'Tipu for Sultan: 5 PARA has begun descent from Point 5287. Halt troops till 9 p.m. till location Spring. No move forward till artillery crunch.'

By 8 p.m., it was time for the 155-mm Bofors to grab the limelight, the big boys taking over from the initial barrages delivered from the 105-mm guns. Red balls of Bofors HEER fire arched across the star-strewn sky with increasing regularity. To pin down the intruders, and curb intervention in the 5 PARA's assault, tracer bullets fired by 1/11 GR[5] left red streaks across the valley spanning the Khalubar Ridge and the Kukarthang-Tharu Ridge. The LMG[6] position next to our tent opened up with a startling rat-a-tat. By 8.30 p.m., all positions, Indian as well as enemy-held, were firing machine guns to deter any assault to their positions under the cover of darkness. At 9 p.m. came the artillery crunch: ten minutes of intense firing on the 300 m x 300 m area.

An artillery officer came on the line to Bhalothia: 'Golf to Sultan: we are now going to obliterate Point 4100.'

Eight hundred rounds of the 160-mm (30 kg shells) heavy mortar, Bofors 155-mm howitzers, 105-mm field guns, 120-mm mortar and MBRLs[7] were fired in 600 seconds. The intruders could flee nowhere as a network of Indian Artillery OPs were directing fire onto them from all four sides. There was no chance of escape this time by fleeing to the reverse slopes of the occupied ridgelines. The entire area of Point 4100 was lit up by the flash of the exploding shells.

At 11.30 p.m., an officer of the 5 PARA came on the line: 'Alpha for Sultan: Enemy is firing from Point 4100. Cannot locate position. Over.'

One of the main reasons why Indian troops could not locate Pakistani positions at night was because the enemy's machine guns had special fittings on their barrel snouts that stifled muzzle flash. At 3 a.m., the mountains fell into a sullen silence. An eerie

---

5. Gurkha Rifles

6. Light Machine Gun

7. Multi-barrel rocket launchers

hush fell over, strangely marking the passage from the earlier overwhelming sounds of war. The war-weary mountains seemed to heave a sigh of relief in the silence.

At 5.30 a.m. came the victory signal: 'Alpha for Sultan: Point 4100 taken. Three cheers.'

We had not slept a wink that night in the battlefield tent. As morning broke over the war-ravaged mountains of Batalik, the soldiers mustered up a magical glass of tea for us. It was time for me to bid goodbye to them as I commenced the climb down to Ganasok with Indrabalan. My mind was already racing ahead, formulating storylines and headlines that I would either punch in the minute I got to the nearest computer or relay the text to my Delhi office over a satellite telephone from Kargil town.

Menu of a Battlefield Mess

An unbelievable food and beverages 'buffet' was laid out in our small tent on the Batalik heights as night set in, but before that dinner, came a special personal service. When our soldiers respect their officers and have the confidence that they will lead from the front and not chicken out, they accord them complete devotion, loyalty, and affection.

In Bhalothia's pup tent that night at 15,700 feet, soldiers of the 12 JAK LI first washed the feet of their CO and then of Indrabalan. When they suddenly started untying my shoes, I thought they wanted their Army-issued hunter shoes back. But, to my surprise, my feet, too, were accorded the same lavishment and honour. I was deeply moved. My good fortunes did end there. That day the supply lines had brought some goodies to the CO's location after weeks of provisioning basic foods and no hard drinks at all.

Just like an Army mess, Bhalothia had the luxury of offering his media guest an astounding battlefield menu: 'Vikram, what would it be tonight—a shot of Red Knight whisky or Old Monk rum? Mutton or chicken kebabs? Egg curry?' asked Bhalothia, an epitome of the finest Army hospitality even at these warring, wuthering heights.

I settled for whisky and mutton. An unbelievable dinner had been mustered up by the Army to raise the morale of its embattled men entrenched in the cold heights. The food had been carried up the ridge lines by sturdy donkeys and Ladakhi porters. In deference to the exigencies of war, the food had been transported in greenish-grey cylindrical casings of 82-mm mortar shells that had been discharged on the enemy. The mortar casings had been washed and recycled for carrying food to the fighting troops.

'There is no crockery or cutlery to go with the food and drinks. This is the very best that I can offer to you at this height and in the middle of the battle. You are lucky as you have landed on a day when food and drinks of this quality have reached us for the first time. The food has come in a tiffin-type style but is carried in the expended mortar shell casings and other make-do carriers. Throughout the war, food has been an issue in the Batalik Sector due to the very long and extended supply lines from the roadheads on the distant Indus River. The food and drinks we are having tonight are like a luxury,' Bhalothia had quipped while describing the availability of alcohol and a grand choice of non-veg dishes that night.

CHAPTER 3

A Shirt That Flashed in the Pakistani Eye

I learnt the difference in artillery shelling impacts, between ground and air bursts, firsthand on 1 July 1999, during my first foray into the high-altitude battle zone of the Kargil War. Shelling claimed an estimated 80 per cent of the casualties on both sides during the Kargil War, of which Pakistani Artillery airbursts registered significant hits on Indian assault troops. Though officer and soldier casualties were also suffered when the Pakistani artillery shelled the valleys of Drass, Mashkoh, Kargil, and the Indus where the Army's bases were situated, bunkers were always available in the valleys, bases, and the rear areas. When shelling was directed onto the roads meandering through the open valleys, the troops, media and civilians could scatter and evade the bombardment or make for the nearest bunker. No such shelter was available to the troops when they climbed the mountain spurs and went up the nullahs to reach the ridgelines where the Pakistani bunkers were situated.

The bunkers for the Kargil battles were situated thousands of feet above the valleys and civilian inhabitation. It was in the narrow confines of the ascent to the bunkers that the Indian troops were severely exposed to the Pakistanis perched on top. By commanding the vantage points, the enemy brought down heavy and accurate artillery fire on the Indian infantry advancing to its bunkers. Only massive boulders and hillsides provided respite from ground-burst artillery shells. The relief afforded by the Kargil terrain proved less effective when the Pakistanis released air-burst shells, which had delayed fuses and were released at a high trajectory. These shells would burst in the air above the soldiers and shower shrapnel on the ground below like gigantic, inverted Diwali *anaars* hanging in the skies. On 7 July, while on my second foray into the high-altitude battle zone of the Batalik heights, I had clung to the cliff like a lizard. But a few days earlier, during my climb up the Tololing Nullah on 1 July, I was forced to crawl like a Monitor Lizard (Goh) amidst the boulders and then slide under them. I also had to scoot like a rat in the short intervals between the landing of shells. It was the classic 'crawl and move' manoeuvre to evade artillery splinters.

I commenced the Tololing Nullah climb with a 15-strong protection team of 18 Garhwal Rifles armed with assault rifles and an LMG. The team was led by Major Kula Nand Sharma, a regimental-commissioned officer serving as the Adjutant of the battalion during the Kargil War. The team had been deputed by the 56 Mountain Brigade HQ to take me to the Area Kaala Pathar-Saddle Point 4700 (15,420 feet) where the Garhwali troops had fought the Pakistani soldiers and were positioned for further assaults on the Drass LoC. The battalion was under the command of Colonel SK Chakravorty, Shaurya Chakra, Sena Medal & Bar, and he was awaiting my arrival at Point 4700.

Point 4700 is part of a ridgeline that lies west of Point 5140 and to the east of the Tololing Nullah. Thc Pakistan Army's 6 NLI (SIKKIS-Saifullah) had fought pitched, bloody battles at the Tololing Complex and Point 5140 in May – June before the Indian infantry and artillery succeeded in clearing these intrusions by 20 June.

Unlike the exhaustive media coverage accorded to the other battalions battling in the Drass Sector such as the 2 Rajputana Rifles, 18 Grenadiers and 13 JAK Rifles, the victories of 18 Garhwal Rifles had been somehow bypassed by the reporters positioned in the Drass Valley. The Garhwal battles had been sidelined in the official media briefings organised in Drass by the Army. Chakravorty, or 'Chacks' as he was nicknamed in Army circles, was naturally peeved. His men were feeling aggrieved. The big media names visiting Drass had ignored personal requests from Chakravorty to grant his men their due recognition and share of media glory. His men were left staring at their wounded and dead comrades. For what? Where was the blaze of glory for their battalion in this supposedly televised war beamed into the living rooms across India? Their anxious relatives back home in the villages would watch the TV reports and be disappointed at not finding any mention of the hard battles fought by the 18 Garhwal Rifles. The battle for credit is intensely contested within the Army as soldiers stake life and limb for a shot at immortal glory. Chakravorty had raised the issue vociferously on the radio set and had been heard by higher HQ monitoring the war-time exchanges in the field. At Srinagar, 15 Corps HQ took cognisance of Chakravorty's misgivings over the lopsided media coverage and despatched an Army man with a camera to Drass. At the same time, they secured permission from Army HQ, Delhi, for me to accompany their man from Srinagar to Point 4700. I was granted permission to take photographs with the Army camera of the Point 4700 battle zone and jot down narratives of the Garhwali troops. I was to stay the night on the Point 4700 heights with Chacks and his brave lads. This was the most unique access to the battlefield permitted to a media person.

The confidence reposed by the Corps HQ in my abilities to weather the Kargil battles was based on my live reportage of operations in Kashmir. I had been on operations with troops to nail terrorists in Kashmir since November 1997. These operations included climbing mountains in North and South Kashmir at night with troops going in for assault and ambushes of terrorists holed up in snow-bound caves and remote hamlets. When the Kargil War broke out, I had told the 15 Corps commander, Lieutenant General Krishan Pal, UYSM,[1] that I wanted to report the war from the line of fire, i.e., by climbing to the ridges intruded by the enemy. I could not imagine myself as just another one of the media persons confined strictly to the valleys thousands of feet below the infantry battles being fought on the ridges. Pal had kept my request in mind. I was given written orders for access to the Kaala Pathar-Saddle-Point 4700 battle zone of Drass.

The permission even surprised the 56 Mountain Brigade Commander, Brigadier AN Aul, UYSM. I would stay at his HQ at Drass during the War and pester him to let me go up with the troops, but he was in no position to clear such a foray. He had his hands full in keeping the media contingent at bay outside the gates of his Brigade HQ, and here I was, wanting access to the battle zone itself! He knew me well enough, though. I had been in the line of fire with his troops during the three-day operation conducted in February 1999 at village Gund Rehman in the Ganderbal *tehsil* of Kashmir.

In Aul's words: 'Vikram kept asking me to let him go with the assault troops into battle. But there was no way I could grant that permission because media persons were being kept away from the battle zones on the ridges. I did not think he would be granted permission for the kind of access he wanted. However, one fine

---

1. Uttam Yudh Seva Medal

day, Vikram came to me from Srinagar. He had in his hand the written permission from Corps HQ to go up with the troops into the battle zone. He handed me the orders, and I then arranged for his climb to the 18 Garhwal Rifles location at Point 4700.'

Aul, whose son, Captain Amit, also fought the War under the command of 192 Mountain Brigade, later retired as Chief of Staff in the rank of Lieutenant General at Western Command HQ, Chandimandir.

The media contingent 'covering' the Kargil War was confined to the Drass Valley. There were media persons from the cream of national and international establishments who were hungering for bits and pieces of news from soldiers coming down from battle and whatever little was being made available to them from the staff officers at the formation headquarters. Media briefings were infrequent at Drass. So, the access granted to me aroused disquiet in the media contingent. But I had earned my spurs by roughing it out in Kashmir during the course of a two-year posting before the war. The Army knew I was not the 'take the evening flight back to Delhi' kind of reporter. That tribe of 'parachute reporters' who eyed a quick, juicy story from the internationalised Kashmir conflict zone and then made an equally speedy exit. On the other hand, I had traversed the remote, anonymous battlefields of Kashmir CI-Ops[2] with the ground soldiers as a 'daily beat' reportage. These thankless operations, which did not always result in terrorist kills, seldom found more than a brief mention in the national media publications emanating from Delhi.

I bid goodbye to the 56 Brigade HQ staff after a briefing on the battle zone on the Tololing heights that I was to access along with the Army man deputed from 15 Corps HQ. I left in an

2. Counter Insurgency Operations

Army Jonga and joined the protection party waiting for me at the administrative base of 18 Garhwal Rifles located in a peripheral village of Drass. I had just brought my essentials from Srinagar to the Brigade HQ and was wearing the only warm, flannel shirt I had. It was a red and green check shirt, a favourite of mine, which my father had brought for me from Germany. I was charged up. My dream of being alongside the troops in the Kargil War was coming true. I was handed over a bullet-proof sleeveless jacket and *patka* helmet weighing a total of 16 kg to protect my chest, stomach, and forehead.

At the beginning of July, the battle situation in Drass was poised for the commencement of major assaults on Tiger Hill and the Point 4875 Complex (later christened 'Batra Top'). The Pakistanis lodged on the heights were on high alert as they were aware of the imminent Indian assaults. The Pakistanis were equipped with powerful binoculars to observe the movement of Indian troops towards their bunkers. At the outset, Major Sharma warned me that the ascent was very challenging even for soldiers who had gone through the three-stage acclimatisation. I had undergone none of that. But we put these concerns aside as war contingencies seldom allow enough time for a non-combatant to prepare and acclimatise. In that era, the Army had not laid down protocols or acclimatisation programmes for media persons, probably, simply because the kind of reportage that I had volunteered for had never been envisaged by the Army's media management cells. The West has a well-honed tradition of embedding journalists with frontline troops, i.e., the proverbial trench reporter's eyewitness account. In India, all this was in a very nascent stage at the time of the Kargil War. I told Sharma that I hailed from the Punjab, was a sportsman, and was determined to make it to Point 4700. We left it to luck and pluck. Whatever eventuality arose during the climb to Point 4700 would be faced as it came our way by reposing faith in the *dekhi jaiye gi* (we'll take it as it comes) attitude. The altitudinal difference between

Drass and Point 4700 was 5,000 feet and the climb was routed through the undulating and boulder-strewn Tololing Nullah.

Soon, we arrived at the firm base of the 18 Garhwal Rifles, where tea was served to us. I met three officers here: Major SK Joshi, SC, SM,[3] Major P Patnaik, and Lieutenant RD Verma. They had just come down from the heights after the battles for Saddle, Tommy and Point 4700. After some scintillating battle *gup-shup* over tea, we took leave from the three officers and resumed our climb. The first of the two bridges we were to cross came soon after. It was a wooden footbridge laid across the tumbling snow-melt stream for the troops ascending the Tololing Nullah. This bridge was crossed without difficulty. The second bridge was a challenge. It was about 20 feet long and comprised two aluminium collapsible ladders fused together and thrown over the steep fall of the snowmelt nullah. It had been laid by the Signals contingent, which was tasked with maintaining the communication cables laid on the ground from Drass Brigade HQ to Chakravorty's location on the ridges. On this precarious contraption, we had to go down on all fours and grip the rungs while cautiously making passage over the swirling, tumbling waters.

Having crossed the bridge safely, we passed by the wreckage of the Mi-17 helicopter downed by a heat-seeking Stinger missile fired by the Pakistani soldiers from the Tololing-Point 5140 ridgeline on 28 May. The forlorn wreckage was lying to our left (i.e. to the west) and on a spur overlooking the Tololing Nullah. Four IAF[4] personnel had died in that Stinger hit on their helicopter, code Nubra 4. Only one of the four Mi-17s in the attack formation had not been equipped with the CMDS[5] that releases missile-diversion flares and Nubra 4 took a fatal hit. The wreckage could

3. Shaurya Chakra, Sena Medal

4. Indian Air Force

5. Counter-Measures Dispensing System

not be seen from the Drass Valley below. Years later, I read from Pakistani accounts of the War that the Mi-17 had been downed by Lance Havildar Muhammad Kamal of the Pakistan Army Air Defence, who had fired a Stinger SAM[6] on Nubra 4 from the Tololing bunkers.

As we stood looking at the helicopter, the first of the Pakistani artillery shells aimed at our team burst close to its wreckage. It was not accurate fire, yet, because it had missed us by quite a margin. The Pakistani Army's Artillery OP was located at Point 5060 (16,602 feet), which was right in front and to the north-west of Point 4700 (our destination). With reference to the Tololing Nullah (our route to Point 4700), the OP at Point 5060 commanded a dominating view of ascending soldiers as the feature was located above and to the left of the nullah.

Artillery officers and soldiers manning an OP are equipped with high-grade surveillance equipment. They are tasked to observe the enemy movements and direct and correct fire from the artillery guns onto the advancing enemy troops. When a shell misses the targeted troops, the OP observes the landing point of the shell and corrects the fire of the guns over a radio set or cable line. The OP directs a series of corrections in the shelling so as to ensure the shells fall on the grid reference tallying with the enemy's movements on the ground. This OP at Point 5060 was a thorn in the flesh of 18 Garhwal Rifles troops located at Point 4700 and those ascending up the Tololing Nullah from Drass. The Pakistani OP's binoculars could virtually pick a button on an ascending soldier's tunic. Our troops had no choice but to get exposed to

6. Surface-to-Air Missile

regular shelling from Pakistani mountain guns, mortars and 155-mm howitzers firing air bursts since the ascent to Point 4700 was possible by only one route, i.e., the Tololing Nullah. The supplies of food, water, and ammunition to the forward Garhwali troops were through this critical nullah.

Shells began to rain down on us in the cool mountain air, including those of the air-burst artillery. 'Vikram, please wear an army olive jacket over your brightly-coloured check shirt or remove it. The Pakistani OP must be thinking a civilian VVIP is accompanying us and is hammering us with a double dose,' Sharma told me in all urgency as he shepherded his team into whatever cover was available in the exposed nullah.

I was pushed to a boulder's side, and an olive-green jacket was handed over to me. I quickly pulled it over my bulletproof jacket to cover the shirt's conspicuous sleeves and collar. Garhwali soldiers lay sprawled next to me. They asked me to lie down and bury my head in the ground. Our fate now rested in the hands of *Dharti Mata*, the Garhwalis said. There was nothing we could do about the shelling. Splinters showered down on us and the whine of flying shells was unmistakeable.

'Sir, it is *kismet* if air bursts don't hit us. We can do nothing beyond praying. Keep faith in Dharti Mata,' was the sage counsel rendered to my numbed ears by a stoic Garhwali. My ears were ringing with the explosions.

I replied to him that I was going to stick it out with the soldiers through whatever contingency might befall us that day, through thick and thin, to witness first-hand their travails in the high mountains of Kargil.

That day, I learnt an old soldier lesson: ground-burst shelling in boulder-strewn terrain is not that hazardous, but air burst can be lethal as it erodes the protective shield afforded by boulders and hillsides. Fortunately, I heard most of the shells that were fired upon us. I say fortunately, because, if one hears the whistle of the shell, it means it has missed you and will explode at a distance. If I had not heard even one of the shells it would have meant it was fired with pinpoint accuracy and had landed right on us. It would have meant curtains for me and the soldiers.

As I lay flat, keeping my fears under control, tiny flowers—bluebells, irises, and daisies, the only flora at those austere and barren heights of Tololing—stared at me, inches from my face. I plucked those with minimal movements as we waited out each bout of the shelling, and I placed them safely in the breast pocket of my shirt under the borrowed army jacket. I sent them to my terror-stricken fiancée, Hemani, later in a letter to Chandigarh from Drass. 'Which fiancée has flowers sent to her from the battlefield?' I had written. I guess I won her for life with those blooms laced with the booms of battle and the novelty of a love flowering at those towering heights. I had been sending her flowers plucked from battle zones in Kashmir, and I would do so again six days later when marooned on the cliffs of the Batalik at Point 4812 on 7 July.

Sharma kept me very close to him. I was directed to keep my neck well down as I lay along the boulders. The air-burst splinters were lethal to the chest of a standing soldier. Sharma was calculating the time between each shell fired at us. The interval was used by the Pakistani OP to correct the fire from the artillery guns as he observed our movements and the locations where we were taking cover. The interval was about 3–4 minutes between shells as the Pakistani Artillery guns reloaded and re-aimed following the corrections received from their OP on Point 5060. In that time gap, Sharma would order us to 'crawl and move' and never run in an upright position or resort to a standing posture. A friendly mountainside, which blinded the Pakistani OP for some time during our ascent, provided much-needed relief from air and ground shell bursts. As an experienced team leader, Sharma was engaged with the task of anticipating the fire correction of the Pakistani shelling and pre-empting it by moving the soldiers away from the target area of the enemy guns.

'The fourth artillery round in a series is the most dangerous. It is the round that comes after the Pakistani OP has fed in repeated corrections to the guns, and the guns are able to land or explode the shell in the air very accurately,' Sharma had explained to me as we waited out the bombardment.

There was no valley bunker for me to retreat into and belt out breathless reportage of the shelling. As the battalion's Adjutant and based in the Drass Valley, Sharma had a good understanding of the media dynamics.

'Vikram, the media persons would catch a soldier here and there, do an interview while he was down in the valley, and file a story. You are the only journalist who has come up with the troops into the fighting zone,' Sharma told me. He added for good measure: 'Now, you know what we face and the pitiful allowances an army man gets for serving in such challenging battle zones. And, yet, ignorant civilians think the army gets too many allowances, canteen discounts and free rations,' he said.

Luck and Sharma's astute leadership saved the day for us.

'The soldiers under my command are like my children. It is my duty to ensure their protection from harm and ensure they go back home safely,' Sharma quipped as we emerged from the shelling zone, relieved that we had left neither a comrade nor a limb behind.

Sharma estimated that the Pakistanis had fired 40 shells directly targeting our small team. At one stage, our progress had been held up for 45–50 minutes when the shelling was at its worst.

From that point, the Tololing Nullah bifurcated with one tributary coming down from the Three Pimples feature and one from the Point 4700 ridgeline. In the ascent beyond this bifurcation, the Pakistani shelling ebbed as our movement was partially obscured from the Pakistani OP. However, the shelling had delayed our advance to Point 4700. Our rate of ascent was about a kilometre in an hour. By late afternoon, acute high-altitude mountain sickness got a grip on me. This can lead to HACO[7], which can be fatal. Soon our rate of ascent slowed down to about a kilometre in 1.5 hours. Climbing in the increasingly rarefied air got tougher and tougher. In the final stages of the aborted ascent, I would walk 33 paces and rest for ten minutes; it was that slow. Then it got worse. I would ascend 20 paces and need to rest for ten minutes. My lips were parched, and my tongue had run dry. It was difficult to manage even a weak laugh. Sharma administered medicines to me, which stabilised blood pressure when afflicted with high-altitude maladies. I sat hunched in a miserable silence. After resting for a while, I would muster up all the energies from my reserves and goad myself to move forward. But then, it was just a few paces up the slope, and I would again grind to a halt. Finally, after a series of such short ascents, though my spirit did remain strong, but my flesh proved too weak to move at its bidding. My body just refused to move forward anymore. There was just nothing that I could do to retrieve my reporting mission from a premature end. We were just 1–1.5 km away from our target destination, Point 4700.

The fact that an army marches on its stomach is an enduring truth of warfare. So is the fact that our Indian soldiers are remarkable. They can gallantly put aside their own hunger and muster up the famous hospitality of their villages in adverse battle situations. Meals would come up the Tololing Nullah slowly from the stressed supply lines. Often, just water, soggy *pooris*, and congealed *aloo* curry. By the time the Garhwali troops halted to let me take some rest, food had been brought up through the

7. High-altitude cerebral oedema

supply lines from Drass. But the soldiers would not eat till their special guest, Vikram Sir, the reporter trudging with them to communicate their stories back home and to a proud nation, had his fill first. I asked them to join me, but they refused. The Garhwali lads sat and watched me eat, a tinge of satisfaction glowing gently on their weatherbeaten faces lacerated by exposure to cold and unfiltered rays of the sun. They were hoping that the food and water would revive me from the dead and that I would be able to reach the destination of Point 4700 with them. They were as keen as me that I should recover from this high altitude induced paralysis and report their unsung heroism from Point 4700. It is another matter that I could not eat much due to nausea/dizziness and the increasing effects of high-altitude sickness. I drank the water gratefully, but my throat would just not swallow the aloo-poori. Through that haze of illness and fatigue, I was touched to the core by the simplicity of these brave-hearts and their shining hearts so full of love. The Garhwali troops with me were hungry after the arduous climb, the stress of shelling and accumulated battle fatigue but they still adhered to rural folk courtesies.

The maladies caused by oxygen-deficient air were aggravated by the 16 kg bulletproof jacket and *patka* helmet that I was lugging on my body. Though I had not undergone the mandatory three-stage acclimatisation, I had counted on my grit and innate stamina to make it to the summit of Point 4700. However, what I had not reckoned for was the huge weight of the bulletproof gear that got tougher and tougher to lug on my body as the altitude increased and the oxygen in the rarefied air decreased.

I failed to reach Point 4700 and join up with Chakravorty, who was waiting so eagerly for me. We were not too far away, but I was reduced to a frozen being by late evening. Realising the gravity of the situation, Sharma got onto the radio set with Chakravorty. We had planned to reach his location by daylight. Now, night was on hand, and it was hazardous for us to move forward, given my health condition. Chakravorty ordered Sharma to turn around and take me down to Drass that night. The Army man from 15 Corps HQ, equipped with a camera, was directed to move forward with the troops and reach Chakravorty's location for taking photographs of the Point 4700 battle zone and the Pakistani bunkers and weapons captured by the Garhwalis.

I made a miserable retreat downhill to Drass, suffering dizziness, headaches, and diarrhoea. An emergency situation arose, and nature's call had to be answered midway down to Drass. Now the question was how to find a place to crap on those steep slopes away from the prying eyes of the hardy soldiers escorting me down? What to use as toilet paper? It had to be a quick decision! There was little time to be lost in a careful consideration of the options! I found an icy stream falling steeply from the Tololing ridgeline's snow. I could not have settled my backside too close to the water as the fall was very steep, and the water gushed in icy torrents. I scratched my head as I squatted after having told the soldiers of my affliction and subtly directed them to exercise patience and not turn their eyes the proverbial 'lady's way'. But it was not a foolproof plan. There was another column of soldiers coming down, and they were regaled by the sight of a backside perched over the waters. Fortunately, they would not have realised it belonged to a media person from a national daily newspaper. They could never have imagined media presence at such heights! As I squatted, having glanced over my back and spotted those smirking looks from bemused soldiers, I pulled out my notebook that snuggled perfectly in my Levi's jeans' back pocket. It was not easy to reach for the notebook as my jeans were pushed down and crumpled over the ankles. I flipped rapidly through the partially used notebook while squatting in the cold. I ripped out pages carrying my notes, jottings and scribbles of stories already dispatched from the front. What a pity, a bit of the archival scribbles of pioneering frontline reportage had to go down the

Tololing drain! There were blank pages left in the notebook that I had planned to fill up had I reached Point 4700 that evening.

We slithered down the nullah as darkness fell. We could not use flashlights as these would have attracted shelling from the Pakistani OP. On our way down, we stopped for some refreshments with the Garhwali troops, and we made it safely to Drass at about 9 p.m.

Many years after the war and having retired as a highly decorated Major General, Chakravorty told me: 'Vikram, had you made it to Point 4700 that day, *maine tumhe gale laga lena tha* (I would have hugged you in sheer joy). My soldiers were so excited with the prospect of a journalist walking up to our location and hearing their stories from the battles. We had so much of the Pakistani war stores left with us: weapons, bodies, sleeping bags, maps, documents, diaries, etc., to show you.'

The 18 Garhwal Rifles was awarded the prestigious COAS[8] Unit Citation after the War, bagging six Vir Chakras, and was bestowed the 'Battle Honour Drass' and 'Theatre Honour Kargil' in 2005.

The Tololing climb made me realise that I needed to travel lighter, without the 16 kg bulletproof jacket and helmet, if I wanted to reach any of the high-altitude peaks the next time. So, when climbing the Batalik heights six days later to Point 4812 and enduring the night in the high altitudes (again without prior acclimatisation), I did not wear any of the said gear. Much lighter on my feet, I made it to the Batalik top and stayed the night in rarefied air at 15,700 feet without suffering bouts of high-altitude sickness. Experience makes one wiser!

---

8. Chief of the Army Staff

(My odyssey up the Tololing Nullah with the troops was recorded in the War Diary of the 18 Garhwal Rifles by Major Sharma with a statement of time, movement from administrative base to objective Point 4700, troop strength and the name of the accompanying journalist.)

A Luxury Toilet of War

Answering nature's call in battle at those heights was never a comfortable proposition, as my predicament illustrates. An example of what constituted a 'luxury toilet' in the War comes from Ganasok in Batalik. A hole was dug into the hard ground with stones piled like a sanger around it to provide a shield from enemy shelling. This was the kind of comfort afforded to senior officers at the 70 Infantry Brigade TAC HQ. As Major General Sanjaya Saran (retired) recalls, his sanger toilet at Ganasok was much in demand. So much so that when Lieutenant Colonel Dinesh Naikwade, CO, Ladakh Scouts, Karakoram Wing, was deinducting from the battle heights and passing through, he would invariably request Saran to let him use the 'luxury' toilet!

Not to forget the brush with death while answering nature's call in the middle of the battlefield. In June 1999, Artillery OP officer Captain Satish Kumar of the 15 Field Regiment and his junior, Lieutenant GS Ghuman, staged forward to Area Spring in the Batalik Sector with 12 JAK Light Infantry troops. Early in the morning as the two artillery officers went to answer nature's call, a Pakistani sniper lay waiting for them. The sniper had sneaked down the slope at night from his bunker. The sniper bullet luckily brushed Kumar's hair before splintering on the boulder in front of the 'field toilet'. The infantry troops retaliated and the sniper fled up the slope. Of course, the two officers did not feel like completing the 'morning task' that day. The nerve-shattering escape had upset their bodies' natural rhythms!

Pakistani soldiers holed up on the Khalubar Ridge heights would follow a routine every morning till Colonel Lalit Rai, CO, 1/11 Gurkha Rifles, decided to make life difficult for them. Whenever the Pakistanis came out to answer nature's call, Rai would get through on the radio set to the 15 Field Regiment's Battery Commander, Major Deepak Dhingra. Rai would feed Dhingra the coordinates of the enemy's toilet and get the Artillery guns to land shells precisely on the squatting enemies. The Pakistanis would curse the Indians and scurry for cover with their pants hastily pulled up over the mess!

CHAPTER 4

Nameless Graves under the Snows

The 25th anniversary of the Kargil War has revived memories of soldiers lost on both sides. But there will be no homes gloomier than those families of the 244 Pakistani officers and soldiers whose remains still lie buried in small, sky-touching corners on India's Kargil heights, forgotten to both nations. The LoC that the Pakistan Army wanted to alter permanently in its favour in the summer of 1999 by invading the Kargil Sector in 'bulges of bunkers' is now marked by a string of unmarked graves stretching from the heights of Mashkoh to Drass till Batalik. The altered LoC desired by Pakistan in 1999, in violation of the 1971 Shimla Agreement, lies buried after 25 years under unmarked graves, three to six feet deep. It marks the rotting remains of Pakistan's interred soldiers.

The string of nameless Pakistani graves across the Indian heights of Kargil underlines the irony of Musharraf's LoC adventurism and tells the tale of not one but 'three LoCs'. The Pakistan Army had attempted to push the LoC of the 1971 Shimla Agreement forward by resorting to an invasion. The Pakistan Army's higher command had war-gamed to extract a ceasefire at the Line of Containment (LoC) held by the Indian Army, which was in a defensive position on the lower heights and pushed as deep as 13 km from the Shimla LoC at certain points. However, the objective was defeated by the Indian Army and the Pakistan Army was pushed back across the LoC of the 1971 Shimla Agreement, barring some shallow intrusions. What was left on the ground to mark the Pakistani forward lines across the Shimla LoC was not the Pakistani flag but a series of graves that constituted, so to say, a 'Line of Cemeteries'. This LoC of graves holds to date.

The graves are entirely anonymous; none of them bear the name of the dead Pakistani soldiers. The nameless graves of Kargil form a line of succession with the hundreds of anonymous graves of disowned foreign terrorists that dot the cemeteries of Jammu and Kashmir since the 1990s. The line of orphaned graves stretching from Jammu to Kargil speaks the grim tale of Pakistan's proxy war of deception.

It will require a massive effort to exhume the Kargil graves, collect the remains, and send them back to Pakistan for DNA tests to match them to their families. Only then will there be a sense of final closure for the grieving Pakistani families, but that seems the remotest of possibilities given the hostile relations between the two nations. The forgotten Pakistani soldiers are amongst the worst victims of the Kargil war.

The Pakistani soldiers buried in India were from the NLI, a paramilitary force operating at that time under the divisional-sized FCNA.[1] They were led by officers serving on attachment from the Pakistan Army. They were Shias and Ismailis recruited from the Northern Areas of Gilgit and Baltistan. They were high-altitude warriors and well-acclimatised for prolonged deployments on

1. Force Command Northern Areas

the Kargil heights. Besides the NLI battalions, regular infantry battalions of the Frontier Force and Sind regiments were also inducted into the Kargil War by the Pakistan Army. The families of these 'orphaned dead' know that their boys have died in the line of duty and have either been buried by the Indian Army on the slopes of the battlefield or are lying frozen forever in some remote, inaccessible crevice.

Rehana Mehboob, the mother of Pakistani officer Captain Ammar Hussain, Sitara-e-Jurrat (Posthumous), 2 SSG-12 NLI,[2] seeks clues to this day as to where exactly his body lies in India. He was killed in an attack on the 8 Sikh fighting patrol on the southwest spur of Tiger Hill in July 1999 along with Captain Karnal Sher Khan, who was awarded the Nishan-e-Haider posthumously. Does her son's body lie in an unmarked grave dug by Indian soldiers, or did he plunge off the heights while fighting and is his body condemned to lie in a frozen abyss in the enemy's land? The then COAS, Pakistan Army, General Pervez Musharraf, had visited her home after the war and had promised that he would get Hussain's body back from India. She met General Musharaff again at an SSG function and reminded him of the earlier promise. However, General Musharraf did not reply to her query during their brief interaction at the function. The forlorn mother still waits for her *bachcha* to come home to Rawalpindi in whatever form his last remains.

Another example of a desolate family is that of Ehsan Ali, a resident of Chipurson Valley in Gilgit-Baltistan. He lost his brother, Naik Ghulam Haider, of the 12 NLI, to Indian Artillery shelling on 7 July in the Mashkoh Sector. The family has no idea of his body's whereabouts since no one has informed them or given them any clue. However, Ali refuses to give up hope. He does not rule out the possibility of a miracle—who knows, a

2. 2 Special Services Group, 12 Northern Light Infantry

casket of his brother's bones may return home one day to finally rest in the company of his forefathers.

The intense battles of Kargil waged across such a long frontier of high and super-high altitudes, defined a war without precedent in the annals of war history. The burial ceremonies of 244 enemy soldiers conducted at heights that ranged up to 19,000 feet during the war were in itself a unique instance of honour, grace, and tragedy under fire. A quarter of a century has passed and now these graves have virtually been forgotten by both the nations and their armies. The troops of the Indian Army now deployed on the heights where these graves are located have little or no idea of their presence and significance.

For the Pakistani parents, widows, and children, only the faintest glimmer of hope exists of the remains of their loved ones or even a symbolic urn of soil from the nameless graves finally reaching home. The bodies ought to have been brought home 25 years back in coffins draped in Pakistani flags and laid to rest in ancestral graveyards following a military funeral. To the dismay of the families, their loved ones lie on those towering citadels of ice and snow in Kargil, slowly merging into mountain gravel with the inexorable turn of the wheels of time. These are *lawaris* graves that no one claims. The relatives who would want to claim them have been numbed into silence. They cannot visit these graves or shower petals or install a tombstone or even read a prayer there. The snows are the white shrouds on those graves where the cold sweeping winds howl in anguish for the most unfortunate soldiers of the Kargil War. The Pakistan Army's higher command has never been able to erase the stigma associated with its refusal to take back the dead bodies of its soldiers after the War despite mediation by the International Committee of the Red Cross and repeated offers from India. The soldiers' bodies did not fit into the deceptive Pakistani narrative that an 'independent Kashmiri *mujahideen*' had staged the Kargil intrusion. When triumphant

Indian soldiers had overrun the Pakistani bunkers, and searched the cold bodies of the enemy, they discovered that they were indeed Pakistani soldiers with identity cards, pay books, letters, battalion records, canteen and mess bills, and war diaries along with a plethora of evidence in the form of the war stores issued to infantry battalions. The retreating Pakistani soldiers had not taken the bodies of their comrades back with them.

The Indian Army's soldiers had faced a piquant situation of having to dispose of the remains of the dead Pakistanis lying on their land. The bodies had begun to rot and stink under the sharp glare of the high-altitude sun as the Indian soldiers consolidated their hold over the vanquished bunkers of the enemy. It was then that the Army decided to render them a decent burial in makeshift graves on the battlefield itself. This was done both on humanitarian grounds and to maintain hygiene. There were some Pakistani bodies lying amongst the rocks and there was no way the Indian soldiers could dig graves at such spots. So, those bodies were entombed in the rocks by slipping them into a cavity and piling rocks over them to protect the remains from wild animals.

Transporting the Pakistani bodies to the base camps below was never an option. It would have been a formidable task as it required eight soldiers to shoulder each stretcher down thousands of feet on narrow, precipitous pathways. Exhausted after the high-altitude battles, no officer leading troops at those heights was willing to commit his men to the arduous task of lugging the dead bodies of the enemy. Neither were the soldiers and officers in a mood to render such a tiresome service to the enemy's dead. The workable solution was to bury the bodies in improvised graves under India's commitment to respecting the enemy's dead and in keeping with the Geneva Conventions.

The media contingents were based in the valleys of Mashkoh, Drass, Kargil, and the Indus thousands of feet below the ridgelines where the unclaimed Pakistani bodies were lying. The Army had only its word to rely upon while briefing the world about these burials as acts of grace under fire. Given the brutal and bloody history of the Indo-Pakistan wars, the global community initially took the Army's statements about the burials with a pinch of salt.

The burials had commenced in the first week of July 1999 across the battle zones of the Kargil War. It was then that the 15 Corps Commander at Srinagar, the late Lieutenant General Krishan Pal, UYSM, handpicked me to climb to Point 4812 (15,700 feet) situated on the southern extremity of the Khalubar Ridge in the Batalik LoC Sector. Pal wanted me to witness first-hand the burial of the Pakistani soldiers and write a report for *The Indian Express.* This would lend credibility to India's claim that the victorious nation had honoured the enemy's dead under severe battlefield stress and had not indulged in primitive impulses of revenge such as mutilation. I was able to accomplish that task after having climbed from the TAC HQ of the 70 Infantry Brigade at Ganasok to Point 4812 on 7 July and witnessed the burials by Muslim, Hindu, and Sikh soldiers of the 12 JAK Light Infantry. The same evening, the Government of India's spokesperson, then Colonel Bikram Singh (later COAS), announced during his daily official briefing in Delhi on the Kargil War that Vikram Jit Singh of *The Indian Express* had witnessed the burials of dead Pakistani soldiers in the battlefield with due accordance of religious rites and honours. It was a poignant privilege for me as the first media person to climb up and witness a moment of grace under fire, a unique moment in the annals of global war history and war reportage. My story of the burials at Point 4812 was headlined by *The Indian Express* and carried in the edition of 11 July. It had taken me two days to get down from the Batalik heights, reach Kargil town and fly back to Srinagar on 9 July.

With a prayer on their lips, our soldiers had laid aside their deep anger towards the enemy and placed the bodies of soldiers of the 5 NLI in battlefield graves in front of my eyes. The 13

Pakistani bodies at Point 4812 were quite fresh and bore bullet and grenade wounds from a close-quarter battle with troops of the 12 JAK LI and did not show the devastating impact of artillery shells. The bodies were found scattered around the 44 bunkers that comprised the Point 4812 Complex. Our troops had collected them and brought them to the spot chosen for the burial. Some bodies were found under piles of stones, hastily buried by the fleeing enemy. The dead enemy soldiers looked quite similar as they were all sporting unshorn hair and unkempt beards and had obviously not bathed for weeks at those austere heights. They were not wearing rank badges.

'We could see their legs and arms sticking out from underneath the stones when we finally captured Point 4812 after a two-day battle. We could not lug the bodies down to the base, and keeping in mind the sentiments of the Pakistani families, the troops of our battalion decided to extricate the hastily-covered bodies and bury the enemy's bodies with religious rites,' the 12 JAK LI's post commander of Point 4812 had told me.

There was both irony and tragedy in this act of grace under fire that I witnessed on the Batalik heights that afternoon. The same pickaxes and shovels (or the war tools as they are known in army parlance) that the Pakistani soldiers had used to build their bunkers over the winter of 1998–1999 were used by the Indian troops to dig the graves of their owners. The Indian soldiers had no other implements to fashion graves from the hard soil and stone of the Kargil heights because the battle task assigned to them was to dismantle bunkers by fire, not make new fortifications at those heights. The Kargil heights are stony, and digging deep is a very difficult task, so the Indian soldiers had to make do with shallow excavations for the burials. The soldiers were weary after prolonged exposure to the high altitudes and battle since the second week of May. At the fag end of the War, they were confronted with the irksome and somewhat novel challenge of fashioning graves from stubborn rocks and soil packed hard and strewn with shale. These were the same rocks that had earlier stood the Pakistani intruders in good stead. They had piled up the abundant rocks and stones to fortify their bunker defences in the face of Indian small arms and artillery fire. These rock bunkers were the mainstay of the Pakistani defences and were known as *sangers*. The rocky fortifications with slits for machine guns also provided the Pakistani soldiers shelter from the icy weather of the exposed heights. Contrary to popular perception, the Pakistanis had not built cement bunkers or fortifications but had relied excessively on sangers to hold the high ground and dominate the peaks and ridgelines. The 13 graves on Point 4812 resembled a row of low, rectangular bunkers fashioned from stones and large enough to accommodate a human body each. The top was left open to lower the body. The bodies were slipped into sleeping bags recovered from the Pakistani bunkers. The bags were zipped up over the heads of the bodies so that they could rest in eternal sleep and lowered into the graves. Indian soldiers shovelled in soil from the top and piled it from the sides to seal it and give it the best possible makeover of a grave on a battlefield so high that the cemetery loomed over the drift of clouds.

The same hands of the Indian soldiers, which until a few hours ago carried assault rifles to kill the Pakistanis, the very same fingers poised on the triggers, were now raised in prayer as they stood at the edge of a small table-top clearing on the Khalubar ridgeline. They may have been enemies out to kill each other just hours back, but when one side had won and the other perished, it was not so black and white. After all, in death, there was no difference left between a Pakistani and an Indian soldier. Both were merely obeying orders.

I read letters recovered from the intruders' bodies, and they told stories of love and loss. There were some pockets that held unspent Pakistani currency from salaries earned while waging war.

A letter from a wife to her husband about their seven-month-old baby, wishing for his speedy return so that the little one would know who her father was; from a father to his son that he had better watch out as Indian soldiers were closing in on Pakistani positions. 'You must take care, *beta*,' the father had written to his son, who now lay dead, the last remains orphaned by his nation and his brave deeds denied by the senior officers who had given him the command to cross the LoC. For those brief moments, it didn't seem to matter that it was a Pakistani father or a Pakistani wife. And so, at a height of 15,700 feet on the Khalubar Ridge, with freezing winds blowing in their faces, 60 soldiers of the 12 JAK LI dug the graves for the enemy soldiers and ringed them with bullet-marked stones before lowering the bodies one by one. The soil freshly shrouding the 13 graves was littered with spent casings of rifle and machine-gun cartridges expended by the Pakistanis and the Indians in the close-quarter battles for the bunkers spread over the Point 4812 complex.

Time stood still that day on Point 4812 as our soldiers, under Havildar Mohammad Iqbal of Kishtwar, bowed their heads, and he read out the *Janazah*. Iqbal was a temporary *moulvi* as the battalion's permanent one was on leave. There were Muslim, Hindu, and Sikh officers and soldiers standing in respect by the graves as the last prayers were rendered. The soldiers from different faiths raised their arms in respect to the enemy's dead and chanted 'Allahu-Akbar'.

It had taken Havildar Mohammad Younis' team of seven men several hours to build the 13 graves. 'The ground was too hard to dig, so we built an enclosure of stones and slipped the bodies into the intruders' sleeping bags,' said Lance Naik Suhrawardy. Younis, Havildar Sonullah Khan, Rifleman Abdul Qadir, Rifleman Abdul Aziz, Rifleman Mohammad Munchhi, and Rifleman Abdul Qayoom, among others, lowered their heads in respect. The first words were the *takbir*: Allahu-Akbar (God is the Greatest).

'During the battle, this was the enemy's war cry,' said Younis. 'Now we are chanting Allahu-Akbar.'

Thrice, the words were chanted, and all three times, the 60 soldiers stood silently, their heads bowed, their hands raised in prayer. And then came the last prayer for the departed souls before Indian hands used Pakistani shovels to dig the earth and fling in the soil to cover the grave. The honourable Indian soldiers had respectfully bid their worthy adversaries a good afterlife.

Within minutes, however, it was all over. The fleeting silence was gone; it was back to the sound of Pakistani shells coming from the Muntho Dhalo area, and the rat-a-tat of the machine guns at Kukarthang. The war was still on. It was as if the Pakistani guns were offering the last salute to their brave soldiers freshly consigned to the soil.

After the burial ceremony, I asked the CO of the 12 JAK LI, Colonel VS Bhalothia, Sena Medal, if he had faced difficulty in convincing his troops to bury the enemy's dead. In war, troops are left seething with rage at the enemy. The victorious side is known to even mutilate the bodies of the dead as they were the ones who had killed their beloved comrades or left them with deep wounds. But India had very graciously and generously ceded small pieces of land in its territory to bury the enemy's dead who had been dishonoured and disowned by their nation and army. It was the wise counsel of the senior officers of the battalion that had introduced a sense of calm in the infuriated soldiers, who had been immensely disturbed by the news of the 'mutilation' of Indian bodies. Our soldiers would go back to their homes and families after the war. Our dead were sent back to their village cremation grounds, and their ashes were immersed in the sacred rivers. But these Pakistani soldiers would never go back home, not even to their ancestral graveyards. They would lie here forever and alone, and their families would never be allowed to visit their graves in India, not even on their birthdays and death anniversaries. Many of the Pakistani families did not even know the precise dates on which their soldier-sons had died in action. They had ended up as expendable, discarded pawns and the real victims of the indulgence in Kargil adventurism by the Pakistan Army's higher command.

Bhalothia was an officer revered by his men as he had led from the front and faced in equal measure all the ordeals that his men went through in the war. So, when he spoke to his men before the burials, they listened in rapt attention.

'We got orders from the Brigade HQ to bury the enemy's dead wherever we found them. The presence of Muslim troops in my battalion made the task simpler. We had to basically take care of the bodies at the earliest and undertake that task in as decent a manner as practical, given that the war was going on and we were stretched to the limits on the heights. Nobody had ever thought that burying the enemy's dead in large numbers would be a task assigned to troops in offensive operations. We are not equipped with the wherewithal for burials when we go into offensive operations as we go into attack with weapons, ammo and food. Yes, had the battalion been in a defensive posture, we would have had a better capability for burials,' Bhalothia had told me.

'I told my men not to hate the dead bodies as these were not of the enemy but of humans. He was an enemy with a rifle in his hands before he was killed; after his death, his rifle is gone, and he has turned into an *insaan* (human). An enemy is an enemy as long as he is alive and not dead. He is the enemy when he can fire at you and kill or wound you or capture your territory. But when an enemy soldier has sacrificed his life for his nation, he becomes a martyr for his nation. He was only a soldier who obeyed whatever orders were given to him. We place a citation in his pocket when his body is sent home to acknowledge his courage in battle. The clan of martyrs is a common one for all soldiers. We are all united by the fact that we are soldiers, whichever side we are fighting on. When the enemy is dead and can no longer fire at you or harm you, then why should you not accord him a decent farewell when his own army and nation are not willing to accept either his role in the battle or his body? In battle, it is a game of wits; the enemy can kill you, or you get the better of him. But finally, when he can no longer harm you, what actions are left with us? Does not our religion or our culture teach us to respect the dead? Should we not bury them according to their religious rites? By addressing my troops thus, I was able to quell their anger and turn it around into an acceptance of the need to bury the bodies with the due honours and religious rites,' said Bhalothia.

Ten days later, on 16 July, when the war was all but over, the Army flew 18 national and international media persons directly by helicopter to a peak at the other end of the war zone. The media contingent was flown to the top of Point 4875 in the Mashkoh LoC Sector to witness another burial ceremony of seven Pakistani soldiers. The Mashkoh ceremony was distinctive, its trappings exotic and conducted in an environment that had just turned peaceful. In contrast, the Batalik burials that I had witnessed had been spartan and conducted amidst the raging war in the first week of July. The Batalik burials represented the limitations of disposing off the dead in an active battlefield.

A special helipad was prepared at Point 4875 for the burial ceremony held on 16 July. This peak had seen pitched battles between troops of the 12 NLI and India's 13 JAK Rifles in the first week of July and was immortalised by the award of two Param Vir Chakras to the late Captain Vikram Batra and Rifleman Sanjay Kumar. The media persons filmed the burial of seven Pakistani soldiers by the Indian soldiers in a curated ceremony. Some of the Pakistani bodies here displayed the impacts of artillery shelling, which had been highly effective in the Drass-Mashkoh sectors.

Since Drass town was nearby, the troops of 13 JAK Rifles, with the assistance of HQ 8 Mountain Division, were able to arrange a regular moulvi, Naik Ikraj Nabi, of the 16 Grenadiers for the burials at Point 4875. The soldiers of the Charlie and Delta companies of 13 JAK Rifles first laid out the bodies on sheets and were provided with *chuna* (white limestone powder) to mark the graveyard with an encircling ring of whitened stones. Pakistani flags were airlifted to this improvised graveyard from Drass to drape the bodies for the ceremony conducted under the glare of a formidable contingent of air-lifted war paparazzi. A special signboard with 'Pak–12 NLI' painted on it in black and white and mounted on a stick was provided to mark the graveyard. The signboard was set against one of the stones placed upright at the head of a Pakistani grave in full view of the cameras. The comrades of these Pakistani soldiers had left their bodies to rot at these heights in their khaki battle clothing. But now their fates had somewhat changed. Before the bodies were lowered into the graves, the Pakistani flags were removed and then soil was shovelled over them. Moulvi Ikraj Nabi recited 'Allahu-Akbar', and Hindu soldiers of the 13 JAK Rifles dutifully lined up next to the graves they had dug and echoed the same chants with the moulvi. The media contingent was flown back to Drass immediately after the two-hour ceremony at Point 4875.

The Batalik burials, in contrast, had been raw ones, conducted with the bare minimum of resources as the roadheads and towns were far away. It took days by foot march to access the Batalik heights whereas the Mashkoh sector lay along the national highway. The vivid difference in the resources made available for burials at Point 4875 and Batalik reflected the larger story of the War. From the beginning of the War, the Batalik Sector had been placed on a lower priority with regard to battle resources and media attention. Priority was accorded to the Drass-Mashkoh sectors as the enemy had to be evicted from the heights dominating the

Zojila-Drass national highway so as to neutralise, at the earliest, the interdiction of vital military and civilian convoys.

Since no *chuna* had been airlifted to the graveyard at Batalik, the Pakistani graves there were accorded the bare minimum by way of finishing touches and ceremonial polish. Bullet-marked stones from the Pakistani bunkers were used instead of *chuna* to mark each grave's boundary on the Batalik heights.

The NLI comprises mainly Shia and Ismaili soldiers from Gilgit-Baltistan. The Sunni-dominated Pakistan Army accorded the lowest priority to their Shia soldiers when it came to recovering their bodies. The bodies of the Shia soldiers, which were taken back by retreating comrades, were dumped on their families in Gilgit-Baltistan in the dead of the night. The bodies were attired in tracksuits and dumped like logs in their family homes. This was done to avoid publicity and maintain the deception of the Kargil invasion. An NLI soldier or two accompanied the bodies. Military honours were not accorded, the national flag was not hoisted, and there were no thunderous gun salutes befitting those who died in the war. The Pakistan Army's higher command feared an exposé and civilian unrest over the very high number of casualties suffered by soldiers recruited from the sensitive Northern Areas. So, it got the families of its high-altitude warriors from the Northern Areas to bury their dead quietly without a proper military funeral. It conveniently left the burden of the remaining burials to the Indian Army.

The few bodies that Pakistan did reclaim were those of officers or Punjabi soldiers or of powerful regiments such as the Frontier Force, which stubbornly refused to abandon their dead. For example, Captain Taimur Malik, TBT[3] of the SSG and attached with the 3 NLI, was killed on Point 5770 (18,930 feet) by troops of the 27 Rajput on 27 June. His father was a retired brigadier of the Pakistan Army. His grandfather who resided in London,

3. Tamgha-e-Basalat

approached the Indian Defence Attaché at the Indian High Commission. The grandfather requested that Malik's body be exhumed from Point 5770 summit and sent back to Pakistan for his final rites. The bodies of the dead Pakistani officer and some NLI soldiers had been honourably buried in the snow at a height of nearly 19,000 feet, atop Point 5770 by the 27 Rajput troops. The grandfather wanted his request to be conveyed to then COAS General VP Malik in New Delhi. This request was accepted by General Malik, and orders were conveyed a month after Taimur Malik's death to the then CO, 27 Rajput, Colonel KH Singh (who retired as Lieutenant General). However, the CO strongly opposed the idea of only exhuming the officer's body and he put it up to his higher HQ that all the Pakistani bodies buried atop Point 5770 be similarly exhumed and sent to Pakistan. The higher HQ agreed to the CO's suggestion. At considerable risk to his troops, as each body's evacuation from Point 5770 required seven to eight soldiers, Taimur Malik's body and those of four Pakistani NLI soldiers were exhumed and sent back to Pakistan. On the body of Taimur Malik, the troops of the 27 Rajput had found letters from his father and mother, with the former motivating his son to become a 'Ghazi' and the latter asking her son to get back, promising him that she would arrange a posting to a better place! They even found a letter that Taimur Malik had written to his father but could not dispatch, and that letter, too, was sent back to his father by the Indian Army as a gesture of goodwill along with his body. Pakistan had refused to take back the bodies of Point 5770 earlier, but the well-connected grandfather and influential retired brigadier had ensured that the lad came back to the family graveyard. In that process, and upon the insistence of the 27 Rajput CO, the four dead NLI soldiers also benefited and went back home for their final burial.

The Musharraf clique of Kargil Generals had vainly sought to wash their blood-stained hands. But no polish could cover the stains of blood marring the rows of medals pinned on the Generals' chests. The ghosts of Kargil would always haunt the Kargil clique. A damned spot that, no matter what lies, denials and misleading narratives it floated, would permanently stain its reputation as a professional army.

I leave the last word on the lost Kargil graves of the NLI soldiers to an irate Pakistani, Tariq Khan, who tweeted on X under the handle @Khantariq1940. In his tweet of 6 July 2023, Khan asked: 'In Kargil, hundreds of soldiers were killed by the Indian Army. Where are their graves? Why are they not remembered and honoured?'

At an icy, windswept battlefield of Kargil towering at 15,700 feet, the spirits of the warring enemies have finally merged. The bullets have ceased, and the LoC does not separate the dead of the two armies at Point 4812 on the southern extremity of Khalubar Ridge, Batalik. At Point 4812 (15,700 feet), a roofed memorial for the 12 JAK LI's Captain K Clifford Nongrum, MVC, was constructed in 2024 by the Dogra Regiment troops deployed at Ganasok. Nongrum's spirit dwells in the soul of the solemn, erstwhile battlefield and merges with those of the enemy. Just yards away from his memorial, among the crags and the granite boulders as big as rooms, lie the 25-year-old slumbering, nameless graves of 13 soldiers of the Pakistan Army's 5 NLI. Nongrum had commanded a column of Charlie Company that assaulted Pakistani bunkers at 3.45 a.m. on 1 July 1999, killing the Pakistanis. In turn, Nongrum and seven of his soldiers lay dead at dawn, having been felled by Pakistani bullets in the deadliest of close-quarter battles for the bunkers.

CHAPTER 5

Rusty Petals in Lusty Letters

Amid the bursts of firing onto us as we negotiated the cliff and crags of the Point 4812 complex on the Batalik heights on 7–8 July 1999, I eyed the tiny wildflowers in hues of yellow, blue, and lilac growing from xerophytic shrubs of the high and super-high altitudes of Kargil. Ridges like the Khalubar receive sparse precipitation during summer, leaving the heights as arid or semi-arid cold zones with limited flora and fauna. Certainly, I saw more soldiers at those heights than wildlife, and the only bones I stumbled upon were those of a 'yak', a domesticated animal kept by the Ladakhis. The wild creatures had either fled the fire or had taken shelter in crevices, caves, and reverse slopes.

Trees do not grow at these heights. Not a bird was to be seen in the clear skies. Nothing flew here except bullets, shells, helicopters, fighter aircraft, and Stinger missiles. There were no warning calls of wild mountain mammals wafting over the chasms or territorial clashes waged over females and barren crags. Here, there were only warring soldiers abusing and taunting each other in the close-quarter battles waged at the heights of madness. The Kargil battlefield of the high altitudes was a desolate place, forsaken that summer by the few wild creatures that could dare those heights. The razor-sharp ridge lines were left to men to war over and proclaim themselves conquerors of barren rock and shifting shale.

There was some natural relief from this austere gloom. There were tiny flowers blooming astride the boulders and rocks scarred by shelling and machine-gun fire. They peeped out from crevices in the ruins of rocks. They were the only visible form of natural life left in the wake of the war's devastation. In the battle-torn fields of Northern France and Belgium during the Great War of 1914–1918, poppies had bloomed irrepressibly as the flower took well to battle-churned ground and cratered fields. Poppies had blossomed unasked, row upon row between the graves of soldiers leading to some of the most poignant war poetry ever written. On the other hand, the Kargil flowers grew alone, some along snow-melt streams, but all were tiny and resilient. They were so small and so dwarfed by the massifs of Kargil that they peered out of the hard ground like colourful, faraway stars.

I picked flowers whenever I got the chance during the War. On a precarious cliff ledge, a flower peeped out from a cleft and looked me in the face. I plucked it, much to the bewilderment and amusement of the accompanying soldiers. I explained to them that I had a fiancée, Hemani, anxiously waiting for me in Chandigarh. We had very little time together in January 1999 when we got engaged before I had to return to Srinagar. A few months later I had proceeded to report the Kargil War from the frontlines. She hailed from a family of lawyers and had no exposure to an army-type of life. She was naturally concerned after reading my reports from the war front. To ease her fears, I would send her flowers in my letters from the battle zone. What I did not tell the battling soldiers on the Kargil cliff was that my letters were also rather lusty, of an impassioned, yearning young man who had bidden farewell to his sweetheart's arms to answer the clarion call of war.

I had seen the bloody battle for Tololing, which had been waged through much of May and June 1999. In my letter to Hemani on 27 June, I expressed my thoughts while reporting the war from the Drass Sector. I drew comparisons with Hemingway's famous novel set in the Great War of 1914–1918, *A Farewell to Arms*, wherein a wounded soldier fell in love with his wartime nurse.

'Well, I keep thinking romantic thoughts that I will throw myself in front of you and take a burst of bullets that are coming your way. And then, you will nurse me tenderly back to good health. Just like, I think, in *A Farewell to Arms* by Hemingway.' Drass had been torn asunder by artillery shelling directed by Pakistani OPs located on the ridges overlooking the town.

The flowers were little bits of life, beauty and hope, transcending the darkness of humanity's ugliest and most unhinged hours when it forsook dialogue and decided to embark on war. When Hemani opened my letters in Chandigarh and found these flowers slipped in, it immediately lent her hope that if flowers could survive the mindless war, so would I. The faint scent of Kargil flowers with their wartime tints evoked the love of the loved one far away, affirming the permanent bonds between the Kargil frontline and the Chandigarh rear.

In that same letter of 27 June, I pleaded with her not to worry herself sick. I referred in the letter to a Grenadier soldier, Dalip Singh, whose story I had written from Drass for *The Indian Express*. The soldier had been struck by four bullets but survived 28 hours to reach the hospital.

'So, my dearest, hop, skip, sing, and make merry; not a moment of youth must go in worrying. Everything is going to be fine. How blessed and lucky we are—see the fate of Grenadier Dalip Singh and our other brave soldiers. So, enjoy every moment of the freedom that they and their families have paid so heavily to give to us,' my wartime letter said.

The soldiers at Point 4812, Khalubar, and those accompanying me during my climb up the Tololing Nullah understood my intent and passion spontaneously. They, too, had anxious ones residing in faraway towns and villages, those who were glued to TV sets and dreading the news the postman or the ominous ring of a telephone call at odd hours might bring them. The romantic spirit of the soldiers was kindled by these flower-picking sessions of mine. The next morning and afternoon of 8 July, as we made our way across the Khalubar Ridge and down to Ganasok, the soldiers would stop and cram my palm with flowers they had picked especially for my letters: 'Sir, here are some flowers I saw and picked for your letters to Hemani ji.'

There was one soldier to whom I needed to give no explanation about the flowers. I owed him my life as he had helped me negotiate the treacherous cliff faces amid exploding Pakistani shells on Point 4812 Khalubar Ridge in Batalik. Havildar Karan Singh saw me picking flowers and got some more. He handed them to me without a smirk crossing his weather-beaten face or passing a sarcastic remark at this person picking flowers on a battlefield. A prolonged exposure to the toughest battlefields of the North Siachen Glacier, followed immediately by 60 days of the Kargil War, had instilled in Karan Singh the understanding that war makes a human behave in strange ways.

I had utilised my leave in January 1999 well. I got engaged to Hemani in Chandigarh. Ever since my return to Srinagar, I would diligently send her flowers from my reporting assignments in Kashmir, including those from operations with frontline troops of the Army. Kamal Kunj Guest House at Rajbagh, Srinagar, where I stayed as a paying guest, had the loveliest array of pink roses on a creeper that climbed right up to the window of my room on the first floor. Clumps of daffodils lined the guesthouse driveway in effortless ecstasy despite the best efforts of the part-time gardener not to tend to them. That was the magic of Kashmir's soil, air, and water. These flowers featured regularly in my letters to her before the Kargil War. Now, I had outdone those voluptuous, flashy, and colourful *Kashmir ki kalis* with the tiny, stoic, understated, and humble beauties that dwelt in the warring heights of Kargil.

Having gotten engaged in January 1999 and on completion of 15 months in Srinagar since October 1997, my heart was torn asunder by a dilemma. I wanted to seek a transfer from Srinagar to Chandigarh and marry her. In fact, Hemani's father had made it clear that the marriage would happen only after my transfer out of Srinagar. On the other hand, I had made a solemn promise to myself that I would complete two years in Srinagar before seeking an exit from the conflict zone.

In my letters of February and March 1999, before the war, I had written to Hemani from Srinagar: 'Sometimes I think of taking a transfer right away. Yet, there seems to be some strange force wanting me to stay on further in Srinagar…I wish I could turn into a Shakespeare and pen down a few immortal lines for you. Maybe, one day, I will manage to. At the moment, would this little poem make do, composed these lines just now…'

Eventually, I did not seek a transfer. Something else was destined—the Kargil War was lurking around the corner to surprise the Army and our nation. The Pakistanis had already stolen into Kargil. The die had been cast and unknown to us, a defining moment of reportage lay ahead for me.

'Which fiancée has flowers sent to her from such a towering battlefield?' I had written to Hemani after I got down from Point 4812 during the war. I guess I won her for life. 'You know, it gives me so much pleasure to love you. When I was picking flowers during my climb to Batalik for the burial story, I just thought about the beautiful smile that would light up your face when you get these flowers. I bet no girl has got such special flowers. Right from the battlefield. I doubt even the more romantic of the Army officers fighting in Kargil would have thought of picking flowers from such a place for their sweethearts waiting for them at home,' were my words for her in a letter dispatched to Chandigarh on 15 July with the war flowers I had picked from Point 4812 slipped gently into its folds.

She had worried herself sick after I went missing at Point 4812 since my plan was to return to Srinagar on 7 July, but I got back only on 9 July, when I rang her up to announce my safe return.

I married Hemani on 27 November 1999 in Chandigarh after I was posted out from Srinagar and joined the Punjab Bureau of *The Indian Express*. She has preserved every rusty petal folded in those lusty letters, just the way I had dispatched them from war.

At the time when I had picked them during the war, the flowers were in hues of yellow, blue and lilac, about 1–2 cm long and growing amongst rocks till 16,000 feet. Years later, as my interest in wildflowers grew beyond their romantic symbolism, I yearned to have the Kargil flowers identified. These flowers were from those heights where no botanist had been; even the Army had not toured these forgotten heights till the enemy occupied them and dealt us a vicious surprise in the summer of 1999. But it was a tricky proposition to have them identified as the Kargil petals had 'rusted' in the folds of the letters. But they still retained ghostly hints of their wartime tints. I sought the expertise of the renowned 'efloraofindia' group of botanists, of whom Dr Gurcharan Singh informed me that these were likely to be of the Astragalus family.

How did these tenacious blooms survive the Kargil winters when tonnes of snow fell on these heights?

'An adaptation mechanism for a special group of plants known as chamaephytes helps them (the Kargil flowers) to survive. These are low-growing shrubby plants with buds above ground and protected by the snow cover. When snow melts, the buds simply grow up to produce leaves and flowers. Since the growing season is short, this adaptation helps plants to flower fast and complete their life cycle. In temperate climates, perennial plants usually have buds hidden at ground level (hemicryptophytes) or buried bulbs, corms, rhizomes, etc. (cryptophytes, geophytes),' was the perspective offered by Dr Singh on my Kargil flowers.

I also learnt that Chamaephytes are low shrubs less than 25 cm tall, with perennating buds above ground level but not higher than 25 cm. Thus, they remain protected by snow in winter and, being very low-growing, are not damaged by winds when the snow melts.

The camaraderie between strong Kargil boulders and resilient wildflowers evokes the words of the late Prime Minister, Mrs Indira Gandhi, who had all her life and political career been a naturalist and wildlife conservationist of great passion.

Expressing her love for the silent dwellers of the high mountains, Mrs Gandhi had, on 12 March 1973, written in her foreword to Major HPS Ahluwalia's book, *Higher Than Everest*: 'No less attractive are the many and changing hues of the barren rocks, so stark and strong looking. And, of course, there are the majestic snow-covered peaks glistening gold and silver in the sunshine, coyly veiled with wisps of cloud. I never cease to be astonished at the sight of wildflowers in the high mountains, their tiny, colourful heads peering out of unlikely nooks and crevices, tenaciously defying the most inhospitable elements.'

Mrs Gandhi had only natural forces in mind when she expressed the resilience of flowers defying the inhospitable elements. In Kargil, these flowers, which bloomed briefly every summer, had defied much more. The streams of melting snow tumbling alongside the flowers had been partially poisoned by the cordite residues of artillery shelling. Their resilience didn't stand a chance when the shells landed right on top of their dainty little heads. In fact, the poisoned waters and snow soon became unfit for consumption by the Pakistani soldiers holed up on the heights. They soon faced a shortage of water as the supply lines from across the LoC were being interdicted by the Indian Army. The Pakistanis could not come down to the nullahs to fetch pails of water as the Indian Army's Infantry was camping along them in strength.

When the war commenced in May, I could not help but observe the stark difference between war and peace. On 26 May, I wrote a small note to Hemani after spending a tortuous night in a bunker in Kargil town. Sitting by the river Suru that morning, I had written, 'This is a small love note I pen while sitting on an old tree's roots in a lovely garden in Kargil. I spent the night in a bunker because of Pakistani shelling. Kargil is an enchanting place, without the shelling. (Even as I write, two shells have been fired. God alone knows where they will land, for it takes 15–20 seconds for the shell to land and explode.) I have picked some lovely flowers for you from this garden. Wild ones, as well as a lovely maroon-purple one from the flower bed. When it does not shell, the only sound is that of the river Suru murmuring, gurgling, and making music that only mountain rivers are capable of composing. A pleasant breeze blows through the place always, and its tranquillity reaches deep into your soul.'

Later that day, I drove down to Drass and witnessed the commencement of air strikes on the Drass ridges by the IAF under *Operation Safed Sagar*. I had rounded off that note enclosing in it, along with the Kargil flowers, a fervent hope and desire: 'Once things settle down, we must together visit the place and share its enchanting beauty, lying on a silent night with the river as the sound of music.'

❦

As I look back upon the flowers I sent to Hemani from Kargil, I realise that the influences of my romantic letters lay in the Western culture of war. Flowers dispatched from the front in letters were a highly evolved form of communication between Western soldiers and their families. I had grown up as a voracious reader of war history. I would consume *Commando* comics, novels, illustrated histories, battle histories, Hollywood films, biographies of great generals, etc., with a relentless passion. There was no Internet in my childhood of the 1970s and 1980s so I consumed every scrap of paper and book on war that I could lay my hands on.

The story of war flowers that lay behind the immortal poem of World War I, *In Flanders Fields*, by a Canadian Army doctor, Lieutenant Colonel John McCrae, had left me deeply moved. The story is that McCrae's friend, Lieutenant Alexis Helmer, had been blown by German bombs on the battlefield of Ypres in Flanders (Belgium) in April 1915. Helmer had to be buried in a makeshift grave close to the trench where McCrae was tending to the wounded. The next morning, as McCrae gazed upon his friend's grave and those of the other soldiers, he noticed the blood-red poppies that had suddenly bloomed in the churned-up soil between graves. Those moments of solitude and reflection upon war deaths deeply moved McCrae, and he composed the famous poem whose opening lines went thus:

In Flanders fields the poppies blow
Between the crosses, row on row

Following that poem's popularity, the poppy was adopted as a symbol of remembrance by the West for its fallen soldiers and those from the Commonwealth nations.

Quite recently, in December 2023, I chanced upon one of the most astounding and moving collections of war flowers while searching an Internet trove of photographs from World War I and II. It led to an essay that I published in the *Hindustan Times* in February 2024 under the title *The Power of War Flowers*. I am reproducing hereunder an extract from that essay to serve as an organic link between the history of the Western war letters and mine from Kargil.

The past speaks to us in many and oft-surprising ways. So it is with preserved flowers, sent many crescent moons ago by battling soldiers in letters....

The poppy is the flower of remembrance for Commonwealth soldiers. In the Tower of London's moat, 8,88,246 ceramic poppies were installed in 2014—one each for soldiers felled by the Great War (1914 – 1918). English writer Anne Louise Avery preserves a rose her grandfather, Charles Brigden, sent to his sweetheart, May, from the trenches of France in 1915 and it still bears a faint, sweet scent. Maz Finch from the UK's West Midlands discovered flowers pressed in her grandfather's Army Bible; he had collected them during WWII battles. The flowers were a tap on Finch's shoulder, a quiet yet powerful whisper from the past.

The greatest and most moving war flowers collection is the emotional legacy of Lieutenant Colonel George Cantlie, Distinguished Service Order (DSO), Mention-in-Dispatches, who commanded the 42nd Royal Highlanders of Canada. He sailed for war in 1914 when his youngest child, Celia, was a year old in Montreal. Though a tough and rugged soldier, he was a very sentimental man. Cantlie was tormented by the thought that he would never see Celia again and she would never know him. Cantlie decided he must do something to make her remember him. So, he sent her flowers from the battlefields of the Somme and Flanders in letters dispatched every day. The flowers were witness to Daddy's eyes misting over as he wrote his brief wartime correspondences: 'From the trenches & shell holes, My dear, wee Celia, With much love and lots of kisses, from Daddy' For Beatrice, his wife, Cantlie picked the last rose of summer from the garden of his French billets on 7 September 2016, and dispatched it to 'My dear B.B.'

Cantlie managed to find enough wild/garden flowers to sustain his dispatches; flowers which were fragile yet standing stubbornly in the shattered fields of France and Belgium. Petals of hope peeping out, come what may, through mud and smeared blood, till a shell landed on a tiny little head. Poppies flushed scarlet as if having drunk the blood of fallen soldiers and turning it into something beautiful. Amid the gloom of trenches and the doom of coffins, there was the bloom of daisies bearing a blush of faraway bosoms. And above, flowers on a wing and a song from McCrae's verses: 'The larks, still bravely singing, fly, Scarce heard amid the guns below.'

A pining Daddy returned in 1917 suffering from battle fatigue, having escaped eternal rest under a cross in some corner of a faraway foreign field. Had Cantlie been another of the soldiers gone with the Flanders wind, the flower letters would have come to notice much earlier. But since Cantlie and Celia lived happily ever after, the world would get to feel a treasure of war emotions more than a 100 years after his return from the Great War. The flower letters remained forgotten, tied in yellow ribbons and retaining ghostly hints of their wartime tints. They were stored in a red-satin box by Celia and upon her death, by her niece, Elspeth Grace Angus.

The collection came the way of Viveka Melki, a sensitive film-maker, quite by chance. Melki's clairvoyant mind—ever conscious, that with the passage of time, and without care, we are doomed to forget—exhumed the Cantlie letters that had been entombed in red satin. Her aesthetic, emotional recreation of the Cantlie letters—the War Flowers exhibition—toured Canada and France to great acclaim. The exhibition was described as a 'collision between the tenderness of emotion and brutality of war'.

Elspeth, who adored Cantlie like Celia, said this about the flower letters: 'What is timeless…is one's own feelings over anything that is sentimental and lovely…anything that moves you, that never changes.'

CHAPTER 6

Irises in a Pak Bunker's Shadows

I had picked irises for my wife, Hemani, from near the Mashkoh bunker of stones that the Pakistanis had abandoned in July 1999. Now it was 5 July 2019, and it marked 20 years of war flowers for us. It was 20 years of marriage, too. These were anniversaries that orbited those of the Kargil War's passage.

Even after so many years the Kargil War resonates with the younger generation in a measure greater than any of the previous wars India has fought. The enigmatic names of the Kargil cliffs, peaks and ridgelines where the battles were fought—Tiger Hill, Shangruti, Meenamarg, Tololing, Three Pimples, Rock Cut, Kukarthang, Jubar, China Nullah, Junk Lungpa, Mashkoh, Drass, Khalubar, Chorbat La, Batalik, Munthadalo, Kala Pathaar, Turtuk, Bajrang Post, Marpo La—to recall a few, have lent the war a phonetic distinction as well as a niche recall in the nation's collective memory.

The imagination of children and the youth was ignited by the courage and infectious spirit of young officers and jawans battling impossible odds in the highest of battlefield snows. One such child was Shikher Choudhary from Rajasthan. He had watched the war on television and was particularly taken in by the victory of 2 Raj Rif[1] over the courageous Pakistanis of the 6 NLI (SIKKIS-Saifullah) entrenched on the Tololing complex during the night of 12–13 June 1999. As images of blood and guts and a triumphant Tricolour unfurling over Tololing beamed their way into living rooms across India, Shikher decided then and there that he was going to be a soldier one day and that, too, with only one choice of battalion in his heart: the 2 Raj Rif.

I met Shikher on Tololing Top on 6 July 2019, after an arduous, non-stop climb with an expedition team from the 2 Raj Rif. He had fulfilled his childhood dream and had been recruited into the 2 Raj Rif. The climb to Tololing in July had been organised by the 14 Corps to commemorate the 20 years of the Kargil victory. Just as the 2 Raj Rif climbed to Tololing to celebrate the 20 years of the War, 18 Grenadiers, 13 JAK Rifles and 1/11 Gurkha Rifles had simultaneously climbed Tiger Hill, Point 4875 'Batra Top' and Khalubar Ridge.

Shikher and I stood next to a small temple that the holding battalion of the Tololing complex in 2019, the 12 JAK Rifles, had installed at 15,000 feet to worship Devi Mata, the goddess that protects the sturdy hill Dogras in battle. For Shikher and the 2 Raj Rif, it was a great moment. The memories that cling to war are intense, and they claw fiercely at the very core of the participant's soul, whether they be of the soldier or of those who anxiously followed the war on TV and prayed for victory and the safe return of the warriors.

---

1. 2 Rajputana Rifles

On Tololing that morning, the 2 Raj Rif's 14-member expedition leader, Lieutenant Sumit K Shadija, pulled out his cell phone upon reaching the summit that stood proudly among the towering ridgelines draped in snow. He couldn't wait a moment longer to punch in his Commanding Office, Colonel Digvijay Singh Parihar's number. Back in 1999, at the time of the war, it was just the Army's cable communication lines, radio sets, or satellite phone connectivity that had linked Drass with the rest of the world for the media and soldiers fighting on the heights. But the BSNL, in its seminal service to the nation, had, by 2019, set up cell phone towers that caught signals from the ridgelines, crags and peaks of the Kargil War vintage. Shadija's call that morning of 6 July was a historic recall and remembrance of the Tololing victory. His CO was in Jaipur and was eagerly awaiting Shadija's call from Tololing. Shadija put the cell phone to his ear and his opening words were, 'Sir, after 20 years, 2 Raj Rif is back on Tololing Top.'

Shadija's words reincarnated the famous sentence that the wartime CO of 2 Raj Rif, Lieutenant Colonel MB Ravindranath, Vir Chakra, had uttered 20 years back over the radio set to his 56 Mountain Brigade Commander, Brigadier AN Aul, UYSM, down in Drass. Ravindranath had spoken on the radio set to Aul at 5.30 a.m. on 13 June 1999:

'Sir, I am on Tololing Top. 2 Raj Rif has completed the task allotted to it.'

To this, Aul, who had been anxiously monitoring the battle the entire night on the radio set, replied briefly to the battling CO:

'Well done! Congratulations! Look after your casualties. Out.'

Ravindranath's terse message over the radio was the one that the entire nation had been waiting to hear. Till now, the narrative of the Kargil War had been of gloom and doom. Following a gruelling battle that claimed numerous lives on both sides, Ravindranath had arrived at the Tololing complex. Despite the freezing cold, many of the casualties were still lying warm in death's fresh embrace. Their blood seeping into the Tololing soil would forever grace this historic mountaintop.

Ravindranath's brief communication had not only led to instant jubilation in the Drass Brigade HQ but was relayed in the quickest possible time up the chain of command to the COAS, General VP Malik. The Tololing battle had, in the words of Malik, turned the tide in India's favour and lifted the veil of gloom and uncertainty that had besieged the military leadership. Tololing had shown everyone that 'lost Kargil' could be wrenched back. After the Tololing victory, there was no looking back for the military's march over the rest of the occupied Kargil heights.

Shadija spoke and went silent. Even the Tololing rocks gazing upon the scene 20 years later must have been moved at the emotions and nostalgia of that moment. There was elation at the memory of a great victory and grief for those whose blood had merged into the Tololing soil and snow. The spirit of valiant soldiers inhabited the restless and deathless air of Tololing that morning.

After Shadija had spoken, the expedition waited for the arrival of the Northern Army Commander Lieutenant General Ranbir Singh and 14 Corps Commander Lieutenant General YK Joshi, who were to fly up in a helicopter from Drass. The two officers were to honour the 2 Raj Rif expedition. I noticed that young Shikher Choudhary was very articulate and bold in expressing his thoughts. He was brimming with a passion for soldiering. Not only had he fulfilled his childhood ambition of recruitment to the 2 Raj Rif, but he had been handpicked for the commemorative expedition by the battalion's officers. As the expedition had climbed to Tololing via the south-east spur, veterans from the Kargil War, Subedar Surender Kumar and Lance Naik Rajinder Singh, Kirti Chakra, had regaled Shikher and the other young soldiers with memories of how Tololing was won 20 years ago. The stories had deeply moved Shikher and the other young soldiers in the expedition. They fully grasped the enormity of what they had seen on TV 20 years ago as children. One of the 2 Raj Rif war stories that has done the rounds over the years as 'langar gup-shup' and is passed down by seasoned subedars and havildars to young recruits to inspire and integrate them into the regimental ethos is of late Subedar Bhawar Lal, Vir Chakra (Posthumous). Legend has it that on the evening of 12 June, before the Tololing attack, Lal had issued a solemn promise in response to Ravindranath's question to his assembled troops:

'I have done so much for you. What can you do for me tonight?'

Lal had promised Ravindranath that come what may, the 2 Raj Rif would host the CO for tea at dawn the next day on Tololing. 'Sir, we will serve you hot tea on Tololing Top tomorrow morning,' Lal had sworn. This was also in response to the CO's query while boosting his troops' morale as to whether they'd made arrangements for tea as it was going to be very cold at Tololing Top.

Lal was killed in action that night. Though he had taken along with him the tea leaves, milk, and sugar in anticipation of honouring his promise to his CO, Lal could not host the tea party. In reverence to his valour and unwavering dedication to the battalion, the CO and his victorious troops had tea served to them on Tololing Top at the dawn of 13 June in Lal's helmet—a tea salute which was no less an honour than a 21-gun salute in other circumstances.

On that morning, after having been energised by these war anecdotes during the climb to Tololing, Shikher told me: 'My message to my country's youth is to join the Army and serve the nation. I want to tell my countrymen to repose unwavering faith in our Army; it stands firm towards the accomplishment of all of its assigned tasks.'

❧

The war had united the people of India in 1999. It had instilled in them a rare vigour of nationalism and patriotism. Shikher's recruitment into the 2 Raj Rif and his words for his countrymen delivered 20 years after the war from the solemn heights of a battlefield renewed the fervour of wartime.

It had been 20 years since the Kargil War, and not a shot had been fired for years by the armies deployed heavily on the LoC. As part of the 20-year celebrations, the Fire & Fury 14 Corps, commanded by a Kargil veteran, Lieutenant General YK Joshi, Vir Chakra, Sena Medal, had come up with the ingenious idea of organising commemorative climbing expeditions.

We had commenced the climb from Drass at 4.36 a.m. on 6 July. It was to be my third climb up the Kargil heights after the two during the war. This time, though, there was no firing directed on us from an entrenched enemy, and I could admire the scenery from the vantage points as I climbed to Tololing. Drass lay sleeping peacefully below.

The 2 Raj Rif expedition had reached Drass much before the 6 July climb and had gone through the required stages of acclimatisation. I was 52 years old and again, had not gone through the recommended three-stage acclimatisation programme. However, I was physically fit because of my daily evening squash games in Chandigarh. I made it to Tololing Top by 10:15 a.m. after an arduous climb. An exertion so demanding that a simple act of bending down to tie one's shoelaces led to panting and instant exhaustion. To give it a more romantic perspective, by the time I was a little over halfway up to Tololing, I had stopped collecting the little wildflowers for my wife. The slopes were slippery, the move to bend and pluck flowers required a strained effort, and it also broke my steady but tortoise-like pace up the ridges. I did reach Tololing Top on foot, the first media person to do so, and much to the amazement of a galaxy of officers from the 8 Mountain Division waiting there. I had started the climb that morning with a contingent of enthusiastic media persons from leading Delhi and Noida based TV channels. The Army had not planned to take or allow any media person to Tololing Top, except for Doordarshan correspondent Nandita Dagar and her cameraman. They were to be flown up from Drass in an Army helicopter for the commemorative ceremonies on Tololing Top and then flown back immediately thereafter. When I learnt of this exclusion, I was left aghast. The very purpose of my coming to Drass for the 20-year commemorative expeditions was to ascend the mountains with the troops as I had done during the War. I quoted my experiences during the War and was able to cajole the Army to let me climb up with the 2 Raj Rif expedition. Soon enough, word spread. Having learnt that I was going to be climbing to Tololing, the enthusiastic Delhi/Noida media persons also sought the Army's permission to join the 2 Raj Rif expedition. A reluctant Army granted permission after a series of medical tests and checks relating to high-altitude health parameters such as blood pressure and blood oxygen were undertaken on all the media personnel at the 308 Field Hospital at Drass.

When the climb commenced in the early morning darkness, I found that the other media persons had extra-loaded themselves with thick winter clothing and heavy climbing boots, though it was July and not all that cold in Drass. It was apparent they had little idea of the weather and what it entailed to climb such high altitudes. In their enthusiasm some raced up like hares in the first phase of the climb, keen to outdo each other and 'reach Tololing first'. However, I fortunately, had my previous experiences to guide me. I had worn light clothing and shoes with rubber studs, which provided a grip and were very easy on the foot. I had learnt that it was vital to climb at a rate where neither one tires prematurely nor breaks a sweat under the clothes. Sweat under layers of warm clothing can cause high-altitude sickness when icy winds at the top lash the overheated bodies of those not accustomed to such exertions. I had learnt the hard way, from my climbs up the Tololing Nullah and to Point 4812 during the War, that it is critical not to weigh oneself down with extra clothing or climbing gear. Climbing the steep spur lines requires a sustained pace as one ridge unfolds after another—the 'false crest' phenomenon—before one reaches the destination, Tololing in our case. I kept my pace slow and steady and climbed with my head bowed in reverence to the mountains. A toffee, two sips of water and a two-minute rest punctuated every 45 minutes of my climb.

The inevitable struck all the other media persons, including the TV cameramen. The media contingent stopped dead in its tracks halfway up to Tololing due to high altitude sickness and exhaustion. They were completely out of breath in the rarefied air, whose oxygen content was getting depleted with each step of the climb. There were no trees to emit oxygen in the Kargil heights, just small, flowering shrubs. Having anticipated this outcome, the Army had arranged for local ponies. The media persons were transported the rest of the way to Tololing on ponies and were brought back to Drass the same evening, also on ponies. Their pleas to the Army to have helicopters flown up to Tololing to ferry them down, as in the case of the Doordarshan correspondent and her cameraman, fell on deaf ears. Having ascended on ponies to Tololing, the thought of descent on ponies down the steep inclines and loose soil was a daunting one. One wrong step by the pony, and the rider could plunge thousands of feet down to an unrequited martyrdom in a battlefield long gone cold.

For those who preferred to walk down from Tololing, the precipitous descent imposed tremendous pressure on the knees. Colonel RS Bisht, a gunner and marathoner, who was commanding a Bofors regiment in Drass, was climbing down and offered to take me along. We steadily slithered down to Drass. In some ways, the descent down the Kargil heights is reckoned to be tougher and more demanding than the ascent up the same tracks. Just short of Drass, we faced a fall that was so steep that the Army had installed a few hundred yards of rope lengths to grip and safely descend a surface of loose soil and stones. It took us two-and-a-half hours to get down from Tololing Top to Drass. There, a beaming Army PRO[2] and media liaison officer, Colonel Rajesh Kalia of 6 PARA, greeted us. As news of the media contingent's difficulties during the Tololing climb had filtered down, Kalia heartily congratulated me on the feat of climbing up to Tololing Top and descending safely in a matter of hours.

'Vikram lifts one end of his handlebar moustache and climbs to Tololing. Then he lifts the other end of the moustache and descends successfully,' Kalia quipped mischievously, much to the amusement of the Army's artillery officers assembled at the HQ of the Bofors regiment on the outskirts of Drass town.

It was an arduous task for the Army to get the rest of the media contingent down the steep slopes from Tololing on ponies that evening. The sure-footed creatures lived up to their wartime reputations and brought everyone down safely. The officers handling the media were relieved that there was no casualty in the Tololing media expedition.

A couple of weeks later, on 26 July, when a much larger media contingent landed at Drass for the Vijay Divas celebrations, many of the enthusiastic media persons put in requests for permission to climb to Tololing. The Army bluntly refused. It had enough challenges on its hands with the VVIP attendance at Vijay Divas. They were in no mood to deal with a set of 'breaking news' hares racing up the slopes of Tololing to eventually require pony assistance halfway up.

A day before the Tololing climb, on 5 July, the Army had arranged a tour of an abandoned Pakistani bunker on the Mashkoh LoC heights at Point 4355 (14,372 feet) for the media teams. Shreya Dhoundial, a doughty media person and Defence Editor for CNN News 18, and I travelled together on a treacherously steep

2. Public Relations Officer

and hazardous drive to this Pakistani bunker in the Maruti Gypsy of the 31 Field Regiment CO, Colonel Thumma Shashikanth. The Gypsy's engine was smoking, and the bonnet was smouldering by the time we reached close to the bunker on the Mashkoh heights. The hairpin bends that the Gypsy negotiated were so steep and broken that there was more than one occasion when a fall into the Safed Nullah, tumbling thousands of feet below, seemed probable. The shrieking, straining Gypsy engine made rough weather of ascending the slopes. We felt that the engine would pack up at any moment midway, leaving the vehicle in danger of slithering back and plunging off the mountain.

We were both quite relieved when we reached the spot near Point 4355. I was tempted to salute the Gypsy for its valourous effort just as the infantry soldiers had saluted the battle-winning Bofors and other artillery guns during the War! We were received by a detachment of the 21 Grenadiers—soldiers whose blackened, sun-burnt faces spoke quietly of the rigours of prolonged deployment in the high altitudes. They were manning a counter-infiltration post dominating the Safed Nullah and guarding against Pakistani infiltration from the nearby LoC.

We climbed on foot for about 25 minutes from the Gypsy track to reach the Pakistani bunker or sanger, a defensive, tactical construction fashioned from huge, piled-up stones. Two machine-gun slits in the sanger had dominated the approach of Indian troops up the Safed Nullah in 1999. The Pakistanis had linked the bunker to a small natural cave on the reverse slope of the bunker. That cave was a shelter for the Pakistanis then as it served to evade direct hits from Indian artillery guns and Infantry battalion support weapons.

This was my second exposure to Pakistani bunkers on the commanding heights. I had accessed the first set of bunkers, including the cave shelter of a Pakistani captain and post commander while the Kargil War was on, at Point 4812 on 7 July 1999 in the Batalik Sector.

Towering right above the Mashkoh Pakistani bunker and to our left was Point 4875 ‹Batra Top'. This was the peak where Captain Vikram Batra, Param Vir Chakra (Posthumous), and the '*Yeh dil maange more*' hero had laid down his life. The bunker and its adjoining area were a living war museum. Unexpended munitions lay scattered in the guise of grenades, machine-gun belted ammunition, and RPGs. We had to pick our way with caution among the rocks and paths to the bunker as there was danger of stepping on an unexploded grenade or RPG. We were ably guided by the Grenadiers who had laid out a marked path for us up to the bunker. They ensured that we adhered to it strictly by standing along the path, like shepherds and warning us whenever a media person was in danger of straying from the assigned track. A precaution well-exercised since unexploded ordnance (UXO), such as landmines and artillery shells displaced by snow and avalanches, to date, caused casualties in the Kargil heights.

The Army did not allow us to get into the Pakistani bunker because of the hazard of UXOs lying inside. But I saw Himalayan or Ladakh rock skinks scurry around in the bunker below. The skinks were too small and light to trigger off a mighty unexploded shell lying in the bunker. These creatures had adapted well to the bunker by using the niches and cavities in the piled-up rocks as shelters for winter hibernation. And there were charming Himalayan irises blooming next to the bunker in that brief window of summer. The Mashkoh heights are, for many months, a towering tomb of snow abandoned by all, except for that winter of 1999 when audacious Pakistani soldiers had stolen in and dared death. The most audacious of the Pakistani intrusions had been that of General Parvez Musharraf who had flown in with his high-level entourage three kilometres across the Mashkoh LoC on 28 March. The 'commando chief' had spent the night with the troops of the 12 NLI (Haideran) at their intrusion base in Mashkoh. It was a historic moment for the Pakistan Army: it was the first time its Chief of Army Staff had addressed troops in Indian territory. He had even taken an aerial recce of the Pakistani intrusions in Mashkoh on that day.

The abandoned Pakistani bunker was in the vicinity of the point where Musharraf had intruded. I ventured to the irises (species: Iris hookerina) blooming in the shadows of the bunker and picked them for my wife, Hemani, in Chandigarh. I indulged in a bit of phonetics by repeatedly letting the lovely word, irises, roll over my tongue with a ballerina's grace. It was an indescribable moment. A flood of war memories—of guns and roses—engulfed me. I could feel some pairs of eyes staring at me, but it didn't bother me at all...I am, after all, a battle-hardened romantic!

The final part of the 20-year commemorative climbs open to the media was staged in the Batalik Sector. On 8 July, I returned with the Army to Ganasok in the Batalik LoC Sector, two decades after my foray during the War. There, in the middle of nowhere, now stood a memorial for the heroic Captain Manoj Pandey, PVC (Posthumous), of the 1/11 Gurkha Rifles. When I came 20 years ago, there were just a few tents of the 70 Infantry Brigade TAC HQ. In its place now stood the full-fledged battalion HQ of the 26 Madras, which was manning the Batalik LoC. A 12-member expedition team of the Gurkhas from Pandey's battalion, including three veterans from the Kargil War, had reached Ganasok and were waiting for the media contingent. The Gurkha expedition was to climb the Khalubar Ridge as a commemorative event to celebrate the battalion's victory. It was on 'Bunker Area', Khalubar Ridge, that Pandey had fought his most glorious battle as 5 Platoon Commander during the night of 2–3 July 1999. Pandey had busted three bunkers before taking a burst from a machine gun in the forehead while attacking the fourth. I told the young Gurkhas in the expedition a story about Pandey and his mum that I had learnt after the war. The axiom of war families is that the braver the army son, the more worried is mum back home, naturally! Even the three Kargil veterans had not heard this story of the officer who had commanded them in 1999. It was a simple story and one that underlined the Indian Army's tradition of officers leading from the front in battle and standing by their men, come what may.

The story was that when the war had started, Manoj's mum, Mohini (now deceased) had told him when she spoke to him on the STD landline phone, 'Manoj, do not venture too forward into battle as you are an officer. Send the jawans ahead.' The young and firebrand officer, who had always dreamt of winning a PVC, had famously retorted: 'Mummy, if you and I are going somewhere and there is trouble, will you, as a mother, put your child in front or will you remain in front and keep me behind? In the same way, the Gurkha jawans are like my children. I will stay ahead when the firing starts and keep my jawans behind me.' Pandey had been true to his word. He had led the charge on the bunkers braving the proverbial hail of fire. His last words to his battling, valiant Gurkhas, as he lay in front of the Pakistani bunkers, were: *na chodnoo* (do not spare them, press on with the attack). The Gurkhas were very moved to hear this story of their valiant officer.

The three veterans also had personal stories to tell me of the war, when on a moonlit night, *khukris* had glinted, blood had shone on stone, and Pakistani heads had come tumbling down the slopes of Khalubar. The valiant Gurkhas coming up the slopes had been undaunted by the withering fire from the bunkers above. The Pakistanis had fled hearing the war cries of the ferocious Gurkhas charging into the enemy bunkers with the blood-curdling war cry *Jai Mahakali, Ayo Gurkhali*. The formidable reputation of the Gurkhas had preceded the assaults on the Khalubar Ridge. One of the three veterans in the expedition was Ganesh Pradhan, who retired in February 2024 with the rank of Honorary Lieutenant. In the wee hours of 5–6 July 1999, rifleman Ganesh Pradhan had run out of ammunition for his INSAS 5.56-mm rifle while engaged in an intense, close-quarter battle to clear the Pakistani bunkers lodged on the Khalubar South Ridge. His Charlie Company's second-in-command, Captain VA Joshi, lent him three rounds of ammunition, and Pradhan unleashed his khukri as he ventured into the bunkers.

'I saw an enemy soldier wearing a tracksuit in the bunker's toilet, and I leapt at him before he could raise his rifle. My khukri, with an angled-down blow starting from the top of the neck, did the job in one stroke. Truly, the khukri is better than a rifle in such body-contact battles,' Pradhan told me on 8 July 2019 at Ganasok.

Pradhan's commanding officer during the War, Colonel Lalit Rai, Vir Chakra, had recounted in a memorable video exposition after the war: 'My short Gurkha lads charged at the tall Pathan Pakistanis and leapt at them with khukris glinting in the moonlight. The charge was fired up with our war cry, *Jai Mahakali, Ayo Gurkhali*, which reverberated in the mountains. I saw Pakistani heads tumbling down the mountain past me as I climbed. I had initially thought these were rocks coming down at me. The Pakistanis panicked in the face of the Gurkhas' ferocity. They fled as they felt that head cutting in the *jhatka* style by the Gurkhas would send them to hell as this method of slaughter was considered *haram* by them. They don't even cut meat in this way. They panicked, and my boys chased them at the high altitudes just like school children playing games.'

Fed on such anecdotes from the war by the serving veterans, the young soldiers in the Gurkha expedition at Ganasok were all fired up.

'The *josh* (high spirits) in our battalion is twice what it was in 1999. Our seniors told us how challenging the fight was. They would share water in a helmet and divide a *poori* among three or four soldiers. A big rock was like God because it protected them from bullets and artillery shells. Their combat uniforms were frayed and torn with overuse, and sometimes, they donned the jackets, socks and other clothes of dead Pakistani soldiers. My message to the youth of our nation is to come together and unite to defeat the enemy like our team of the Gurkhas who fought in the Kargil War,' a young recruit, Rifleman Shuvas Shrestha, said as he gazed up at Pandey's bust at the Ganasok War Memorial.

It was time for the media contingent to depart for Hanuthang on the Indus River, from where we would leave for Leh. I wished the Gurkha lads well and hoped that the battalion would win another PVC[3] or AC[4] to add to the brace of the highest gallantry awards it already possessed (a PVC and an AC) as its most distinguished silverware. Another one of the nation's highest gallantry awards would lend the 1/11 Gurkha Rifles a peerless distinction in the Indian Army and take them a notch higher than the 'Bravest of the Brave'.

There are just six units of the Indian Army that have been awarded two of the highest gallantry awards that include at least one PVC. The distinguished units are the 1 Sikh (4 Mechanised Infantry)—two PVCs, 13 Kumaon—PVC and an AC, 17 (Poona) Horse—two PVCs, 8 JAK LI—a PVC and an AC, 1/11 GR—AC and PVC, and the 13 JAK Rifles—two PVCs.

---

3. Param Vir Chakra

4. Ashok Chakra

CHAPTER 7

Death Before Dawn: A Rustle in the Autumn Leaves

It was a long road to get to the point where one could pen down these lines and push them through the newspaper bureaucracy for a limited publication in Jammu & Kashmir:

> Concealed behind a tree, Naik Gyan Prakash of the 13 Jammu and Kashmir Rifles (13 JAK Rif) heard what he thought was the usual rustling of the autumn leaves. A mortar flare lit up the pre-dawn darkness, and Gyan Prakash saw the shaggy mane of hair protruding from a ditch five yards away... One jawan unearthed a charred, spongy mass, which he smelt and stretched to verify if it was indeed a chunk of roasted human flesh. No such luck, though, for it turned out to be some oily, organic matter.

Dawn had just broken out into the clear skies over village Gund Brath on the outskirts of Sopore in North Kashmir on 12 November 1997. A young foreign terrorist lay dead at our feet. Our team from *The Indian Express'* Srinagar Bureau, comprising Muzamil Jaleel, Photographer Javeed Shah, and myself, had been granted unique access to an encounter between the terrorists and the soldiers of the 13 JAK Rif. It was a journalistic expedition to ascertain the flesh, blood and hair of the battle between terrorists and the Army in the Kashmir villages. There were so many such battles that the media had long lost count of them.

Our reportage marked a departure from how such encounters were reported till then—under such bland headlines as: 'Four terrorists/militants killed', two soldiers wounded in an encounter'. Such reportage had turned banal and routine in Kashmir, so frequent were these dangerous games being played in the remote corners of the valley.

One way of reporting encounters was reflected in the tendency of sections of the local press to frame it in a human rights perspective, alleging atrocities committed by troops and collateral damage to the home, hearth, and livestock of the civil population by the Army's use of overwhelming firepower available to it through infantry battalion support weapons. The locals would refer to the outlaws as militants/mujahids. At the other end of the media spectrum was the 'guided tour' style of encounter coverage. A convoy of Army vehicles would depart from the Badami Bagh cantonment of 15 Corps HQ, Srinagar, or the Tourism Reception Centre, Srinagar, to the encounter site in the rural areas or towns. On arrival, the media would be kept at the fringes of the outlying third cordon, and interviews would be conducted with Army officers and soldiers who had participated in the encounter under the watchful eye of the PRO from Srinagar. It was a prepared script which gave nothing away beyond the standard details, the courage of the soldiers, and the effort to cause minimum collateral damage. The reporters from the national media would refer to the outlaws as 'terrorists' and 'Pakistani mercenaries'.

There was a special arrangement in place for defence correspondents who flew in from Delhi. Some of them were sons/

daughters or close relatives of serving or retired officers of the Armed Services. They would pull strings at Army HQ, Delhi, or with the Ministry of Defence, or milk regimental connections and get VIP treatment on arrival in Srinagar. These defence correspondents would be taken to operational zones exclusively but were kept away from the inner fighting zone. They would, however, be provided with a far greater degree of access—as compared to Kashmiri media persons—to the information collected by the Army from the documents recovered from dead terrorists, signals intercepts, links to Pakistan, etc. In other words, the wards of the defence services would bag the 'exclusive' Army stories from Kashmir.

Between both the narratives running parallel to each other, there was a yawning gap. There was a paucity of detail as to how exactly the fighting took place in the dangerous built-up areas, what level of resistance the terrorists had put up, what kind of heavy weapons the Army deployed to knock down houses, how the Army searched each house and battled the risk of a terrorist hiding in a closet, beneath the stairs, in the wood stacks, or the umpteen hiding spots afforded in human habitation. No media person, however esteemed his access to the Army, had ventured to report an eyewitness account from within the inner cordon of fighting or at the 'line of fire'. Such a style of war or conflict reportage has a tradition with a long lineage as far as the Western press goes, but in Kashmir, neither the Army nor the local media nor the 'parachute' corps from Delhi had any such inclinations.

When I landed in Srinagar in the third week of October 1997, I was determined to be a war correspondent in the truest sense of the profession. I was very curious and full of zest. I wanted to be with the troops in the line of fire and bring to the readers a scintillating first-hand account of battle. Kashmir was full of such opportunities, but they had gone abegging. Kashmir was a conflict zone that had international exposure, and it afforded a war correspondent a varied choice: encounters in villages and towns, in the high mountains and forests, ambushes, heavy artillery firing on LoC bunkers, and high-risk patrolling along the LoC to maintain its sanctity. If a correspondent was willing to take the risk, Kashmir was a paradise for proxy war/conflict reportage.

The Army was initially befuddled by my request: I wanted to accompany troops in the encounter's firing zone. Neither had any such request come in before nor did the Army have well-laid-out procedures to allow the media into the firing zone. The first question the officers in charge of the media at 15 Corps HQ asked me was, 'Who will be responsible if you suffer a loss of life or limb during the operation?'

Pat came my reply: 'I will sign any indemnity bond, and the Army bears no responsibility to my family for any such loss. If I am wounded, please get me to hospital, if I die, please send my body home. That is all I ask of you.'

The officers soon realised I had a grasp of military matters and was very passionate about being a war correspondent. Fortunately, the then 15 Corps Commander, Lieutenant General Krishan Pal, developed an affinity for me very early on, and he cleared all hurdles for my pioneering foray into the battle zone. Lieutenant General Pal knew what a thankless, strenuous, and endless task his soldiers performed in the field hunting terrorists embedded firmly with the local populace. He was keen that their extremely risky battles be given due recognition, and that the nation's awareness of the Kashmir conflict go beyond the dull headlines that reported nothing beyond an anonymous soldier answering his call of duty. Once I had won Lieutenant General Pal's confidence, the officers subordinate to him at the Corps HQ also put aside their misgivings. It was a very special honour, as I was not the son of a retired or serving general officer or air marshal. I hailed from a family of IAS[1] and IPS[2] officers, who are generally not viewed too favourably by Army officers!

The wheels of the Army's bureaucracy in Srinagar began to turn in my favour. Late in the evening of 11 November 1997, I got a call on the office landline phone from a colonel at the operations branch of 15 Corps HQ. A battle was underway at village Gund Brath, Sopore, where the Army had surrounded a group of terrorists. Night had fallen, and the terrorists were under siege from the troops. The officer at 15 Corps HQ told me to wait till a confirmation came from his side. The scene of the encounter was a good 65 km away from Srinagar. In those days, there were no cellphones or even pagers, and contact with the Army was only through the BSNL landlines. I waited in my office for the call as the night grew deeper. It was cold, and we had no dinner as the hotels and *dhabas* had all shut down early in the Srinagar of 1997. We finally decided to shift to the residence of our photographer, Javeed Shah, who had a landline at his Srinagar home. Shah offered us a solid dinner of mutton and rice, and we waited for the Army's confirmatory call granting clearance to proceed to the encounter site. Finally, we got the call from the officer around 11 p.m. Our team had been cleared for the encounter at Gund Brath as it was still underway, and the Army was yet to clear the village of the last terrorist. We were asked to reach the encounter site before daybreak when the troops would launch the final assault on the trapped terrorists. Unlike the standard Army facilitation of 'encounter reportage', there would be no convoy to escort us to the encounter site and guard us. We were comfortable with that. Our spirits were lifted by the prospect of reporting a battle in Kashmir from a different perspective and as a purely journalistic endeavour. It was very risky, but it fired our spirits. A front-page

1. Indian Administrative Service

2. Indian Police Service

story was all that we dreamt of, no matter what hazards lay in our odyssey ahead.

In the dead of night, we set off from Javeed's Srinagar home at about 2–2.30 a.m. for the 65 km drive to Sopore and beyond to the Gund Brath village. There was no vehicle on the road, not a soul, not a dog crossed our path. A few kilometres outside Srinagar, we ran into a security checkpost on the Srinagar-Baramulla highway at Parimpora. They were quite astonished when I spoke to them after rolling down the front passenger seat window of Javeed's Maruti 800. I told them authoritatively that I had permission from 15 Corps HQ. They examined our ID[3] cards certifying us as accredited journalists. The determined tone and tenor of my voice brooked no interference to our expedition. The cops, in due reverence to the Army's permission, waved us on from the checkpoint.

As the checkpoint receded in the distance and darkness engulfed the road with the Maruti headlights cutting white beams through the looming colonnades of poplar trees, Jaleel quipped that my personality and Army moustaches had saved the day for us!

'Vikram, had you not been with us, the security force personnel at the checkpoint would have made life very tough for us in the middle of the night as we are Kashmiri journalists. Also, the Army would never have given permission to us had we wanted to go for an encounter in this fashion.'

I was new to Kashmir, but my colleagues, Muzamil Jaleel and photographer Javeed Shah, had readily agreed to accompany me for the encounter. Jaleel was an accomplished reporter with a penchant for breaking exclusive stories from the length and breadth of the valley. He went on to bag national and international

3. Identification

awards for his reportage and essays on Kashmir. Shah was one of the best news photojournalists of Kashmir. However, the access to the inner zone of an encounter was a first for Jaleel, and as a professional journalist, he was very excited. Shah drove his white Maruti 800 steadily as we sat quietly, peering into the sides of the highway as the headlights cleared the darkness ahead. It was bitterly cold as we raced along the fabled poplar-lined road and through the Kashmiri countryside as captured in many Bollywood movies. But the excitement and tense situation ensured that we almost didn't notice the cold. Adrenaline was racing through our veins. Had we been intercepted by terrorists, it would have been curtains for us. There were no swift or quick reaction mobile units of the Army patrolling the highway at night who could have come to our rescue. As we neared Sopore, we were stopped at various Army checkpoints. Had it been anyone else—civilians or the local media—the Army would have impounded the car and questioned the occupants severely, perhaps even dealt out a sound thrashing. There was an unwritten curfew in place at these unearthly hours, and anyone violating it was automatically a suspect. However, the checkpoints had been informed in advance about our passage and vehicle number by the Army's higher headquarters, and we were cleared quickly by the burly Dogra soldiers brandishing assault rifles. We reached Sopore safely and, after a trying search in the darkness, located the 13 JAK Rifles HQ on the city's outskirts.

At the gates, we were warmly welcomed by alert Dogra soldiers and ushered into the presence of Major Mukherjee. He offered us a cup of tea, but I was keen to get to the operational site lest the action was over by the time we reached. Time was of the essence because it would be dawn in the next hour. We sped off to Gund Brath village, where the CO of 13 JAK Rif, Colonel Jasbir Singh, was located in the outer cordon and monitoring the operation from the ground. The officer leading the men in the front was the Alpha Company Commander, Major S Vijay Bhaskar, who later was awarded the Vir Chakra during the Kargil War. The battalion, 13 JAK Rifles, was awarded two PVCs for the Kargil War, including the one for the late Captain Vikram Batra. The PVC winner had also served in the Sopore area hunting terrorists through 1997–99 before being inducted into the Kargil War zone.

Death had, however, beaten us in the race to Gund Brath. The Army had managed to kill only one terrorist, and that, too, just before we reached. The rest from a group of four had managed to escape into the night, taking advantage of the darkness, support from the locals and familiarity with the terrain. The troops took us to where the lone body lay face down in the autumn leaves and mud with a hole in its head caused by the entry of a heavy bullet from an army self-loading rifle of 7.62-mm calibre. Shah took photographs of the dead terrorist. Colonel Singh and Major Bhaskar briefed us on the encounter. I took leave from them and ventured into the smoking village. A couple of houses lay in ruins, demolished by the Army's firepower. No one from the Army stopped us nor were there any guided tours conducted by Army officers. The officers of 13 JAK Rifles were under instruction from 15 Corps HQ to let the journalists' team from Srinagar see things for themselves. The roosters had begun to crow hesitatingly as I picked my way into the rubble. My eyes picked a plethora of details in the pastoral setting torn asunder by violence. The peasants had fled the village and their homes. I understood then and there the meaning of the expressions 'Kashmir – a troubled paradise' and 'Kashmir – a paradise lost'. I had come across these expressions so often in the mainstream media's reportage of Kashmir prior to my Srinagar posting.

Having satisfied myself after an unhindered, unescorted view of the smouldering houses, I returned to the waiting officers. They had been joined by their brigade commander, Brigadier MPS Bajwa of the 192 Mountain Brigade headquartered at Pattan. He was the officer who later commanded the assault on Tiger Hill during the Kargil War and was awarded a Yudh Seva Medal. Bajwa had a very firm handshake. As was his wont, he would try to pull the unsuspecting person towards him in a handshake, which was more of a violent yank than anything else! I was unsuspecting of his habits and had violently lurched forward upon clasping his hand that morning in the frosty fields outside Gund Brath. But he had a merry twinkle in his eye. After Brigadier Bajwa had briefed us, we bid adieu and raced back to Srinagar. The army part was done with; the next and more daunting part of the challenge of reporting the encounter lay before us! We had to ensure our story appeared in the newspaper that would be published the next morning from Jammu.

Brimming with excitement, I briefed the Jammu editorial desk of *The Indian Express* upon our return to Srinagar. I told the Jammu desk that Jaleel and I would be sending a story that evening along with Shah's photographs of the dead terrorist and the encounter-hit Gund Brath village. We were planning to write in a narrative style that lent a different perspective to these daily battles. I had already thought of a headline for it: 'Death before Dawn: Flesh and Blood of an Encounter'. However, my enthusiasm was dampened soon enough by the newspaper bureaucracy. The Jammu desk asked me how many terrorists had been killed in the encounter. On hearing my reply that only one terrorist had been shot, the editor in charge at the Jammu desk expressed disappointment. 'Where is a story worth publication if just one terrorist has been killed?' he asked with some bored hums and haws interspersed with tongue clicks loud enough to be audible over the tenuous STD line. Anyway, I was determined enough and weathered the desk's cynicism by promising to bring a fresh and novel perspective to the daily reportage of Kashmir encounters. My story was reluctantly listed that same evening by the Jammu desk for publication the next morning of 13 November 1997.

During the day, Jaleel and I thought long about the story we were going to write. We finally got down to writing it in the evening, spinning a long narrative that read more like a war novel by Hemingway. It was a very cold November with night temperatures plunging below freezing point. The rest of the Express Bureau reporters left by 8 p.m., leaving both of us hunched over the computer. In those days, we would transmit stories from Srinagar to Jammu via the modem linked to the office landline BSNL connection. There were frequent power cuts, so Jaleel had to get the diesel generator in action to keep the desktop computer and modem functional. It was a newspaper working under the duress of a conflict zone.

At about 10.30 p.m., Jaleel positioned himself next to the generator on the ledge outside the window of our first-floor office at Hotel Remano near the Zero Bridge on the river Jhelum in Srinagar. The generator was kept outside on the ledge as that was the only way to keep the dense diesel fumes out of the office room. Jaleel had to hold onto the generator so that it would not fall off the ledge while vibrating. Some of the fumes still entered the room and swirled around like tear gas. I was typing the narrative into the computer, taking pains at the same time to impart a creative flourish to the copy. That took time. Both of us were aware that if we did not file the story that night, the Jammu editorial desk would get a handle to kill the story on the bland pretext that publication on the day next would render the story stale and a day late. As we were stationed in Srinagar and our only means of communication with the Jammu desk was via the lone STD connection, there was little we could have done to influence such decisions taken on the other side of the Banihal tunnel.

When I finally got the copy done, it was a long one of 1,500 words. Though both of us knew in our hearts that it was way too long for a full accommodation in a newspaper's weekday pages, we had written it with a prayer on our lips. Hope springs eternal and we hoped for some miracle to occur overnight and see it through in a full flourish the next morning.

Then came the next challenge. The story had to be sent via modem to the Jammu editorial desk. However, the modem was not efficient for transmitting data. We kept dialling the Jammu desk on the modem, but it repeatedly failed. Both of us were nauseous from inhaling the noxious diesel fumes from the generator, but we refused to give up. Finally, the story was transmitted late that night to the Jammu desk.

Those icy nights of sending stories via the modem with the indefatigable Jaleel perched on the window ledge have never ever left me. The challenges of Kashmir and Kargil have stood me in good stead ever since. Whenever I faced a journalistic challenge in subsequent years, I always recalled the Srinagar nights to overcome them. The latter-day problems seemed trifling in comparison.

The next day, we eagerly waited for the newspaper that was published in Jammu and airlifted to Srinagar or sent by road if the flights did not operate due to inclement weather. Jaleel and I had failed to hit the front page of the J&K Newsline, the local news supplement of *Express*' Jammu and Kashmir edition. Our narrative, hanging on the slender thread of 'one terrorist killed', had been cut almost a third to 635 words. Shah was even worse off. His pictures of the dead terrorist and the smouldering ruins of Gund Brath did not find publication. The story appeared in the inner pages of J&K Newsline, *The Indian Express*, Jammu edition, without a photo of the encounter. It never made it to any of the other editions of the newspaper throughout India. Though the Jammu desk and the big bosses in New Delhi had been left unenthused by the encounter story, our readers in Kashmir were very appreciative of the unique encounter narrative.

It was published on 13 November 1997, under the dateline, Gund Brath (Sopore), 12 November 1997, with the joint byline of Vikram Jit Singh and Muzamil Jaleel and introduced by the headline: 'Death Before Dawn: The Flesh and Blood of an Encounter'. I reproduce it verbatim:

Just before the break of dawn, the youthful militant started his 50-yard crawl towards death from the smoking spent shell of the house that had helped him keep army jawans at bay for nearly 14 hours.

Concealed behind a tree, Naik Gyan Prakash of the 13 Jammu and Kashmir Rifles (13 JAK) heard what he thought was the usual rustling of the autumn leaves. A mortar flare lit up the pre-dawn darkness, and Gyan Prakash saw the shaggy mane of hair protruding from a ditch five yards away. He had just about nudged his companion, rifleman Gurdial Singh, when a lightly built 'foreign' militant panicked in the sudden glare of light to make a desperate dash.

The dark shadows of the tree had hidden the two jawans well. They opened fire when the half-crouched militant with his AK-47 swinging in a deadly arc passed within two yards. The heavy high-velocity bullet of the SLR blasted through the back of his head, flinging him on the damp grass.

It all started yesterday when a local informer pressed a slip of paper into an army officer's hand at 2 p.m. in Sopore. 'Message Army Camp Seeloo. Please go, Gund Brath. There is militants in the House of Haji Rahim Tantry. The house of sister (of) sarpanch Gund Brath.' Major Bhaskar of the 13 JAK Rifles, along with 20 jawans, rushed to the concrete-brick target house in the deserted village and had a preliminary cordon in place. Apprehending trouble, the villagers had fled their homes by noon yesterday. A J&K Newsline team, acting on late-night information, reached the village an hour before the first light today to report live the climax of the encounter.

'We issued appeals through the loud-hailer asking them to surrender,' said Colonel Jasbir Singh, commanding officer of the 13 JAK Rifles. 'The response was a hail of AK-47 fire accompanied by the throwing of grenades.'

The solid house, which was under siege by two rings of the army cordon, withstood the rifle fire from the security forces. Darkness was coming in fast, and the army decided to direct rocket fire on the house. The army arsenal, which included the Russian-made automatic grenade launcher, light machine guns, and rocket launchers, boomed through the night.

Frequent flares released by army mortars augmented the moonlight as the defiant resistance from the now-smoking house saw bursts of AK-47 fire and grenade attacks whenever there was a lull in the fire of the jawans.

Army rocket fire knocked the stuffing out of the house, and one militant fled the blazing hideout after midnight to take refuge in the adjoining house before crawling to his death.

With daylight, the army sent in a search team of 11 villagers from nearby Seeloo to check if any resistance remained. Shovels were used to sift the smouldering rubble, but the two bodies the army expected to find were not there.

The search was a macabre one. One jawan unearthed a charred spongy mass, which he stretched and smelt to verify if it was indeed a chunk of roasted human flesh. No such luck, though, for it turned out to be some oily organic matter.

'The other two militants that we had expected inside must have fled the house before the preliminary cordon was put in place,' explained Brigadier MPS Bajwa, commander of the 192 Infantry Brigade.

Badly burnt four AK-47s, a Chinese-made rocket launcher, and some grenades were retrieved from the remains of the house. One jawan suffered splinter injuries.

As the guns fell silent, Gund Brath resounded to the familiar calls of the hens, cows, and ducks who had a field day in the absence of their owners. It was an Orwellian animal farm. A half-empty plate of rice in a deserted house captured the plight of the locals, caught between two warring sides.

CHAPTER 8

Pandit Blood on the Safapora Snows

Kashmir was gloomy in February 1998, not just because of the greyish blanket of cold that enveloped the vale's countryside. It was the kind of seemingly still, depressing meteorology that protagonists in classic English novels unfailingly commented and complained about. But there was foul murder afoot in the Kashmir countryside. The solemn trees stood naked. The famed flames of the Chinar's autumnal leaves were long gone, and spring's verdant blush was still a couple of months away.

A big group of 10–12 foreign/local terrorists aided by four to five local OGWs[1] had massacred 23 pandits in Wandhama village a few days ago, on 25 January 1998. The victims included toddlers, and one baby left clinging to his mother's bloodied chest. Enjoying a firm grip on local intelligence and fully cognisant of the laxity of the Army's 5 Sector Rashtriya Rifles in the Wandhama area, the terrorists had struck with complete immunity that night.

1. Over-ground workers

They had been confident that there would be no Army presence in the Wandhama area at night, and they could carry out the massacre without any danger to themselves. The murderers had moved from room to room, shooting at all the inhabitants in the three to four pandit houses. Their aim was not to convert them to Islam at gunpoint but to kill and terrorise the entire state. There was no pandit left even to wail in Wandhama, save a boy, Vinod Dhar, who had hidden behind a pile of cow dung cakes and seen a psychotic serial murder movie playing out before his eyes. A movie that will not leave him till the time he goes to his own pyre.

The Wandhama massacre was one of several such killing sprees of the minorities that took place in Kashmir and south of the Pir Panjals in the Jammu region during that horrific phase of the 1990s and early 2000s.

The massacre on 25 January had left the Army embarrassed. The wanton butchery sparked a national outrage. It shook India to the core of its secular nationhood. A worried prime minister Inder K Gujral, along with his principal secretary, NN Vohra, flew down in a helicopter to Ganderbal on 28 January to take stock of the situation. The pandit massacre loomed as a major threat over promising signs of a return to normalcy. An elected state government was in place. The VVIPs, along with the chief minister, Farooq Abdullah, and the governor, General KV Krishna Rao (retired), joined the mourners at Wandhama on the same day. They were received at the Ganderbal helipad by the GOC, 8 Mountain Division, Major General JBS Yadava, Vir Chakra, whose formation's area of responsibility included the Wandhama village. There had been a lapse on the part of the Division's 5 Sector Rashtriya Rifles HQ—it had failed to keep the sensitive Wandhama village housing a significant and threatened minority under regular surveillance and patrolling.

'After briefing the dignitaries on the critical situation, I assured them that within a month, the Wandhama killers would be dealt with under the law of the land. True to that assurance, and within a month of the massacre, the Army had nailed 11 of the 12 terrorists responsible for the massacre,' recalled Lieutenant General Yadava.

The Wandhama massacre was no ordinary incident of terror and brutality; its execution lay at the centre of the ISI's[2] politico-strategic aims.

'The operational situation in Kashmir had changed and to the ISI's disadvantage because of relentless operations launched by the security forces. The state was fast returning to normalcy, and a freshly elected government under Farooq Abdullah was at the helm. 26 January was Republic Day, and the Winter Games at Gulmarg were to commence from 27 January, which would have signalled to the international community a robust return to normalcy in Kashmir. Hence the timing of the massacre on 25 January and that, too, in the VIP Assembly constituency of Ganderbal, which was the Abdullahs' pocket borough. The ISI was desperate to destabilise the valley and convey to the international community that the situation was far from normal and contradictory to the reassuring message the Indian Government wanted to convey by staging the Winter Games. So, to divert focus away from the continuous losses suffered by terrorists and portray a scenario where the government's writ did not run, the ISI executed the Wandhama massacre. The pandits were targeted as a means of ethnic cleansing and promotion of communalism. To the Kashmiri populace overall, the message was that it was the terrorists who were calling the shots. The operational instructions that I got after the Wandhama massacre from the 15 Corps Commander Lieutenant General Krishan Pal, with whom I spoke every evening, were to restore peace in the area and facilitate the elected government in carrying out its mandate. Based on his

---

2. Inter-Services Intelligence

instructions, I issued operational orders to 70 Infantry Brigade,' recalled Lieutenant General Yadava.

The first operational move initiated after the massacre by 8 Mountain Division HQ was to realign the area of responsibility of 5 Sector Rashtriya Rifles and 70 Infantry Brigade and get the latter formation to take charge of the Wandhama area. The 70 Infantry Brigade was a reserve formation for Ladakh's 3 Infantry Division and its permanent headquarters were at Khalsi, Ladakh. The brigade's primary orientation was towards the defence of far-east Ladakh. However, it had been pulled out by the then 15 Corps Commander Lieutenant General JS Dhillon and brought down to the valley in 1997 to plug gaps in the CI-Ops grid to the north of Srinagar. The Brigade was commanded by a daring and dynamic paratrooper officer, Brigadier RK Shivrain, who later retired as a major general.

The wheels of justice had begun to turn. Local informers working for the security forces tipped off the Army and pinpointed the location of the Wandhama terrorists. The murderers of the pandits were hiding in improvised structures of wood and polythene sheets and remote natural caves on the Safapora heights outside Ganderbal and just 3 km from Wandhama village. The terrorists would use goat tracks to come down from the heights at night and obtain food from the villages. The Safapora heights were a remote, hostile terrain where there was minimal human presence. There were many caves here where the terrorists could hide and monitor the situation below them without incurring a high risk of detection. The Wandhama massacre, according to the diaries and other documents seized from the killers later, was planned three to four months prior to its execution on the night of 25 January.

The stage was set for an extraordinary assault by the infantry troops in the Safapora mountains. The spilt blood of the pandits would be avenged in an epic battle in the high snows.

Outlining the operational plan for the Safapora heights, Yadava recalled the details from the briefing notes he preserves to date: 'It was a fantastic operation. Two columns of 3 Kumaon (Rifles) moved in from the east up the Krushanar, Middle Spur-Tragbal, and Baba Salehrishi area and climbed to the highest feature, Point 3297 (10,816 feet), from where the Kumaoni troops rolled down to the villages. Two columns of 9 Dogra moved in from the west after scaling to Point 3138 (10,295 feet) and then rolled down from there. When 9 Dogra was moving up Bodnar, Doodhnar, and Gujjarnar, it had come under fire from terrorists. Once the operation got underway, the terrorists broke radio silence, and we were able to pinpoint their location through electronic surveillance. The brigade's third battalion, 17 Bihar, was deployed in a huge cordon at the base of the heights. Two columns of the 13 Rashtriya Rifles (Kumaon Regiment), a battalion which was operating in the ORBAT[3] of HQ 5 Sector RR, was placed under the command of HQ 70 Infantry Brigade as a reserve element for *Operation Safapora*.'

By surprising the enemy with the least expected and most difficult approach to the caves in the high mountains, *Operation Safapora* foreshadowed the subsequent eviction battles of the Kargil War. The Army had faced setbacks during its initial frontal assaults on the Kargil bunkers in the summer of 1999 but found success when it reoriented its assault plans and executed them from the least expected and most difficult approaches to the Pakistani bunkers sited in the high and super-high altitudes. The 70 Infantry Brigade HQ moved back to Ladakh in late 1998 under the command of Chandigarh-based Brigadier Devinder Singh and was successful in executing an operational manoeuvre to evict the Pakistan Army from extensive and deep intrusions in the Batalik LoC Sector.

---

3. Order of Battle

'The operational plan for the Safapora assault was to climb to the highest points (Points 3138 and 3297) at night and then roll down onto terrorist hideouts from above. Initially, the CO, 3 Kumaon (Rifles), Colonel Sudhir Uppal, was not very enthused about the tactical salience of the operational plan, but I was convinced it would work. I offered Uppal that I would personally accompany him and the troops in their ascent to Point 3297. That offer settled his doubts, and although I did not accompany the troops up the mountains, the operation was launched with vigour and confidence. The troops of 3 Kumaon (Rifles) hit the terrorists at first light on 13 February 1998, and a battle raged in the snow of 4–5 feet as the latter tried to flee. Possibly, four escaped or were burnt alive in the caves while six terrorists were accounted for by 3 Kumaon (Rifles) and 9 Dogra,' recalled the Dehradun-based Major General Shivrain who commanded 70 Infantry Brigade during *Operation Safapora*.

Seven Harkat-ul-Ansar terrorists were nailed after being taken by surprise in the major operation launched by the 70 Infantry Brigade between 12 – 14 February. Four more of the Wandhama killers were brought to book in later operations. The assault teams had climbed up from the most difficult and unexpected routes and rolled down on the terrorists sleeping peacefully in the main cave with just one sentry on duty outside during that February 1998 operation. The other caves on the Safapora heights were systematically smoked out using Russian thermobaric weapons that sent flame balls of 1,000 degrees centigrade into the depths of the natural recesses, leaving scorched, unrecognisable remains of terrorists or unlucky wild animals inside. The fear of being burnt alive in a 'crematory fire' was a very real one for the terrorists holed up in the caves due to their jehadi beliefs. The army had calculated that the use of the thermobaric munitions would scare the living daylights out of the terrorists, and they would flee the caves and come into the open, where the troops would find it easier to nail them. To add to these thermobaric weapons were the Carl Gustav 84-mm rocket launchers that discharged high-explosive rounds into the cave depths. The caves became death traps for the terrorists, with the rocks fragmenting under the army's firepower and splinters flying inside with lethal effect. From the main cave that served as the terrorists' hideout, the army found a stockpile of rations that would have ensured that the terrorists could have subsisted for another 15–20 days.

After the 11–12 November 1997 encounter at Gund Brath village situated in the valley's plains, *Operation Safapora* lent me the maiden opportunity for live reportage of army operations in the high mountains. It would serve as a stepping-stone for my live reportage from the super-high altitudes of Kargil some months later.

Safapora turned out to be a reporter's voyage into absolute uncertainty. At about 4.30 p.m. on 13 February, the landline phone in my Srinagar office at Hotel Remano rang. It was the missive I had been waiting for ever since I had landed in Srinagar in October 1997. It was Lieutenant Colonel AK Ghosh, GSO 1 (OPs), at HQ 8 Mountain Division, Sharifabad.

'Vikram, your request has been granted to report army operations live. We are carrying out a massive operation on the Safapora heights ahead of Ganderbal to nail the killers of the Wandhama pandits. Please reach the HQ of 70 Infantry Brigade at Saloora at the earliest.'

There would be no army convoy to take me to Saloora from Srinagar. I donned whatever woollens I could after making a dash to my paying guest accommodation in Rajbagh and made Godspeed for the taxi stand at the TRC, Srinagar, which is situated on the river Jhelum. The taxi drivers, otherwise keen to make a quick buck in the tourist-forsaken valley, were not willing to budge an inch in the direction of Saloora, which lies ahead of Ganderbal. That area at night was reckoned by the locals as a hotbed of foreign terrorists coming down the infiltration route from the Kupwara

LoC to Bandipore and then to Ganderbal. The Ganderbal area was a staging ground for terrorists to further disperse to the Srinagar periphery or move down to South Kashmir. Terrorists were active at night in the deserted Ganderbal countryside while the Army withdrew its presence or put up ambushes at particular spots. For taxi drivers, a drive into Ganderbal was fraught with the risk of encountering the 'foreign mujahids'.

However, I was determined to reach Saloora, come what may. The risk to my life was a secondary consideration to me. I had grown up reading about the careers of war correspondents such as Winston Churchill, George Orwell, and Rudyard Kipling. The British had a long tradition of true-blue war correspondents who wrote eyewitness accounts from the trenches while facing bullets, shoulder to shoulder, with the soldiers. I wanted my writings to echo that distinctive character of war reportage on Indian battlefields. But on that cold, grey February evening, even getting to the Safapora fighting zone was a daunting challenge. My organisation had little interest in backing my ambitious forays into operational zones. It had not placed a committed taxi at my disposal or even offered to reimburse the fare when I took taxis into the Kashmir battlefields. My bureau chief in Srinagar had tight control on the army 'beat', and my arrival in Srinagar and proclivity for reporting operations live had not left her either particularly enthused or encouraged. It had been enough of a task for me to convince the Army to permit me into the operational epicentres. I was, thus, alone, working in a new, unfriendly zone and out on a very long limb when it came to live reportage of Kashmir battles. My parents back home in Chandigarh knew little of my reporting adventures. My father was afflicted with Pick's frontotemporal dementia (similar to Alzheimer's disease). My mother was a stoic lady who kept her fears bottled in her heart and diverted her concerns with rigorous readings of the scriptures. They could never have imagined what their son was venturing into. Fortunately, my reporting forays did not end up with my folks having to deal with a body bag from Srinagar. My father was spared the tragedy of shouldering a young son's remains from Kashmir to the pyre.

Out of the blue, an autorickshaw driver answered my prayers after I was turned down by each and every taxi driver at the TRC. Night had set in by now. The doughty fellow agreed to take me 21 km to Saloora in his rickety contraption. He was a squat man with a bullish physique, attired in a Kashmiri cap and sporting a trimmed beard. At the back of my mind, a vague suspicion arose but I glimpsed a purity of intention in his eyes. He was just a professional going about the task of earning his daily bread and willing to take an extraordinary risk in this case. But he had a price for that. I agreed to dish out a princely sum of ₹250 to him when my total monthly salary at the time was ₹10,000 with no extras and allowances thrown in. We had to drive through 21 km of deserted countryside before we reached the Saloora Brigade HQ. It was dark. We were like tiny fish navigating in a vast ink bottle. At times, I glimpsed the lights of passing villages. They glimmered like distant stars from a remote galaxy. Anything could have happened that night during that autorickshaw odyssey. No one would have heard our screams or shouts for help had the terrorists intercepted us on those deserted, broken roads where I did not come across a single vehicle in the 21-km stretch. The autorickshaw driver knew the precise route to Saloora. We did not exchange small talk on the way. It was grim business. Only the racket of the autorickshaw's engine broke the silence. We did not even comment on the prolonged spell of gloomy weather to relieve the tension. I did not mention the purpose of my surreal excursion. The pandit issue was a sensitive matter in Kashmir and I did not want an impassioned argument to derail my passage to Saloora. The autorickshaw driver, the thorough professional that he was, and true to the vocation of his life, never asked me a question. He was quiet, calm, and stoic. He might as well have been an army driver, manoeuvring his officer›s vehicle through a minefield.

I had driven through much of Kashmir as a child on family holidays in the summers of the 1970s and 1980s. We would drive through Ganderbal on our way to Kangan for trout fishing with my father's dear friend, Flying Sikh Milkha Singh. My father, Man Mohan Singh, was a poet, author, and a Punjab cadre IAS officer (1962 Batch). Back then, I could never have imagined that one day I would drive through this area in an autorickshaw, in such circumstances.

We reached Saloora safely. It was difficult to find villagers to guide us to the Brigade HQ as the streets were deserted. Soldiers bearing AK assault rifles rushed out from the Brigade HQ and surrounded us. Fortunately, they had been intimated of my arrival but were expecting some hotshot reporter in a swanky taxi, not someone in a humdrum autorickshaw. They were taking no chances. Terrorists could have surprised them by travelling in an autorickshaw. I settled their harsh, tense questions by showing them my ID card. I gave the autorickshaw driver a warm, grateful hug and paid his charges of ₹250. I hope to trace him down in Srinagar one day and shower on him all the gratitude and affection that has welled up in me all these years for his having ferried me through the devil's gate.

Terrorists would fire at night at the Army, so the Brigade HQ was deliberately very dimly lit. I was given a quick meal under a lantern's light in the tent housing the officers' mess. The meal was hosted by a gracious and sharp-witted Brigade Major (BM), Major M Indrabalan, who later played a heroic role during the Kargil War in the Batalik LoC Sector as the most forward and versatile of all the war BMs. He nearly made it to the esteemed rank of Lieutenant General and retired in 2023 as a Major General. He was not a regular infantry officer but had been commissioned into the Corps of Engineers. After a briefing by the BM at Saloora on the ongoing operation, it was time to depart to the battle site.

From Saloora, it was a drive of 12 km to the Safapora base, where the Brigade Commander had staged forward to monitor the operation on the spot. Major Indrabalan bundled me into an army QRT[4] of three vehicles with headlights off as there was the danger of terrorists firing Pika machine guns and RPGs or blasting the vehicles with IEDs[5] on those dusty, broken roads connecting villages to Safapora. The roads meandered along the mountains and were vulnerable to terrorists holed up in the forests and caves. To increase my safety, I was placed in the middle vehicle. The drive was extremely tense as we went slowly through the countryside without headlights, not knowing if bullets would break through the vehicles' non-bullet-proof exteriors or if the earth would heave us up in an IED/mine blast and leave our remains hanging on the gloomy trees. The two soldiers sitting with me in the back of the truck armed with assault rifles were silent; they were straining their eyes in the darkness to discern the danger of a lurking ambush. The reaction time in case of an ambush would be minimal, so the soldiers were focused on picking up any sign of danger at the very earliest. We were not on the hunt of my childhood days when we would beam a powerful flashlight on wild animals who could not strike back. We were the hunted now, driving in pitch darkness, and those hunting us could hit us hard. As a *shikari* in my childhood and youth, I had always felt courage had never been really tested while shooting down animals and birds, though I had a fair share of encounters with danger and death in the jungles of Punjab, Himachal Pradesh, and the Terai. Here, I was now hunting men, and those men could hunt me. This was true shikar; the other side had an equal chance of staging a surprise and

4. Quick Reaction Team

5. Improvised Explosive Devices

discharging formidable weaponry on us. I sat quietly through the jolts of the QRT drive to Safapora, not wishing to disturb the tense soldiers and distract them from the vigil. A stray dog ran across the dusty track as a fleeting phantom and I sensed the soldiers tense up. I carefully observed their body language and the way they held their rifles in anticipation of returning the fire in case of an ambush. It was an eerie feel of the nocturnal battle theatre of Kashmir. The QRT drive did not encounter an ambush, and we reached a point just off Safapora village. The Brigade Commander had set up an 'ops room' in a small hut. I was greeted by Brigadier RK Shivrain. My first glimpse of him was cast in the dim light of the hut. From the mountains above us, the periodic reverberations of assault rifles and machine guns firing into the night reached us. The dull boom of a rocket launcher would periodically intersperse the automatic fire. He was a handsome man, a paratrooper officer, and a gentleman from the old school. He struck me as one of those army officers of such bearing and pedigree that they effortlessly commanded the loyalty and obedience of men in battle. In that gloomy hut, Brigadier Shivrain could well have been an officer fighting India's first war over Kashmir in 1947–48. I learnt that his CO of 6 PARA in the 1970s was Colonel Balwant Singh Sandhu (retired). It was a small world indeed—Sandhu had been my father's childhood friend and an eminent mountaineer.

'Vikram, we will send you up the Safapora mountains at first light,' Shivrain told me, after explaining the ongoing operation on a map.

I retorted, 'Brigadier Shivrain, thank you. But I have not come here to drink soup with you. I am here to be with your fighting troops at the point of contact with the enemy on the Safapora heights. These are the orders of the 15 Corps Commander, who has cleared my reportage from the battlefront.'

Shivrain nodded silently, sensing the conviction and passion coursing through this young reporter's blood. I told the Brigadier:

'I go into the operation at my own risk. The Army bears no responsibility to my family. All I ask of you is to send my body back home or get me to a hospital if suffer injury.'

The Brigade Commander got onto the radio set with Colonel Bharat Khurana, the CO of 9 Dogra. He informed him that a reporter from *The Indian Express* would be joining his Dogra troops fighting on the Safapora heights that night to cover the battle in situ (live). A seven-man patrol of the 9 Dogra under a JCO[6] was summoned down from the Safapora heights to Shivrain's ops room. I bid adieu to Brigadier Shivrain and climbed the Safapora heights with the 9 Dogra patrol. It took us about 90 minutes to climb to the battle zone towering above the vale of Kashmir. I spent the night with the troops manning the cordon around the terrorists. A few *shakarparas* were shared with me by the battling soldiers. The night was an icy February one. A soldier lent me a thick jacket, which I draped over my knees as I took position with the troops behind the rocks. In the very distant night, the lights of a slumbering Srinagar tucked into quilts and warmed by *bukharis* winked invitingly at us. At the slightest *harkat* or movement, the detachment LMG next to me would loosen off a few bursts into the night. The troops were on high alert to prevent the terrorists from sneaking through the cordon and making their way further up the heights or sneaking down the nullahs to a hideout in the villages at the base of the mountains.

At 12.30 a.m., under a silvery moon, stones slipped and rattled. Something was coming down at us from the mountaintops. The rattling of stones perfectly matched a childhood memory. I recalled the hunts in the Shivalik foothill jungles when we would position ourselves in a ravine. Wild boars and barking deer flushed by beaters from their lairs would run down the ravines. The sounds of the stones displaced by their fearful hooves as they plunged

6. Junior Commissioned Officer

unwarily towards the hidden hunters were exactly the same as the ones I heard that night on the Safapora heights. It took a while for the Safapora mystery to unfold. The Dogra troops had picked up the movement, but they had evidently recognised it as of its own troops.

From the darkness, soldiers of the 3 Kumaon (Rifles) emerged wearing big, white snow boots. They were dragging down the *asli shikar* from their operational zone on the Safapora heights. The booty was the bodies of five Wandhama terrorists of the Harkat-ul-Ansar with ropes wound tight around their feet. The Kumaoni troops were in no mood to sling the bodies on their shoulders or put them on stretchers. The bodies sliding down the mountainsides on ropes held by the Kumaoni's had dislodged stones leading to those eerie sounds akin to 'ghosts riding down Safapora on horses'. The attrition of stone as they were pulled down hundreds of feet of bare mountain had stripped the terrorists of their winter clothing. Their stark-naked bodies glimmered in the silver moonlight. They only had shoes and socks on—a spectacle that would remain etched in my memory forever. I would once again see those naked bodies on 15 February at the media briefing at the Safapora base. But this time, white sheets enveloped their naked bodies. Their own clothes had been left in tatters and shreds on the descent from the Safapora heights the other night. The spirit of the murdered pandits could finally rest in some peace. A promise made to the prime minister of delivering swift retribution to the Wandhama killers had been kept by the Army.

After the night with the troops on the Safapora heights, the next day, on 14 February, I went further up with the troops of 9 Dogra's Charlie Company under the command of Major Rajesh Bhaskar, Sena Medal (who later retired as a brigadier). The task assigned to Charlie Company was to hunt down terrorists who had escaped above the snow lines. We trudged up the inclines the entire day in a tactical approach, scanning the mountainsides and ridges for fleeing terrorists. I was wearing a 16 kg bulletproof jacket to shield my chest and stomach and a similar *patka* helmet to shield my forehead. I realised what it meant to be a soldier lugging such cumbersome weights and fighting in the toughest terrain. We did not encounter the terrorists but were hit by a blizzard in the late afternoon. The winds were driving the snowflakes so strong that Major Bhaskar's cap and epaulettes flew off. We hugged the mountain sides to keep ourselves stable. The winds threatened to fling us off the mountains. There was no retreat for the troops due to the blizzard. Orders were orders. The task was to seek and destroy terrorists. So, our 9 Dogra search party proceeded in the blizzard, sticking to rocky outcrops and taking rest whenever the winds and driving snowflakes turned too aggressive. By the early evening, orders were relayed to Major Bhaskar on the radio set that I was to be sent down to Safapora with two soldiers accompanying me. The rest of the troops moved further up under Major Bhaskar but found no terrorist after that. Major Bhaskar courted success later when 9 Dogra was moved to the Drass LoC sector in the year 2000. He was awarded a Sena Medal for his bold recce of the enemy-held feature of Point 5353.

I was put up for the night of 14/15 February 1998, with the company commander of 13 RR, who was occupying a school building near Safapora. The next morning there was a press conference to be addressed by Major General Yadava. A huge contingent of media persons from Srinagar had been brought to Safapora in a convoy by then Army PRO, Major P Purushottam. It was a major briefing for the media as the terrorists killed were the killers of Wandhama. The Army was anxious to redeem its tarred reputation.

The bodies of the terrorists I had seen on the Safapora heights were put up for display along with the weapons recovered.

The media contingent included my *Express* bureau chief from Srinagar. Before embarking on his briefing to the media, Yadava told Purushottam that he was very keen to meet this journalist of *The Indian Express*, who had gone into the Safapora operation with the troops. I was, at that moment, speaking to Shivrain and the young 3 Kumaon (Rifles) officers who had fought the battles and writing down the minute details of the operation. I was summoned to the GOC's presence. He looked very carefully at me and offered me a warm handshake.

'I am very happy that you ventured with the troops and saw the challenges they face first-hand. We want more journalists like you,' Yadava told me.

I was left beaming with pride.

Back in Srinagar that evening of 15 February, I filed a brief, to-the-point news report of four to five paragraphs revolving around the fact that the main Wandhama killers had been shot by the Army on the Safapora heights. I had reserved my eye-witness account of the battle for a very detailed narrative as a Sunday features section story, which I submitted to the head office in Delhi within the next few days. The feedback that I got from Delhi was that my battle narrative had been liked immensely by the then-big boss at the *Indian Express* and that it would be published in the Sunday Magazine edition of the newspaper, which was circulated across India. That solemn assurance was never put to print by the Delhi *Express* office, and the blood-and-guts story of an operation in the high Safapora snows and the blow-by-blow account of the shooting down of the pandit murderers never saw the light of the day in the *Express* pages. Another story of mine had been killed by elements hostile to me in the *Express.* However, I had fortunately preserved the script in long-hand and written in ink on sheets of A4 size, white printing paper. The Safapora operation was a trailer to the Kargil battles that followed 15 months later. The armies of Western nations officially acknowledged the unrivalled valour and tactical acumen displayed by the Indian Army in the super high-altitude theatre of the Kargil War. Those tales of Kargil valour are well known to our countrymen also, but they should also know what lay behind the bland newspaper headline of 16 February 1998: 'Wandhama killers shot by Army'. The troops fighting unsung on the unknown Safapora heights had operated under extremely testing conditions of steep inclines and snow-bound terrain. I reproduce below verbatim the Safapora battle narrative that I have preserved and should have found publication in the *Express* 26 years ago:

❧

From Shock to Surprise, Army Avenged Pandit Massacre

The Army had set a life of 90 days on the killers of Wandhama's Kashmiri Pandits. It seemed well on track to keep its vow when it shot six Harkat-ul-Ansar militants in a 750-soldier, 48-hour operation that went sweeping up from the Valley's plains to the snowy peaks at 14,000-15,500 feet.

It was 8 p.m. on 25 January 1998, when the killers had entered the first Pandit house at Wandhama. Eighteen days later, at exactly the same time on 12 February 1998, troops of the 3 Kumaon (Rifles) under Colonel Sudhir Uppal were snaking up 5,000 feet in moonlight to ambush militant hideouts from the rear. At 8.30 p.m., 9 Dogra troops, under Colonel Bharat Khurana, were trudging up three nullahs to complete the encirclement of the terrorist hideouts. Meanwhile, the troops of 17 Bihar were placing a wide cordon around the base of the mountains where the terrorists were hiding.

The 70 Infantry Brigade had been tasked to track down the Wandhama killers and clean up the Ganderbal area. The Safapora Heights were just 3 km away from the ill-fated village of Wandhama. First contact was made by the Ghatak (Commando) platoon of 3 Kumaon under Lieutenant Paul. In the first light of dawn, at a height of 11,000 feet, stood 12 phantom-like figures in waist-deep snow. The appearance of 12 men at that height at the crack of dawn initially startled the lone sentry on duty outside the terrorist hideout. The first sighting blew the bugle for a battle waged over a few kilometres of snow, ridges and ravines.

The terrorists' sentry overcame his shock and rushed into the improvised shelter where four others were sleeping in comfort. The hut was constructed of logs and polythene sheets. There were potatoes and carrots for a meal cooked in 'Dhara' brand refined oil over a kerosene stove. There were custard powder and coconut biscuits for a sweet tooth and 'Liril' and 'Pears' soaps for warding off overpowering body odour. 'Colgate' toothpaste and toothbrushes for morning ablutions. Sleeping bags for comfortable snoring at those icy heights plus 'Vaseline' cream for warding off skin dryness.

Till now, the hideout had afforded a tactical advantage to the terrorists. They could monitor the movements of security forces in the Ganderbal area sprawling below the Safapora heights. Goat tracks were used at night to go down to the villages for procuring food. For some of these terrorists, it was the lure of women. But the tide was turning on them as the 3 Kumaon troops closed in on the hut.

From the hut, five terrorists rushed out and were armed to the teeth. They scampered for a passage over the peaks. They had been rudely woken from slumber and taken by complete surprise. They were not in a position to confront the Ghataks, who were a decidedly different proposition than the unarmed pandits they had slaughtered days back. The precise location of their hut hideout had been leaked by villagers acting as informers for the Army. The credible intelligence provided to the Army by the villagers proved a battle-winning factor.

The Ghataks opened fire initially at 300 m, pumping a fusillade of bullets at the fleeing terrorists from AK-47 rifles.

Sliding, running, and crawling through the snow, the Ghataks closed the gap to 50 m. Ducking behind trees and boulders, the two sides freely emptied magazines with the Ghataks also deploying LMGs. This fire was interspersed with the hurling of hand grenades, though the effect was dissipated due to the snow. What added a touch of the bizarre to the bloody battle at close quarters was the exchange of filthy abuses. Punjabi epithets were preferred by both sides. The exchange of abuses not only expressed the intense hatred between the adversaries but sharpened their killer instincts. The motivation levels in the Ghataks were at their peak in the theatre of the Safapora snows. Here, the adversaries were abusing each other in plain sight. It is not uncommon for terrorists and Army officers to exchange abuses over the radio sets by coming onto the same frequency.

The battle took a decisive turn when the fleeing terrorists were manoeuvred into a bowl-shaped ravine that ended in a drop of thousands of feet. By this time, Lieutenant Paul's Ghataks were joined by the platoons under the command of Lieutenant Manjit Singh Bhau and Lieutenant SK Singh, who had cordoned off the battle area. Peering over a rock face, Lieutenant Bhau saw below him the 'Captain' of the Harkat-ul-Ansar's death squad, the Al-Badr. He was firing the much-dreaded Pika General Machine Gun at Lieutenant Paul's platoon. The burst of fire from Lieutenant Bhau's AK-47 rifle tore through the side of the fair-skinned, light-bearded controller of foreign terrorist operations in the Ganderbal sector. The diary recovered later from the 'Al-Badr' Captain revealed complex coding systems and his address in Pakistan. And his revelatory entry: 'We have killed 23 kafirs (pandits) today.'

The dead 'Captain's' comrade lunged for the Pika and resumed fire on Lieutenant Paul's platoon. Lieutenant Bhau then undertook a daring action: he went sliding down the slope loosening off the last rounds of his rifle magazine before coming to a stop behind a tree stump, yards away from the unaware militant who was firing the Pika. The terrorist's feet were towards Lieutenant Bhau. The daring officer placed a hand grenade near the terrorist's feet and rolled away. The blast at such close quarters mangled the legs of the terrorist. The young officer then yanked the pin from another grenade to deliver the coup de grace.

The sun was advancing to its zenith on 13 February 1998 when three terrorists crossed a spur to the right of Lieutenant SK Singh's platoon. Havildar Bhagwat struck first in the battle of wits and quick reactions. The first of the three militants downed was the one who must have felt the bullet pass from armpit to armpit before the report of the rifle's fire reached his ears. He was, by then, spewing blood from his ear and nose. His two companions lugged him down 30 yards but left him thereafter with an AK assault rifle in his hands. The soldiers kept a safe distance and took potshots at what they assumed was a wounded, incapacitated terrorist. But he was dead and had been left as a decoy to delay the advance of the soldiers on the remaining two terrorists. Borrowing a 7.62 mm SLR[7] from one of the jawans, and one that packs a cannon punch, Bhagwat blew a hole the size of a cricket ball at the back of the terrorist's skull. The bullet had entered through the right eye by making a small hole, then tore and mangled through blood, tissue, and bone as it revolved at high speed, and finally exited from the back of the skull by tearing it open.

The two other terrorists did not last long after that. The Kumaoni soldiers shot one after tracking his blood trail. He had been shot through the stomach, and his spilling blood and innards had left a telltale red carpet strip on the snow. The last of the five terrorists shot by troops of the 3 Kumaon was crawling and slithering through the snow as a Kumaoni bullet pierced his chest. This wounded terrorist's last stand was upon the banks of a

7. Self-loading Rifle

snow-fed brook that he could not cross. He fired his last rounds and rifle grenades before a volley of fire brought the curtains down on another one of the Wandhama killers. The swathe of blood left in the wake of the fleeing quarry had finally come to an end in widening pools of blood. The terrorists lay still in the Safapora snow, the gunfire ebbed, and silence resumed its rightful reign over the mountains. Soon, the snowflakes would begin to fall and these etchings of blood, too, would fade into oblivion.

Darkness was creeping over the peaks as the weary Kumaoni soldiers settled into position in the Safapora heights. The deep nullahs in the distance reverberated with the fire of machine guns, rocket launchers, and thermobaric munitions targeted at the caves where the remainder of the terrorists were suspected to be hiding. The terrorists would use the night to make a desperate break from the cordon of 3 Kumaon and 9 Dogra. Huddled in blankets with a few dry *rotis*, water and jaggery balls, the soldiers peered into the inky darkness for signs of fleeing terrorists.

The last of the six terrorists was shot by troops of the 9 Dogra as he scampered out of a cave and made a beeline for the peaks. The cave was set on a steep cliff, with the darkness going several yards into the cavity. He did not get too far once he abandoned the cave.

From the diaries and documents recovered from the bodies of terrorists, the slain outlaws included a 'Captain' of the Harkat-ul-Ansar's Al Badr squad named Ali Shahir along with two other Pakistanis, Jameen Qaisarani and Sarjullah. The other three killed terrorists were local cadres of the Harkat-ul-Ansar. Shahir was the commander of the Harkat operations in the Ganderbal area. Four terrorists were believed to have escaped the cordon of the Safapora operation or had been burnt in the caves due to the firing of thermobaric munitions by the Army.

From the terrorists, one Pika general-purpose machine gun, six Kalashnikov rifles, eight hand grenades, six rifle grenades, and 20 days of rations were recovered.

CHAPTER 9

The Hunting of Armed Men

There is no hunting like the hunting of man, and those who have hunted armed men long enough and liked it, never care for anything else thereafter.

—Ernest Hemingway

The irrigation channels servicing the paddy fields of Kashmir's Gund Rahman village were quite unlike the shallow ones of the Punjab. As children, we would peer into the gurgling waters surging from tubewells into the shallow channels and take delight in spotting a bullfrog or a non-venomous water snake. Sometimes, the harmless snake would be bludgeoned by the burly Punjab farmer, much to the excitement of the children. The Kashmir channels were four to five feet deep and fed off the snow-melts brooks. They ran like trenches across the agrarian tracts and were as wide as a man's shoulders.

It was the end of January 1999, and I had long given up my passion for hunting defenceless wild birds and animals. I was in Kashmir's Gund Rahman village, on a hunt of armed men, those who could hit back very hard and enjoyed the advantage of surprise. They were more dangerous than the worst of the man-eating tigers. The Army was hunting for them by searching each room of this sprawling village. The initiative lay with the holed-up fugitives. They would open fire first. In those initial bursts of fire from assault rifles and Pika General Machine Guns, the Army usually suffered the bulk of its casualties. After that, the terrorist was as good as dead because he had given away his location by opening fire. If he opened fire in the darkness, the muzzle flash of his rifle barrel would give away his hideout.

The Army's 56 Mountain Brigade had laid siege over Gund Rahman village of Ganderbal tehsil outside Srinagar. It had been tipped off by an intelligence source that a group of Hizbul Mujahideen and Al-Badr terrorists had taken refuge in this village since the night of 31 January 1999 and were being sheltered by a section of its inhabitants. Three infantry battalions operating under the command of HQ 56 Mountain Brigade had cordoned off the village that night to ensure the terrorists could not escape. The first gunfire contact that night with the terrorists was made by troops of the 15 Assam, but the Army could not secure a kill in the darkness. The stage was set for a systematic search of the village from the dawn of 1 February till the last light of 3 February.

I was granted permission by HQ 8 Mountain Division to report the operation 'live', and I reached Gund Rahman on the morning of 1 February after a 40-minute drive from Srinagar. All the villagers had been herded into a huge group. I saw the troops systematically check their identity cards to ensure no terrorist dumped his weapon and slipped the Army dragnet by posing as a villager. Gund Rahman was described by the Army officers as a 'difficult' village, for it would offer the 'mujahids' the hospitality of food and a warm bed. Not a single tongue would wag before the Army and betray the terrorists' presence and hideout locations.

The Army officers had sensed from the villagers' glib denials that a long and hard search of each of the 200 houses of Gund Rahman lay before them.

The Army operation required that the villagers be moved out of their homes so that the terrorists would be isolated like fish gasping for breath out of water. Also, the cordon-and-search operation would be severely hampered if villagers were roving around as troops went about their arduous tasks. The troops would move from house to house, haystack to haystack, woodpile to woodpile, cow shelter to cow shelter, and closet to closet. If villagers were present during the search, they would form crowds and obstruct the troops, shield the terrorists and even suffer collateral damage in the crossfire. So, when the troops went in for the search operation, it was only them in uniform and a specially picked search party of villagers, who came to be infamously known as 'human shields'. Once all the villagers had been removed following announcements from the mosque, the logic was that it left only terrorists inside the village and presented a clear, unambiguous target for the Army's search teams. The troops were searching ready with a hair-trigger response, and there would be no time to verify a target before opening fire. The one who fired first won the round in the close-quarter battles conducted in the built-up areas of Kashmir.

On the first day of the operation at Gund Rahman, I was met by the Brigade Commander, Brigadier Amar Nath Aul, UYSM (who later retired as a Lieutenant General). None of us knew that in just three months, his brigade would be moved overnight to Drass to fight the epic battles of Kargil. Brigadier Aul was a man given to circumspection when it came to the media. He was not enthused by the idea of my going into the inner cordon where the troops were in contact with the terrorists. He had never seen this kind of reportage in his career. He had positioned himself on the fringes of the outer-most of the three cordons the troops had placed around Gund Rahman. The posse of Kashmir media persons, mostly photojournalists working with the Srinagar dailies, were being briefed by him outside the cordons. He expected me to join their company, but I politely told him that my purpose was to be with the frontline troops. He eventually had to assent to my entry into the inner cordon of the battle zone as I had the clearance from the HQs of 15 Corps and 8 Mountain Division. He summoned a bulletproof jacket for me. I was handed a black scarf to place under the bulletproof *patka* helmet. I bid him adieu and reached the search parties, moving from house to house.

I had been with the troops searching the Gund Rahman houses fruitlessly for about 90 minutes. There was no sign of the terrorists. An eerie, uneasy silence hung over the village. Not a rooster crowed, or a cow mooed. I could not even spot an inquisitive village dog. And, then I saw Brigadier Aul stride into the village. Under the operational safety protocols, the Brigade Commander normally does not enter the inner cordon as he leaves the hazardous task to the battalion officers and troops. The Commander's task is to conduct the battle from a safe vantage point and exercise command and control keeping in mind the operation's larger picture. The battle situation can change and evolve rapidly.

Yet, Brigadier Aul had been unable to contain himself after seeing me off into battle. He strode into the village surrounded by his security detail comprising 20 troops of the 18 Grenadiers (the battalion that won Kargil's Tiger Hill in July 1999 along with 8 Sikh). He joined me, and after a brief exchange on how the operation was proceeding, we went down the narrow streets of Gund Rahman. The morale of the troops rose as their Commander was with them, keeping an eye on the operation from ground zero and leading from the front. It was a gamble, and a hazardous one, that Brigadier Aul had taken by entering the operation.

As we entered a street that had the village mosque on the right side, we immediately came under fire from assault rifles. The terrorist/terrorists had cunningly hidden in the religious shrine to exploit its sanctity. We pressed ourselves close to the walls on the left side of the street and opposite the mosque. The volleys of fire missed us and struck the walls above us. The troops retaliated immediately with bursts from their automatic rifles. There was a locked barber's shop right next to where Brigadier Aul and I had taken cover. We were ringed by the burly Grenadiers in a semi-circle. But we were still in the open, and the Brigade Commander's life was a very important one. The Grenadiers acted swiftly. They broke the lock of the barber's shop with their rifle butts and pushed us both inside into a dank, dark room where we could barely make out the outlines of the shop's interiors. Some of the Grenadiers also came inside the shop with us. It was an eerie room of mirrors as the firing went on outside. The door was banged hard on us by the rest of the Grenadiers, who took up position outside the barber's shop. By firing at us, the terrorist/terrorists had given away his/their positions. He/they fled the mosque soon after as he/they wanted to escape the increasing retaliatory fire and tightening cordon. After 15–20 minutes in the barber's shop, we came outside after the Grenadiers gave the signal that all was clear.

Brigadier Aul's security detail escorted us to a safer location in the village outskirts and, within 20 minutes, came up with tea for both of us, served in dainty white cups on a tray! They also served us apple slices in another tray. From where they had quickly conjured these goodies in the middle of the battlefield defied comprehension. Brigadier Aul savoured the tea and apples without batting an eyelid and left the village. I went back to the troops who were searching the houses.

Bursts of assault rifle fire again broke Gund Rahman's deceptive silence. The troops had nailed the first of the terrorists. He was a young, bearded man who had slithered into an irrigation channel running through the houses on the periphery. He had taken position by lying flat on his back with his AK assault rifle on his chest. He was shot in that very position by alert troops before he could initiate the exchange of fire. I saw him lying there with his rifle at rest across his chest, blood oozing like fresh, gurgling springs from multiple bullet hole entry marks on his upper body. He looked strangely peaceful in death, like a tired peasant from a Van Gogh pastoral painting who had settled for a nap in the channel to avoid the searing sun. The first of the man-eating tigers of Gund Rahman was down.

The irrigation channels coursed through the rice fields and ran along the village periphery. Armed men could lie flat on their backs inside the channels that virtually served as trenches in such encounters. They were effectively sheltered from ground-level fire. Anyone who poked his unwary head into the channels was in danger of being shot by an armed man lurking inside. During the Gund Rahman encounter, blood flowed in the channels, not water. The channels traditionally irrigated tonnes of rice to service the staple Kashmiri food of *goshtaba* (minced mutton balls). But in a vale torn asunder by conflict since 1989, the channels would periodically transform into the trenches of a proxy war.

Nearing dusk, the same day, a section of troops of the 1 Naga led by a subedar extended the search to the outhouses in the fields of Gund Rahman. I was with them. A small hut loomed in sight at a distance from the village. The troops sensed it was worth a search because, throughout the entire day, they had managed to shoot only one terrorist from a group of six. Where were the other five? Proceeding in a tactical approach, we were about 35–40 yards away from the hut. The search party that I was accompanying did not have a civilian search party or 'human shields' to search the hut before the troops entered. I was with the subedar, and we were inching towards the house in fading light, taking cover of whatever tree or ground contour was available. A window opened halfway in the hut. Kashmiri houses and huts have multiple windows, and a terrorist commands the advantage of a first-fire initiative from any of the windows that he determines will lend him a tactical advantage. This terrorist was not the standard one equipped with an AK assault rifle.

All of a sudden, the air around us was cut into ribbons. The clear, decisive sounds of Pika (a belt-fed general machine gun) fire from the window exploded like firecrackers. The air around me buzzed with flying projectiles like angry hornets going 'whizz, whizz'. The further one is from the point of discharge of a bullet, the less one hears the explosion of gunpowder that releases projectiles down the rifle/machine-gun barrels. The target hears only the whine of projectiles whizzing by. If he hears them, it is good! Even though I was wearing a heavy bulletproof jacket and patka, there were too many parts of my body that were vulnerable to the Pika fire from such a range. The legs, neck, face, arms, shoulder and a part of the forehead were not protected by bulletproof gear.

'*Saheb*, dive into the ditches (irrigation channels). The terrorist has opened fire at us with a Pika,' the subedar shouted at me.

I needed no prodding. We were in the open and exposed to a high rate of fire. Contrary to popular notions and filmy depictions, when fired upon in a surprise attack, troops do not stand up and bare their chests. They scamper for the nearest cover to save their lives and choose the right moment later to retaliate. Or lie low till the danger has passed. The Pika can strike at ranges beyond 1,000 m. Most of the well-equipped terrorist modules operating in Kashmir had a Pika in their armoury. The Pika was also an infantry battalion weapon for the Pakistan Army and was deployed to deadly effect from the machine-gun slits of bunkers dominating the Kargil heights in the summer of 1999.

I ducked and sprinted in as low a crouching posture as my spine could manage to the very inviting channel 15 yards away to our right. We dived headlong into the channel and were soon bunched together, keeping our heads well down. Luckily, we did not suffer a casualty in the opening Pika bursts because the channel was close at hand, and the terrorist's hand was not that steady on the Pika. Firing automatic weapons accurately and avoiding needlessly long bursts is a professional art. The terrorist continued to fire but stopped, realising his quarry was safe in the 'trench'. If he wanted to survive, then he had to flee that outhouse at the earliest, as he had exposed himself by opening fire with the Pika. He knew the army was out there in great strength.

It was nearing darkness, and we stayed put in the channel. The Naga troops were alert to the contingency of terrorists advancing towards the channel and firing bursts down at us. But the Pika-wielding terrorist did not seem inclined towards prolonging the encounter with us. The subedar then ordered the troops to start inching their way towards safety. He was a seasoned man and realised that if his troops attempted an encirclement of the outhouse that night, there would be casualties in the darkness. We crawled in the channel for a few hundred yards, came out, and made our way cautiously to the safety of the Army's outer cordon placed around Gund Rahman in the agricultural fields. The outer cordon was manned by troops of the 15 Assam, a battalion that had recently de-inducted from its tenure in the Siachen Glacier and had been placed under the command of 56 Mountain Brigade in the valley. It would soon leave the valley and move to a peacetime cantonment for a well-deserved rest and refit. I drove back to Srinagar in my Maruti 800 that night to return before dawn the next day when the troops would again commence searches of the houses. At night, the Army's search parties withdrew from the village, and troops placed a tight cordon around it so that the holed-up terrorists could not escape under the cover of darkness. Through the night, the troops of 15 Assam would fire speculative, probing bursts of LMGs into the village at the slightest sign of movement so as to keep the terrorists pinned down in the village and pre-empt an escape.

The narrow escape from the Pika terrorist in the outhouse that evening had underlined the criticality of civilian search parties for Army operations. I was forbidden from taking a camera into the Kashmir operations as there were sensitive aspects to the Army's on-ground methods of dealing with terrorists embedded within hostile populations. The vexed issue of 'human shields' was one of them. Their use in warfare attracted trenchant criticism from the Kashmir media and human rights organisations. The Army's logic was that a holed-up terrorist would not shoot a civilian searching the house. The 'human shields' would exit each house and reveal to the Army where precisely the terrorist was hiding. If they were to lie to the Army, they faced terrible consequences. There have been deaths of these 'human shields' in encounters, attributed later to 'civilians caught in crossfire'. Some civilians searching houses at the Army's behest have been caught in the fire unleashed by the terrorists on troops. On occasion, the Army even described them as 'volunteers' in the operations, but certainly, that was stretching it too far. The work of 'human shields' searching houses as a precursor to the troops' entry was hazardous in the extreme. If we had a search party or 'human shields' accompanying us that evening, the fate of the terrorist could have been very different. The 1 Naga troops would have stood at a safe distance and sent the civilians into the hut first.

I reached Gund Rahman the next day, much before dawn. The fallow fields, aching with the pain of winter, bore a layer of ice. I joined the troops and officers of 15 Assam. I was waiting for the troops of 1 Naga and 25 Rajput to enter the village once the light got better. As the officers of 15 Assam recounted tales of their tenure in the Siachen Glacier to me, the troops were firing LMGs continuously into the village. I left the 15 Assam outer cordon and joined the search parties. But that day—2 February 1999—went without a fire contact with the hiding terrorists. Not a bullet was exchanged in back-breaking searches throughout the day. Would such an effort find mention in the media, ever? What to say of the media, the Army itself has based its CI-Ops system of awards and promotions on the number of terrorist kills and weapons recovered.

I repeated my routine the next day, 3 February, reaching Gund Rahman from Srinagar before dawn. By mid-day, the troops located another terrorist and search parties of the 1 Naga and 25 Rajput encircled the house in which the terrorist was hiding. A barely visible black AK rifle barrel peeped out of a window and opened fire at the rate of 60 rounds a minute. The bullets sent soldiers and officers standing a mere 15 yards away, diving and pushing for cover as hell broke loose. Troops from all directions opened fire on the house. Frantic orders and yells from officers and JCOs for control punctuated the firing as soldiers next to the house were in real danger of being shot in the crossfire. No one knows who is firing and from where in such situations. The enemy's bullets can pop out of the proverbial closet while the troops are on a hair-trigger response. This is a complication encountered frequently in close-quarters combat in built-up areas where a density of troops under different commands has been tasked to target a handful of armed desperados who could be hiding just about anywhere.

Along with troops of the 1 Naga, I rushed into a house which shared a common wall with the one in which the terrorist had taken position. We climbed the staircase and entered the loft of the house. We lay flat and slithered across the wooden floor to peer down into the adjoining house from the triangular openings in the loft. I saw the terrorist right opposite in the other house looking up at us through a window. He opened fire at us, and the assault rifle bullets went screaming through the low, sloping roof of the loft. In the first few moments under fire, one hardly realises where the bullets are striking. The wooden loft got chipped with the bullets. The troops retaliated with seven or eight Naga soldiers discharging bursts from their assault rifles at the window from where the terrorist was firing. The terrorist ducked and retreated into the depths of the house, and we could no longer see him.

Around those two Gund Rahman houses, there was an uproar. There was shouting, firing, and abuses directed at the terrorist. We, in that loft facing the terrorist's direct fire, soon came under fire from the left flank of the house. It was from troops of the 25 Rajput or what is called 'friendly fire'. Casualties to troops from 'friendly fire' are not that rare in such encounters. There were such mishaps in the Kargil War, too, when Indian Artillery shells and IAF bombs fell in the wrong spots on the steep, narrow ridges and nullahs and struck their own troops. The 1 Naga troops with me used all the lung power at their disposal and interspersed it with some choice army regulation abuses: 'O *bhaiyon*, stop the firing! It is us in the house. You will kill us!'

The sheepish Rajput troops stopped firing in our direction. They had not seen who was firing and from where. It was a perfect melee. The Rajput troops had assumed that the firing in the general area of the loft was from the terrorist, and they had pressed their triggers in that direction. It was a close call, caught as we were in the crossfire of the terrorist and the troops of the 25 Rajput. In close-quarter combat, no one resorts to the 'doctrine of no first use'!

Once the troops of 25 Rajput were clear as to the specific house in which the terrorist was hiding, the crossfire stopped, and a measure of control was restored. The target was left literally doddering on its foundations with troops opening fire on it with infantry battalion support weapons in the guise of the 84-mm Carl Gustav rocket launcher (meant for knocking out tanks in conventional warfare) and the Automatic Grenade Launcher (AGL). The civilian search party or 'human shields' were sent into the house after that to locate the terrorist's body among the rubble and smouldering ruins. We waited outside the house, waiting for news of a sure kill. After about 30 minutes, the civilians came out running, ashen-faced. There was no body or wounded terrorist in the ruins. Incredibly, the terrorist had survived the heavy pounding and had jumped into the next house and then the next one like a monkey skipping across gardens. Terrorists were known to be nimble in built-up Kashmir areas. Their lives were dependent upon it. Surrounded by regular infantry troops, outgunned and outnumbered, their only chance of escape lay in luck and a Houdini-like agility to escape when under fire.

Their quarry had, once again, escaped. It was the third day of the search, and the Army had only one kill to show for the Brigade-level operation. With a sense of apprehension, the soldiers turned to search the haystacks dotting the courtyards of houses. They had to remove every bale in case the terrorist had burrowed deep into them. No army officer wanted the terrorist to escape by hiding in the haystacks, but no one wanted a repeat of the incident of November 1998 when a Pakistani terrorist had jumped out of a haystack and shot two soldiers. The lofts in the houses, stacked with firewood and cattle feed, had to be painstakingly dismantled and dislodged from the roof. The memory of the disaster in a Budgam village was fresh when a terrorist burrowed deep in the firewood stacked in a loft had opened fire, killing an army jawan and two civilians searching the loft.

It was late afternoon of 3 February. The troops had been in a constant operational mode, either searching for the elusive 'needles' or manning the three cordons around Gund Rahman. Fatigue had set in, and troops were of the view that the rest of the six terrorists had somehow escaped. And then, there was a dramatic finale to the flagging search operation.

Motivated by their officers and inspired by the presence of Brigadier Aul in the periphery of the operational zone that afternoon, the troops renewed their searches with vigour. It was the last shot at finding the elusive 'man-eaters' of Gund Rahman.

Search parties went through an isolated and inky dark hut. They were searching for a long-haired Pakistani terrorist who had been glimpsed in the village, engaging in 'shoot and scoot' guerilla warfare tactics. They reckoned that by now, he must have run out of ammunition. But they missed him. The troops hurried on, for they had another 50 houses to search before sundown on 3 February. Burrowed neck-deep in *bukhari* coal in that inky-dark hut with another sack to conceal his head was Idris Khan, code Saifullah, an IED bomber armed with an AK-47 rifle, four full magazines, grenades, and an automatic pistol.

Luck finally ran out on Saifullah. A civilian searcher sent back into the same inky dark hut ran his hand over the coal stack. The hand encountered a bunch of shaggy hair. He ran out to alert the troops. Within no time, more than 150 troops threw a noose around the house before bombarding it with an automatic grenade launcher. A daring CRPF[1] officer deployed with his contingent at Gund Rahman had joined the search. He volunteered to deliver the coup de grâce. The Army troops carry IEDs with them in search operations like the one at Gund Rahman. These are wrapped in innocuous-looking white cloth. The CRPF officer sprinted to the window of the hut and chucked in the IED. The blast was volcanic. The hut's tin roof was hurled high into the air and, on its descent, settled on the top of a poplar tree next door. It was an unforgettable spectacle—the oddity of a rusty tin roof wobbling on the top of a tall tree bearing faintly-lime leaves. It symbolised what violence had done to the quaint and idyllic pastoral life of Kashmir—how green was my valley once. The body of Saifullah was pulled out of the rubble at 5.45 p.m., 3 February 1999. Following this, the Gund Rahman operation was terminated as darkness set in that day. Two terrorists had been killed, and the rest had escaped. Rounds running into the thousands had been

1. Central Reserve Police Force

expended. The army had been supported in the outer cordons by the police, CRPF, and the BSF.[2] A logistical exercise that ran into lakhs of rupees for the skins of two desperadoes trained cheaply by Pakistan to engage and bog down a formidable conventional formation.

None of the Gund Rahman villagers had tipped off the Army on the hiding places of the terrorists and had lied consistently to the last man, woman, and child. 'We have not seen any mujahid,' was the standard refrain. Yet, two bodies lay at their doorsteps, which they could not account for.

In a different search operation in Yangoora village in March 1998, some villagers had gone a step further. Some women had locked the house from outside and told the soldiers it was empty. A cynical Lieutenant SK Singh of the 3 Kumaon (Rifles) had broken open the door to be greeted with a hail of fire from four terrorists inside. He was lucky. He got away with three bullets in the shoulder. It took him years of convalescence to recover from those wounds inflicted by the deception of the locals.

My live reportage of the Gund Rahman encounter was confined to the JK Newsline supplement of the Jammu & Kashmir edition of *The Indian Express* on 8 February 1999, under the headline: 'Ultras elusive as needles, death in every haystack for jawans'. The story was not carried in any other edition of the *Express* across India. The published report had no mention of my personal experiences during the Gund Rahman encounter. In fact, I wasn't even sure it would be published so I heaved a sigh of relief when it was carried in this limited edition. The Gund Rahman encounter story was run by the *Express* with a blurb: ‹Live from firing line. That was a bonanza under the circumstances and a

2. Border Security Force

cause for a quiet celebration. Given the hostility towards me in the top echelons of the *Express*, the report could easily have been 'killed', as is the parlance in newspaper circles for not carrying inconvenient stories. My Delhi boss was not keen to build my profile as a pioneering frontline correspondent. Hence, my live reportage from Kashmir's firing lines would not be showcased in all the *Express* national editions.

◂ *Remains of an animal that was eaten by the Pakistani soldiers at Point 4812. (Photo by the author)*

War Correspondent Vikram Jit Singh (the author) climbing to the Khalubar Ridge, Batalik, from the Tactical HQs of 70 Infantry Brigade at Ganasok, Batalik on 7 July 1999. (Photo by Major M Indrabalan) ▾

▴ *The author in a bunker previously occupied by Pakistan Army's Captain Qamar of the 5 NLI, the Point 4812 intrusion post commander. (Photo by Major M Indrabalan)*

Right to left: The author, Major M Indrabalan, Colonel VS Bhalothia and troops of the 12 JAK LI in a stone bunker at Point 4812. ▸

The Tricolour and the JAK Light Infantry's Regimental Standard flutter proudly atop Point 4812. The author with the victorious troops and officers. (Photo by HQ 70 Infantry Brigade)

The author in a tricky spot on the treacherous, western cliff face of the Khalubar ridge (15,700 ft), and coming under fire from Pika UMGs and RPGs from Pakistan Army soldiers lodged on the flanking Kukarthang ridge. (Photo by Major M Indrabalan)

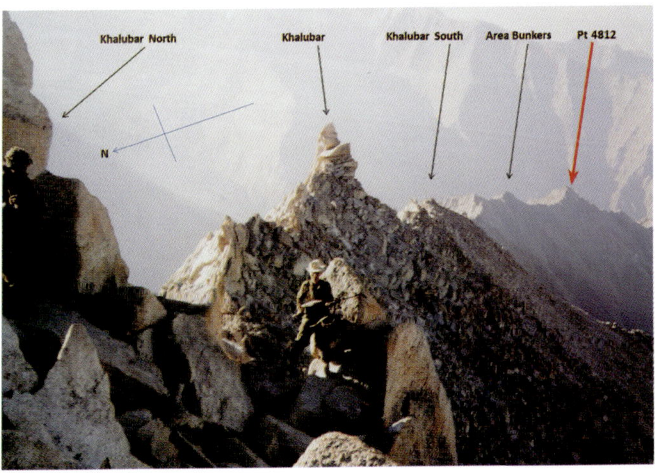

The red arrow points to the steep western cliff face of the Point 4812 on the Khalubar ridge. (Photo by Lieutenant Colonel Amul Asthana)

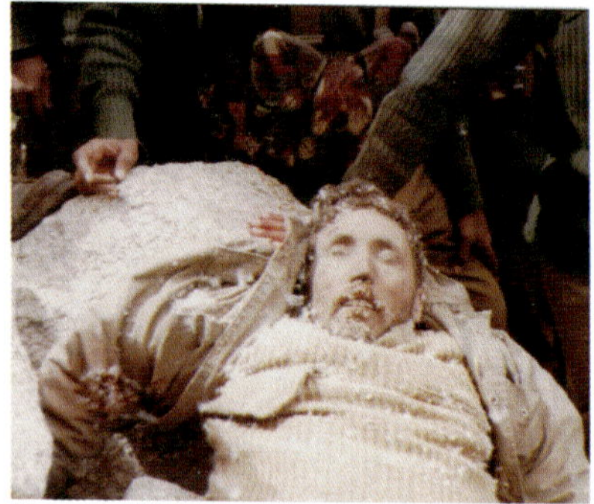

An unidentified dead soldier of the Pakistan Army's 5 NLI is taken up for burial in an improvised grave of stones by soldiers of 12 JAK LI at Point 4812, Khalubar Ridge, Batalik, on 7 Jul 1999. (Photos by the author)

Soldiers of 12 JAK LI stand in silent homage with bowed heads at the graves of enemy soldiers at Point 4812, Khalubar Ridge, Batalik, on 7 July 1999. (Photo by the author)

Soldiers of the 13 JAK Rifles buried 7 Pakistani soldiers of the 12 NLI at Point 4875, Mashkoh, on 16 July 1999. (Photos by AP)

Lieutenant Rishi Singh dispersing ashes of Captain Jintu Gogoi on Kaala Pathar (16,165 ft), Batalik, during the war in July 1999. (Photo by Major P Rajnarayan)

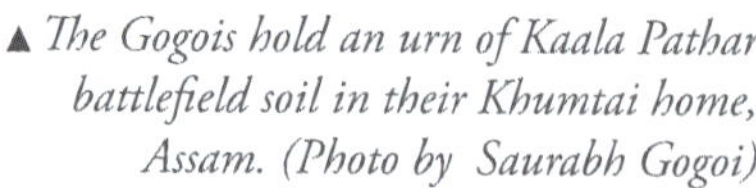

▲ *The Gogois hold an urn of Kaala Pathar battlefield soil in their Khumtai home, Assam. (Photo by Saurabh Gogoi)*

A red 'matka' holding Captain Jintu Gogoi's ashes dispersed on Kaala Pathar during the War. (Photos by Major P Rajnarayan)

Delphinium brunonianum blossoming at the Kargil battlefield of Gun Hill—Point 5140. (Courtesy Indian Army)

Yellow roses bloom over a stream of Tololing nallah, Drass, in July 2019. (Photo by the author)

Rhodiola tibetica blossoming at the Kargil battlefield of Gun Hill—Point 5140. (Courtesy Indian Army)

On return from World War I, Lieutenant Colonel George Cantlie with Celia in Montreal, 1917. (Photo from the Elspeth Angus Collection)

A letter that the author wrote to his fiancée, Hemani, from Kargil along with flowers on 26 May 1999. (Photo by the author)

Flowers sent in a letter to Celia by Lieutenant Colonel George Cantlie from the French front, 1916. (Photo by the Canadian War Museum)

◂ *The author with Kargil veterans of 2 Raj Rif, Subedar Surendra Kumar and Havildar Rajinder Singh, KC, during the commemorative climb to Tololing, 6 July 2019. (Photo by Arpit Seth)*

◂ *The author with Lieutenant General YK Joshi, 14 Corps Commander, on Tololing Top, 15100 ft, on 6 July 2019. (Photo by Arpit Seth)*

▴ *The temple maintained by the 12 JAK Rifles at Tololing Top (15,100 ft), July 2019. (Photo by the author)*

▴ *The Tricolour flutters proudly atop Tololing (15,100 ft) on 6 July 2019. (Photo by the author)*

The author interviewed Rifleman Shikher Choudhary of the 2 Raj Rif on Tololing Top, 6 July 2019. ▼

▲ *What was the handkerchief doing around the Pakistani neck? Was it the handiwork of the famous Gurkha khukri? Battle for Khalubar ridge, Batalik, 5 July 1999. (Photo by Lieutenant Colonel Amul Asthana)*

▲ *The author with his Maruti 800 car and journalist Khursheed Wani in Srinagar, March 1999.*

▲ *An assault rifle casing from Jaggerpora encounter, August 1998.*

The author with Naib Subedar Ganesh Pradhan of the 1/11 GR in July 2019. Pradhan had cut the head of a Pakistani soldier with his khukri during combat in July 1999 on the Khalubar ridge after he ran out of bullets. ▼

▲ *Hooker's irises blooming next to the abandoned Pakistani bunker at Point 4355 (14,288 ft), Mashkoh, on 5 July 2019. (Photo by the author)*

The author with 70 Infantry Brigade Commander Brigadier RK Shivrain after Operation Safapora on 15 February 1998. ►

▲ *Lance Naik Kripal Singh of the 17 Garhwal Rifles with his wife Vimla Devi and son before the Kargil War.*

▲ *The naked bodies of the terrorists covered with white sheets on 15 February 1998. They were responsible for the massacre of 23 Wandhama Pandits in January 1998. (Photo by HQ 70 Infantry Brigade)*

Brigadier Amul Asthana's sketch with his hand-written note inscribed at the bottom depicts donkeys ferrying computer, generator and diesel during Kargil War to the battlezone of Yaldor.

The red arrow points to a Pakistani bunker in a war-time sketch done by a subedar of the 1/11 Gurkha Rifles to pinpoint location for direction of artillery fire.
Courtesy Brigadier Amul Asthana (retired)

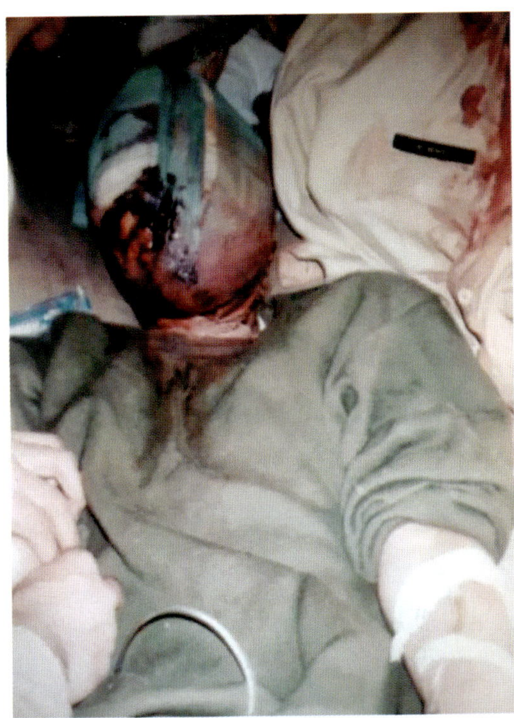

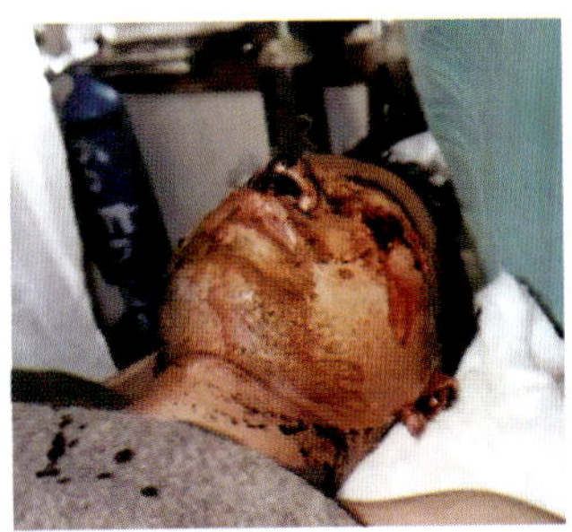

Captain Rommel Akram, Sitara-e-Jurat, 6 NLI, just after an Indian sniper round pierced his left cheek and exited from his left earlobe. Rommel with the scar left by the wound just after the Kargil War in September 1999 (below).

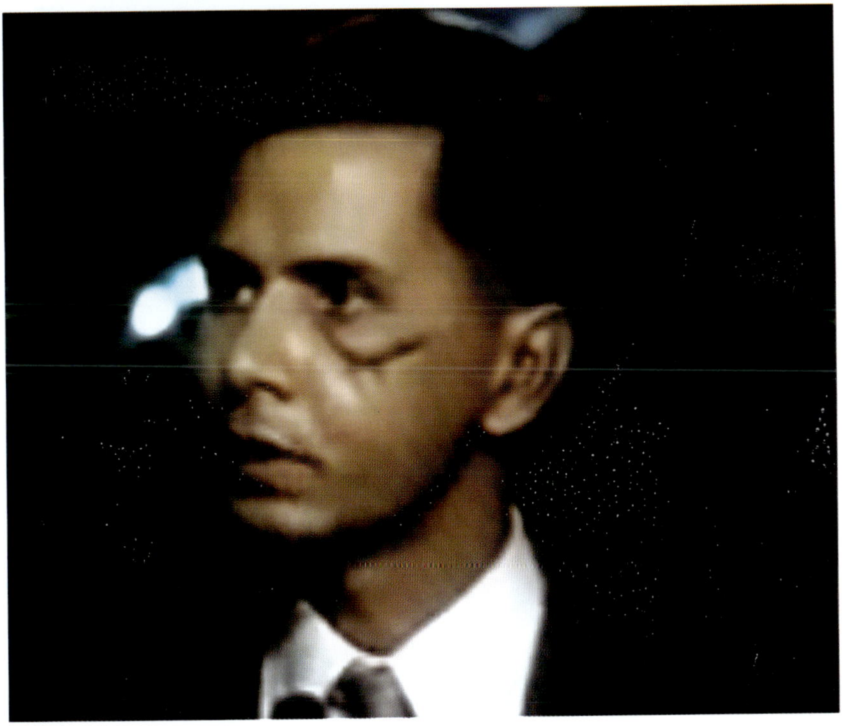

Pakistan Army COAS General Parvez Musharraf with (from left) Lieutenant General Aziz Khan, Major General Javed Hassan, Lieutenant Colonel S Amjad Shabir, Brigadier Masood Aslam and Lieutenant General Mahmud Ahmed after flying 3 kms across the LoC in the Mashkoh Sector on 28 March 1999. (Courtesy Brigadier S Amjad Shabir)

Pakistan Army COAS General Parvez Musharraf with Lieutenant Colonel S Amjad Shabir and Major General Javed Hassan across the LoC. Musharaf stayed the night with the intrusion troops of the 12 NLI. (Courtesy Brigadier S Amjad Shabir)

Pakistan Army COAS General Parvez Musharraf with Lieutenant Colonel S Amjad Shabir (to his right) and Major General Javed Hassan (to his left) in Indian territory, 3 kms across the Mashkoh LoC. (Courtesy Brigadier S Amjad Shabir)

Photograph of small lake in Indian territory across the Drass LoC. It was taken by one of the recce patrols of the 6 NLI in October1998 to survey features for exploitation in the coming winter. It was used as a landmark on the map and ground to ensure that the recce party's assertions were correct. (Photo by Captain Rommel Akram)

Photographs of the ascent to Point 5353 on the Indian side of the LoC in the Drass sector which was taken by one of the recce patrols of the 6 NLI in October 1998. The Pakistan Army still holds onto this intrusion post which commands a wide, unhindered view of the Drass National Highway and the Lamochen post. (Photos by Captain Rommel Akram)

CHAPTER 10

No Kills, Where Is the Story?

My passion for reporting encounters live required me to exit the office at all kinds of odd hours and that too, without any warning. I would dash off at a moment's notice lest I reach the operation site late and miss out on the action. It provoked a lot of dark humour, pokes, and jokes at my expense among colleagues in the Srinagar Bureau of *The Indian Express*.

Having never witnessed such a pro-active approach to live operational reportage in Kashmir from any of the national or international media persons, my esteemed colleague, Muzamil Jaleel, took it upon himself to warn me: 'Vikram, if you keep going for these encounters, the mujahids will kill you.'

I replied to Muzamil: 'The militants may kill me, but they will not change my intention to go for encounters.'

My intentions, my disregard for death, were rooted in the philosophy of the Sikh Gurus, especially Guru Tegh Bahadur ji, who had lived by the belief that the fear or threat of death would not deter him from the pursuit of his ideals.

The risk of death or grievous injury was an omnipresent one while reporting Kashmir. Often, I would drive out from Srinagar alone in the very early hours to reach an encounter site in remote Handwara or Vilgam—places so remote that the villagers would tell me no Kashmiri journalist had ever come to their village. I would not know if I would return to Srinagar alive or in one piece.

The other challenge was to get the story published in the face of the editorial desk's constant refrain: 'Where is the story? No militant was killed in the operation you reported live. How is the operation worth reporting if no militant died?' Kills, kills, and more kills. The Army relied on the metric of terrorists slain to evaluate the performance of a battalion or the higher formation in the proxy war. So, it was with reportage in Kashmir. News value was a function of the number of people dead. The news of four terrorists shot was guaranteed a front-page placement. A four-day-long operation in the worst of built-up areas or the high mountains but without terrorist kills or Army casualties was destined for oblivion in popular consciousness.

For a reporter on the ground, who went into an operation without knowing if there would be any kills at the end of the day, live reportage was marked by complexities, exploration of new ground in conflict journalism, and entailed immeasurable risks. In my case, the challenge was further knotted by the fact of suffering inimical relations with the editorial hierarchy perched comfortably on the commanding heights—onwards from *The Indian Express*' Srinagar Bureau and peaking at New Delhi's Bahadur Shah Zafar Marg. The exception in the hierarchy was Vipin Pubby, the then Resident Editor of the *Express* in Jammu, who stood by his forward correspondent to the extent of his limited powers.

The result was that I drew a series of 'failures' or blanks in my live reportage of troops in those operations where the net result did not fit into the newspaper's limited expectations. The newspaper did not want to waste space on such 'zero kill' operations.

The failure to get my stories published even in the limited Jammu & Kashmir edition of the *Express* underlined the many disappointments that I, as a war correspondent, faced in the field. It is not all as glamorous a pursuit as some young reporters may imagine it to be. Firstly, it took persistent, tedious efforts to convince the Army to let me accompany them. If the operation threw up nothing worthy of a news report or narrative, one just put it aside and went back to the office waiting for the next opportunity. Secondly, it was hard to explain to the officers of the Army who had given me unprecedented access to the operation as to why there was no report about it in the newspaper the next morning? After all they had worked hard during the operation, risked their lives and had given me no guarantees that there would be 'kills' at the end of the day. It was not an easy task to approach them again and request access to yet another operation. After many tries and operational opportunities gone to waste, one encounter would materialise finally with the results 'worthy' of being published in the newspaper. Thirdly, there was no one who had gone through similar reporting experiences and who could counsel or guide me through the novel challenges. Neither did the army have the benefit of experience or clear procedures/guidelines to handle a correspondent of my inclinations. It was all about learning on the job and rectifying my own mistakes. The endeavour of war and CI-Ops reportage in Kashmir, with all the sincerity required for the pursuit, was a journey down a long, lonely road.

I recount below five such forays as a frontline correspondent in Kashmir which never got published in the newspaper I was employed with.

Three Days in Captivity

In June 1998, the HQ of 1 Sector Rashtriya Rifles (RR) at Khanabal, Anantnag, had planned a major operation to nail terrorists of the

Hizbul Mujahideen hiding in the Khiran bowl of the Shangus Valley in South Kashmir. The Khiran bowl was a densely packed inhabitation, an old abode for terrorists and remained squarely in the army's crosshairs. Brigadier RS Mehta (later Major General, AVSM, VSM), an Armoured Corps officer of the 16 Cavalry, was commanding 1 Sector. He sounded me out for the operation. He left the details very guarded but asked me to pack clothes for a few days and proceed to his HQ, a 45-minute drive south of Srinagar on the national highway. The condition imposed on me was that I was not to let anyone know of my destination, not even my office hierarchy. I put up a vague excuse in the *Express* bureau office and made haste for Khanabal. From there, I proceeded along with Brigadier Mehta, who later commanded the Baramulla LoC's 19 Infantry Division and retired as a major general, to Khundru, where the HQ of 7 RR (Punjab Regiment) was located. Once I was safe in his 'custody', Brigadier Mehta outlined in brief the contours of the impending operation as we drove through the countryside with the Pir Panjals looming silently over us in all their majestic beauty.

The next order for me was to stay put at Khundru till further directions were given. The Army was mindful of the fact that if rumours were to leak out that a war correspondent was roving around at the 7 RR HQ at Khundru, the terrorist early-warning network would sense an imminent operation in the 7 RR's Area of Responsibility. So, for the next two days and nights, I was confined to the beautiful surroundings of the 7 RR's HQ campus with apple trees and plenty of flowers in the garden. I had nothing to do during the day, except chatter with the orderlies and gardeners, so I got to know virtually every little flower and ripening apple. At night, there were drinks with the then 7 RR CO, Colonel Ajay Saxena, and his subordinate officers. A go-getter officer commissioned into the Brigade of the Guards, Saxena was driven by a burning ambition. He got embroiled two years later, in 2000, in the notorious Pathribal fake encounter following the massacre of 35 Sikhs of Chittisinghpura by terrorists on the eve of the US Presidential visit to India. However, Saxena weathered the Pathribal blot on his career and rose to the rank of major general before retiring. He passed away a few years ago in Mumbai.

Saxena and his genial wife, Sushma, were very fond of Brian Silas' rendition of evergreen Bollywood tunes on the piano. The immortal Kishore Kumar tunes wafted through the Khundru garden those two evenings I was there, a charming distraction from the daytime boredom.

During the second day of my undercover stay at Khundru, I was made privy to the intricacies of the build-up to the Army operation. I was summoned to a small room in the interior of the 7 RR HQ. Here, a Kashmiri with a dishevelled look and fear written large on his face was waiting. He was the informer or the 'source' of the army. He was from the Khiran bowl, where the terrorists had holed up. The army officers under Saxena put him to sustained questioning to assure themselves that his tip-offs were credible. The key factor was that the Sector (brigade)-level operation involving elements of three battalions—7 RR, 3 RR (JAK Rifles), and 13 Mechanised Infantry (18 Rajput)—had to be launched at night to the remote village only when it was certain that the terrorists were present there. Having satisfied themselves with the source's credibility, clearance was given by Brigadier Mehta for the operation's launch at 11 p.m. the next night. If the source intelligence was not credible, the Army would end up wasting its time and resources on a wild goose chase rather than ending the day with bodies of terrorists laid out at their feet like tiger trophies collected by the maharajas of yore.

I was to march 5.5 hours through the mountains of coniferous forests with a column of 7 RR under the command of Major PS Rathore. There was another column with us under the command of Major Katyal. The task was to hit the Khiran bowl located in the Shangus Valley before first light, cordon it off from the top downwards, and then move in for a classic house-to-house search. The march to the village was to be undertaken in absolute stealth. The army had, at that time, very rudimentary night-vision devices at its disposal. There was, firstly, the hazard of terrorists setting up IEDs on our route or an ambush with Pika machine guns, RPGs and AK assault rifles. Slumbering hamlets on our way were to be skirted cautiously and left none the wiser of the onward march of army columns. Virtually every hamlet harboured terrorist OGWs. Were the OGWs to detect the movement of army columns in the dead of night, the warnings would be relayed across the hamlets. The terrorists would flee their hiding place and make for hideouts in the high mountains before the army columns reached from multiple directions and placed a tight cordon around the target area. The terrain was broken and forested, which suited the terrorists. They had lookouts from the villages posted on the hillocks, and often lady folk would tip off the terrorists on the approach of army columns during the day. Village dogs were the pillars of the terrorist early-warning system in the night. A dog, upon detecting movement, would break out into hysterical barks, jerking out the OGWs from sleep and alerting them to army movements in the neighbourhood. All in all, the Shangus Valley was a difficult area for army operations, given the deep support the terrorists enjoyed within sections of the local populace.

Mindful of the above hazards, we walked to the target area that night in absolute control of our mouths, like ghosts stealing from the graveyard. A stone dislodged harshly by heavy army boots would occasion a startled pause in the column's momentum. With bated breath, we would strain our ears to catch a nervous bark or a sign/sound of alerted villagers. After a few minutes of a halt in absolute silence, the march would resume. We got to the top of the mountains overlooking the Khiran bowl just before the first light.

However, the four terrorists had got an inkling or a tip-off on the army's major operation. As the army columns firmed up on top of the bowl, we saw four terrorists escape the village and flee up the slopes on the opposite side. The troops were given orders to open fire with MMGs and LMGs, but the distance was too far, and the cover afforded to the terrorists by rock and bush was formidable. We saw the last of them disappearing over a ridgeline, which was glinting softly with the first rays of dawn. All this time, Brigadier Mehta, who was a workaholic to the core, was up and awake at his HQ and monitoring the operation by logging into the radio frequencies of the three battalions in the operation. Later, Brigadier Mehta learnt that the terrorists had escaped from Khiran that dawn and found refuge in nearby Srigufara, another habitation that supported terrorists and had been the location for a bunch of Army casualties, including a major of the 13 Mechanised Infantry.

Seeing its quarry escape from under its nose, an irate Army descended on Khiran. Colonel Saxena drove into the village in a roaring, throbbing Jonga before noon, its seats upholstered in a maroon corduroy finish. It was time for a search and 'questioning' of the villagers. It got worse as it became apparent to the tense, frustrated troops that the quarry had managed a Houdini act. The Khiran inhabitants put up a poker face and claimed that they had seen no militant. I witnessed some rough and ready methods employed by Colonel Saxena to extract the truth from the wily OGW suspects. The truth was seldom offered on a platter by the OGWs. Sometimes coercion worked, sometimes cash. But all the efforts were in vain that day. Dealing with the OGWs at Khiran that morning was like closing the stable door after the horses had bolted. I drove back to Khundru with Colonel Saxena in his Jonga that afternoon. The road was an exceptionally broken one and notorious for springing IED attacks on Army vehicles. We got to Khundru safely, and I was given a lift by officers of the 3 RR to the Khanabal HQ of 1 Sector RR, where my Maruti car was parked in secrecy.

I got back to Srinagar after four days. My absence had not been sanctioned by the head office at Jammu. Having been sworn to secrecy by the Army, I had plunged into the uncertainty of this proxy war reportage, not knowing how long the operation would last. I was admonished by my boss. Worse, I had 'nothing to report' as there had been no kills during the Khiran operation. I vainly tried to explain the complexities of Army operations on the ground. But I was firmly told to find something else to report. 'No terrorist was shot during this so-called operation. Where is the story? Find something else to despatch,' was my boss' parting shot over the telephone.

I was warned that any more such reporting adventures without due sanctions from the head office would attract disciplinary action in the future.

A Dive into Paddy Fields

In August 1998, the mother of all Kashmir encounters took place in village Jaggerpora in the Kupwara District. Foreign terrorists, along with local ones, had infiltrated in strength and had taken shelter in the village. They were a group of 16, including Afghans, Pakistanis, and one Sudanese. The Army's 7 Sector RR, headquartered at Drugmulla, had thrown a dragnet of 21 RR, 4 RR, and 24 RR around Jaggerpora. The BSF had also been called in to eliminate the group. The village was ringed by maize fields. On the first night of the encirclement, the Army lost 4 RR's Captain Tarun Kumar, Shaurya Chakra, and his radio operator, AM Sawant. They had engaged in a hand-to-hand fight in the maize fields with the terrorists who tried to escape the village by penetrating the cordon. Both their wives were carrying their first child.

The Afghan terrorists were formidable. They had jumped onto the hatch of a BSF armoured vehicle in Jaggerpora's lanes and attempted to drop a grenade inside. But a gallant, speedy counter-fire by the late Captain Mandeep Singh and troops of 4 RR had nailed the terrorists mounted on the vehicle before they could open the hatch. Captain Mandeep died a year later in the first wave of *fidayeen* attacks that commenced as the Kargil War raged in 1999. In a major fidayeen attack on his COB[1] on 6 August 1999, at the Chak Nutnus village, Kupwara, Captain Mandeep and five of his soldiers laid down their lives.

After two days of operations at Jaggerpora, the Army had shot 12 terrorists. I was very keen to get into this mammoth operation. But clearances were not coming from HQ 15 Corps. I was finally able to get through to the 15 Corps Commander, Lieutenant General Krishan Pal, on the evening of the second day of the encounter. He cleared the hurdles and gave me the requisite clearance. He asked me to reach Jaggerpora before first light the next day as that is when the troops would re-commence search of the village. In the dead of night at 2.15 a.m., I left Srinagar in my Maruti 800. It was a 150-minute drive to Jaggerpora, located in the interiors of Handwara tehsil and a hotbed of foreign terrorists. Those were the days when there was no counter-infiltration fence on the LoC, and the passage of men and war stores from POK[2] under the cover of artillery shelling was not difficult. There were dumps upon dumps of weapons and ammunition in the Kupwara district that terrorists could rely upon to arm themselves to the teeth. Terrorists even fired rockets armed with a solar timer on the house of the CO of 21 RR (The Guards) at Handwara in 1998. The rockets had been tied to trees at night and aimed at the CO's house. The terrorists fled after that. As the first rays of dawn hit the rocket, the solar

1. Company Operating Base

2. Pakistan Occupied Kashmir

device set them off. Fortunately, the rockets went through the top of the house and did not harm the CO and his wife asleep in the rooms below. I was shown the gaping holes in the top portion of the house by the CO, Colonel RS Chauhan, who later died in the IED blast on 21 August 2000, along with Commander, 7 Sector RR, Brigadier BS Shergill, and Signals Naik Jose.

I had never been to Jaggerpora. Relying on luck and with a bit of pluck, I drove off into the deserted night roads from Srinagar, snaking my way to Jaggerpora in North Kashmir. There was not a soul on the roads, except the security force pickets. As I neared the Handwara area, the scene got more desolate. Not even a dog crossed my car. The final stretch was a maze of broken, dusty countryside roads. The Handwara countryside must have constituted a spectacle of immeasurable charm at sunrise in the halcyon days of Kashmir. It was bewildering and intimidating in the last hour before dawn on that day in the summer of 1998. I located Jaggerpora and drove straight into the village square at 5.15 a.m. To my surprise, no Army cordon stopped my entry on its outskirts, nor did I meet any soldiers inside the village.

Jaggerpora was smouldering after two days of the fiercest of encounters. These fights were unlike the ones two decades later when the Army came into possession of very advanced surveillance technology that allowed the troops to pinpoint the location of the terrorists and cut down on casualties. In 1998, the encounters were the classic battles of the streets and rooms where raw courage and wits tilted the scales. The terrorists fought hard and did not concede an inch. They would mock the Army's calls to surrender and the end of the battle only came when their bodies were pulled out of the smouldering fires and rubble. The remains of the terrorists made for a horrific sight: limbs torn, faces mangled beyond recognition, and the bodies roasted like potatoes pulled out from a winter bonfire. It's a saving grace their mothers were not there to see them laid out at the encounter site. Their assault rifles would get badly charred and bore a piteous resemblance to the once-feared glories of Kalashnikov firearms.

There were fires raging in some Jaggerpora houses as I stepped out of my car and walked into the lanes. Houses had been burnt down and shelled during the operations. There were no villagers. It did not seem there were any terrorists left in Jaggerpora; it was so silent. Strewn in the ashes and dust of Jaggerpora's lanes were thousands of empty casings of rifle cartridges. I picked up two as battle souvenirs and exited the village, thinking it was all over and I had missed the action. The empty casings were a consolation; at least I would have something to show for my Jaggerpora reportage! I left for the village Panzgam in the Kupwara District, where another operation was underway involving the troops of the 19 RR (Sikh Light Infantry). Little did I know what the smouldering Jaggerpora had concealed as I had stood in the village square looking askance at the deserted, wounded houses. Four terrorists were still there and holed up in the ruins. They were smoked out and shot later the same day to a total of 16 'man-eaters' for the army's Jaggerpora bag. Unwittingly, I had been alone and completely vulnerable in Jaggerpora that dawn.

As I drove towards Panzgam, which was 30 km north-west from Jaggerpora and connected by dusty, broken countryside roads, streams of villagers came down the road. They were fleeing from Panzgam. I stopped them and sought directions to Panzgam, which was a few kilometres away. They were shocked and horrified that a stranger would be seeking directions to a village whizzing with bullets and under the shadow of death. They thought I was an innocent traveller, lost in the proverbial woods.

'Sir, you don't know, there is massive firing going on in Panzgam. An Army operation is underway there. You cannot go there. It is out of bounds for civilians. Come with us. We will shelter you in a nearby village till firing stops at Panzgam,' a fleeing villager told me.

His face comes back to my mind vividly as his fellow villagers gaped at me. He was not very tall, fair-skinned with light eyes and hair, and his peasant's brow bore a furrowed look. He was well-intentioned, and I was touched by his simplicity and concern for my welfare. I told him that the Panzgam operation was precisely my destination and that I was a newspaper reporter from Srinagar. Upon realising that they were dealing with a journalist as mad as a hatter, the villagers gave up on me and resumed their flight to deepen the distance between themselves and the Panzgam firing.

As I approached Panzgam on a narrow village road that meandered above lush paddy fields, the scene was completely forsaken by living creatures. A chaos of firing bellicosity began to engulf my ears. Bullets whizzed above my car in the crossfire as I reached the outer houses of Panzgam. The troops and terrorists were not firing at me specifically, but there was such a heavy volume of fire from all directions that my car got caught in it. The firing got too hot to handle as the bullets, shells, automatic grenade launchers etc., were screaming and shrieking all over. My luck had held out till now and I decided not to risk it further. My car was in danger of being hit. At the same time, I was determined not to reverse the car and flee Panzgam. I decided to wait it out and the only option left for me was to abandon the car and get out of the crossfire.

I abandoned my car on the road and dived for safety into the paddy fields about six feet below. Here, I spotted a Kashmiri house in the distance. I crawled and ran in a crouching posture to the house. On reaching there, I startled three women and two children inside. They were shocked beyond words at my urgent knocks on the door. They let me in, and after getting over the initial terror at my entry, they offered me Kashmiri tea and buns. The hospitality of the Kashmiri peasants is remarkable, and the generosity they extended to a stranger under those trying circumstances touched my heart. They had never seen a journalist venture so far into the interiors of violence-hit North Kashmir and that, too, a non-local, from Punjab. They implored me to stay back in their house for my own safety.

After about 45 minutes, there was a lull in the firing from Panzgam. I was keen to get into the operation before it was 'all over' like Jaggerpora. If I could not witness the actual shooting of terrorists, my bosses would have a ready excuse to junk my report from the spot as they had done in the past. I thanked the women and made my way back to the car. It had escaped the crossfire. I drove slowly into the heart of Panzgam, turned a corner, and came face to face with three Sikh troops of the 19 RR. They were even more shocked than the women had been earlier at my entry in a Maruti 800 in a war-hit village. The situation turned extremely tense. They had their fingers on the 7.62-mm SLRs mounted on their shoulders and aimed at me. I had been given clearance by the Corps HQ for the Jaggerpora operation. But no one knew beforehand at Panzgam that I would make my way to its ravaged heart. In the far-flung rural areas of Kashmir, a journalist venturing into nerve-centre of an Army operation to report the proceedings was something that the soldiers could never have imagined.

I gently braked and brought the car to a standstill. I sat in the car without making the slightest movement and looked back at the soldiers with a calm, steady gaze. I was aware that one nervous twitch on my part or a gesture misinterpreted by the tense soldiers would lead to the nervous squeeze of three triggers and a barrage of hard-nosed 7.62-mm bullets my way. My hands turned sweaty as they held onto the car's steering wheel. I kept sitting still, waiting for the soldiers to relax. It worked. They did not open fire.

Very slowly and deliberately, and while maintaining eye contact with the tense troops, I leaned my head out of the car window and shouted at them in Punjabi: '*Main Srinagar to patrakar haan.* Corps commander *Sahab ne bhejya hai* (I am a journalist from Srinagar. I have been sent by the corps commander).'

I dismounted from the car and walked to the three soldiers, whose tension was visibly ebbing after having heard my authentic Punjabi. I showed them my *Express* identity card. They were still somewhat unconvinced.

What on earth was this reporter doing here?

Fortunately, I had a copy of *The Indian Express* lying in the car and showed them my bylined story written a few days earlier.

However, they did not let me proceed further into the village. I was asked to get in touch with their company commander, Major Pandey, who was in the middle of the village, commanding the operation. I requested them to inform Major Pandey of my arrival. However, they did not have a radio set, and they would not budge from the spot assigned to them in the cordon. The turbaned trio suggested that I go to the nearby Vilgam village, where the 19 RR's Adjutant was based. The Adjutant would get in touch with Major Pandey on the radio set and secure my clearance for the operation. Realising I had hit a dead end, I retreated to Vilgam, which was south of Panzgam and another 12-km drive. I reached Vilgam and found the adjutant, Major Sahni, outside his field tent. He turned out to be from my old school, St John's High School, in Chandigarh. But that did not help very much in securing clearance for my entry into the Panzgam operation. Major Sahni was asked by his boss, the 19 RR Commanding Officer, to seek clearance from higher HQ, i.e., 28 Infantry Division, at Kupwara.

Staff officers at the Kupwara HQ were not at all keen to let a journalist into the Panzgam operation. They had other thoughts in their mind. That evening, the Army had scheduled a media briefing to showcase the Jaggerpora success of 16 terrorists shot along with recoveries of weapons. The GOC, 28 Infantry Division, Major General VG Patankar, was to address it. His staff officers were keen to get *The Indian Express* to report the media briefing and carry a glowing picture of the GOC. Major

Sahni was given orders on the radio set by the Division HQ to direct the *Express* journalist sitting with him at Vilgam to proceed to Kupwara town for the briefing. I refused. I told Major Sahni that given the timing of the media briefing and its clash with the ongoing encounter at Panzgam, I would prefer being with fighting troops rather than sipping tea and nibbling *paneer pakoras* with the GOC. However, the staff officers at the Division HQ were equally adamant. Orders were repeatedly relayed over Major Sahni's radio set to get the journalist to reach Kupwara as soon as possible. He was under no circumstances to be permitted entry into the Panzgam operation. I was equally determined to be in the field with fighting troops. A stalemate ensued, and Major Sahni was caught squarely in the middle. The day was coming to a close, and I had a long drive back to Srinagar. Realising that clearance would not be forthcoming from Division HQ, I bid adieu to Major Sahni with a promise to renew our school bonds when on leave in Chandigarh. I drove back to Srinagar that night with another 'empty bag'. I skipped the media briefing by the GOC on the Jaggerpora operation. A media statement would be released later by the PRO at Corps HQ and I would avail of that to report the 16 kills.

My father's words from another era consoled me: 'When out on a *shikar*, it does not matter if you return home with an empty bag; the reward lies in the challenges and tests of your pursuit; in the patience and resolve you exhibit in the face of disappointments.'

After Permission, the Admission

There were occasions when I secured permission directly from the 15 Corps Commander, Lieutenant General Krishan Pal, after getting through to him via the Army Exchange on the landline telephone. The direct permission helped me save time and get to the encounter location speedily before the action got over. Going through the rigmarole of formally seeking sanction through the media cell of the Corps HQ did not work in situations when encounters broke out suddenly in the Kashmir hinterland.

In June 1998, an encounter erupted near Manasbal in North Kashmir. I requested the Army Exchange to put me through to the Corps Commander and he came onto the line immediately. Pal gave me the go-ahead and told me that he would speak to the 5 Sector Rashtriya Rifles (RR) Commander to let him know that I would be joining the troops at the point of contact with the terrorists. I speedily drove out from Srinagar at 2 p.m.

Permission secured, the challenge ahead was to get into the encounter safely. As I reached the encounter village, there was total confusion in its neighbourhood. There was firing within the village and in the maize and rice fields outside it as some of the terrorists were believed to have fled into the agrarian patches. I parked my car under a tree on the outskirts of the village. Before I knew what was happening a volley of assault rifle fire hit the top of the tree. It was not aimed at me, but I was, inadvertently just caught in the crossfire. I left the car and walked into the village streets.

The challenge was to locate the company commanders of the battalions fighting inside the built-up area of the village and inform them that I was going to join the troops with the permission of the Corps Commander. In the melee of operations, the 5 Sector RR Commander was nowhere to be seen. Had he passed on the orders from the Corps Commander to his company commanders that a journalist would be entering the firing line? It was a tricky situation as no one from the battalions fighting within the village knew me as they were from 5 Sector RR (I had never been on an operation with the 5 Sector RR). The troops and officers could never have imagined a legitimate journalist would pop out of nowhere. When responses from both sides are on a hair-trigger, an unknown person within the operational area can invite hazards upon himself. The firing exchanges within the village kept shifting. I somehow managed to safely navigate through this firing and melee but without meeting any officer I could join up with. Finally, I managed to find a way out to the other side of the village. Here, I got a bit lucky as I ran into troops and young officers of the 3 Kumaon (Rifles) and their Commanding Officer, Colonel Sudhir Uppal. I knew them all and they were elated at seeing me in the middle of the battlefield. The 3 Kumaon (Rifles) was under the operational command of 70 Infantry Brigade and the battalion was fighting in the village along with the troops of 5 Sector RR.

Uppal took the wheel of his Jonga and, with me sitting beside him, drove into the agrarian fields. To our right side, the Kumaon troops were moving through the fields in search of the terrorists, a scene reminiscent of a line of beaters flushing grey and black partridges towards shikaris poised on the flanks with double-barrel shotguns. We did not find any terrorist in the fields and the operation was called off by the early evening. I bid adieu to Uppal and his young officers.

By this time, the 5 Sector RR officers had located me and they insisted that I have a cup of tea with them at their Manasbal HQ. I agreed but by the time we finished with the tea and an animated round of discussions on the terrorists and their activities, darkness had set in. After seeking directions to the Baramulla-Srinagar highway from the 5 Sector RR officers, I left. Soon enough, the broken village roads of the Manasbal hinterland had me confused in the pitch darkness and I realised I was lost. There were no milestones or road signs to lend direction in the deep countryside. I kept going round and round in circles and was so lost that I could not even find my way back to the HQ of 5 Sector RR!

There was not a soul around. After 90 minutes of wandering around in my car, I spotted some lights in a village hut. I stopped my car and knocked on the door. The Kashmiri peasants were warm and helpful. They put me on the right track to reach the highway, which I hit at about 9 p.m. before reaching my Srinagar accommodation safely by 10 p.m.

Down and Out on Farkian Top

The Kashmir LoC was very active in the summer of 1998. It was so 'hot' in army parlance that old villagers residing on the LoC swore they had not witnessed such artillery firing even in the 1965 and 1971 wars. I had been reporting from Srinagar the daily dosage of shells and other war munitions fired across the LoC onto targets in POK and the casualties suffered by villagers and soldiers on our side. The scale of firing would be reflected in the daily situation reports issued by the 15 Corps HQ. The Army would also come out with periodic statements of Pakistan Army targets destroyed, such as an ammo dump or a battalion/brigade HQ. I sought clearance from HQ 15 Corps at Srinagar to report live the firing from infantry bunkers located right on the hot LoC. I was cleared for a two-day stay at 28 Infantry Division HQ at Kupwara, from where, if the opportunity presented itself, I would be inducted into the LoC operations at the discretion of the Division's GOC and the Brigade Commander on the LoC.

It was June 1998, and Kashmir was warm. My room at the Kupwara Division HQ was a comfortable one, and the officers' mess was luxurious with thick carpeting and intricate woodwork. It was cast in the style of an Alpine retreat in the Swiss mountains. The staff officers were welcoming and hosted me with many drinks. But they subtly tried to dissuade me from venturing to the LoC bunkers. I was determined and sought an audience with the GOC after his staff officers did not get me permission to move to the LoC. I had a one-to-one discussion with the GOC, Major General VG Patankar. I told him that I wanted to spend the day and night with the LoC troops where the firing was the heaviest and write a detailed narrative on what the LoC battles entailed.

All that the citizens of the country knew about LoC firing was an idea of its intensity (number of shells fired) and the number of casualties, targets struck, etc. Major General Patankar had four brigades—104, 53, 268, and 109—on the LoC under his command. He listened patiently to a young reporter's impassioned pleas. He voiced his admiration for my spirit but remained non-committal on my request. On my insistence, he finally gave me clearance to visit the HQ of his Keran brigade, the 268 Infantry Brigade, which was caught in the thick of LoC firing and located at Farkian Top on the Shamshabari Ranges. The rest, he said, with reference to my movement further from Farkian Top to bunkers on the LoC, would be left to the discretion of the man on the spot, the Keran Brigade Commander, Brigadier Bahukhandi. I was to realise later that the GOC had no intention of letting me stage forward to the LoC bunkers; the visit to Farkian Top was just a foil to get an extraordinarily insistent journalist off his back and, at the same time, keep the Corps HQ satisfied as it had granted me permission for the LoC foray.

I drove to Farkian Top in my Maruti from Kupwara. It took me three-and-a-half hours because of really bad roads. The final stretch was a broken, winding mountain road throwing up tonnes of dust. Pakistani shells were landing on the mountainsides flanking the road and exploding in huge sprays of greyish dust. An odd army truck overtook me or went past me down to Trehgam. Upon reaching the 268 Brigade HQ, I was ushered into the presence of Brigadier Bahukhandi. He offered me lunch but remained non-committal on my request for forward deployment on the LoC. It would have been a memorable lunch on those heights amid the shelling, except that I sensed that the Army would not let me go forward. Disappointment was again welling up in me. I befriended the Brigade Major, Major Marrya, who was also from Punjab. I sat with Brigadier Bahukhandi and Major Marrya at lunch but got nothing more out of them, barring a generalised briefing on heavy artillery cross-firing. I attempted to steer the conversation towards clearance for a reporting stint in the forward bunkers and made it plain that the foray would be entirely at my own risk. But Brigadier Bahukhandi blocked my moves deftly. He was under orders from the GOC not to let me proceed further from Farkian Top. They were not the classic risk-takers.

Brigadier Bahukhandi's son had come to visit him, and the officer was preoccupied with that. He bid me adieu after lunch and retired to his personal quarters. It was time for me to leave and head back to Kupwara. I was desperate. My dream to be on the LoC and report live what I had been doing second-hand through daily LoC situation reports in Srinagar was in danger of being ground into the dust of Farkian Top. On my way out of the brigade officers' mess and to my car, I requested Major Marrya to let me have a last shot at requesting Brigadier Bahukhandi. He warned me and said it would be of no use. But he showed me the way to his commander's residence. I presented myself at the commander's residence. He was having a small nap but came out, a bit chary and weary. He politely nixed my final gambit and turned his heel on a despondent reporter left gaping at his doorstep. I drove back to Kupwara via the broken roads of the troubled frontier like a bedraggled, dusty dog on the retreat with the tail firmly between his legs. It was a crushing failure for me.

Not a word of my two days in Kupwara and Farkian Top would find publication in the *Express*. There was nothing worthwhile to report except failure. But I gathered the bits of my shattered dreams, lying scattered at Farkian Top, and hope bloomed again. A year later, I would realise my LoC reportage dream at a level far higher than what Farkian would ever have offered me. During the Kargil War of 1999, I was the only media person allowed twice into battle on the LoC heights in Drass and Batalik under the enemy's intense shelling. I managed to stay a night in a tent at 15,700 feet in Kargil under fire from the Pakistan Army. I was glad I had never ever given up on my reporting dreams, whatever may have been the crushing rejection handed out to me by the GOC and the 268 Brigade Commander on Farkian Top.

On a Wild Goose Chase

It was campaign season in Kashmir for the 1998 Lok Sabha elections. I had not purchased my Maruti 800 by then and would use taxis at the rate of ₹300–400 per trip to report the election rallies in outlying villages of the valley. My organisation did not reimburse a single one of the taxi bills that I incurred during the course of my forays into the countryside. But I was more than compensated for the steady depletion of my modest salary by the heady experience of reporting Kashmir from the deep field.

Having attended an election rally addressed by Chief Minister Farooq Abdullah way ahead of Ganderbal at village Wakoora on 24 February 1998, I was on my way back to Srinagar when I came across a heavy army presence near the village of Saloora. The 70 Infantry Brigade Commander Brigadier RK Shivrain, along with his officers, was standing by the roadside. I knew them all as I had accompanied the brigade's troops earlier that month to the Safapora heights to nail the killers of the 23 Wandhama pandits. I left my taxi and walked to the officers.

Shivrain was a relieved man. His alert troops had foiled a plot by the Harkat-ul-Ansar to target the cavalcade of Abdullah and his son, Omar Abdullah, who was the National Conference candidate for the Srinagar Lok Sabha constituency with IEDs. One of the IED terrorists had been shot by his troops just 30 minutes before Abdullah's cavalcade had passed by Saloora on its way to Wakura.

The terrorists had entered the Sofi *mohalla* of Saloora on 23 February and had prepared two IEDs to be planted on the road on which Abdullah's cavalcade would be travelling. Tipped off by a source, troops of the 3 Kumaon (Rifles) had cordoned off the Sofi Mohalla at 9 p.m. during the night of 23/24 and started the house-to-house search at 7. The search was unsuccessful and was on the verge of being called off when a schoolboy quietly informed the troops that the two terrorists were hiding in the hay stacked on the top floor of Abdul Gaffar Sofi's house. It was the last house in the Sofi Mohalla. Terrorists opened fire on the advancing Kumaoni troops injuring five of them before jumping into a nullah at the back of the house. They ran towards the jungle and marshes of Nambal. One of the injured soldiers, Naik Urba Datt, chased the terrorists into the nullah and shot dead the Harkat 'company commander', Husama Hassan. However, in retaliatory fire from the terrorists, Datt laid down his life. (He was posthumously awarded the Shaurya Chakra on 26 January 1999. The gallant lad hailed from Pitthoragarh in Uttarakhand and left behind his bereaved parents, Rama Devi and Ram Datt.)

The other terrorist, identified later as Janed from radio intercepts, fled towards the nearby Nambal jungle and marshes. The Army had recovered one IED, fuse wire, detonators, a Kalashnikov rifle, two magazines, and 22 rounds from Sofi's house. The two diaries recovered from the body of the six-foot-tall Humana revealed him to be a Pakistani from Malakand. He was the radio operator and message relayer for the Harkat operations in the Ganderbal area.

The Army had informed a grateful Abdullah when he was crossing Saloora en route to Wakoora of the threat to his life that had been averted by alert troops.

When I met Shivrain outside Saloora, he was gearing up to nail the terrorist who had fled towards the Nambal jungle and marshes. He was launching the 9 Dogra into the marshes for a combing operation under the command of its CO, Colonel Bharat Khurana. I was completely unprepared for the opportunity that had come my way out of the blue. I was wearing calf leather shoes and formal, grey flannel trousers. The outfit was appropriate for an election rally and media questions to the CM after the political speeches but just not suited for the mud and marshy terrain of the marshes. What I needed was duck-hunting gear. What I did have was plenty of experience of duck shoots in the northern plains that entailed wading into marshes and rivers in the thick of winter and an intense passion for the outdoors.

I sought Shivrain's permission to accompany 9 Dogra for the 'seek and destroy' mission of the terrorists hiding in the wetland. The Army was anxious to nail the terrorist because these ones were experts at IEDs and could target VIP convoys on the broken roads in election season. Without batting an eyelid and without seeking any reference to higher HQ for clearance, Shivrain said: 'You are most welcome to go with the troops.' He was well aware of my capabilities, and he also knew that I enjoyed the confidence of his top boss, the 15 Corps Commander, Lieutenant General Krishan Pal.

I disposed of the waiting taxi on the spot by paying him Rs. 300. I was given a bulletproof jacket and patka to strap on, and we bid adieu to Shivrain. The wetland was dotted with marshes and broken by stands of poplar trees. Migratory common teals and mallards were flushed out of the waters as the burly soldiers trudged through the marshes. They poked the bushes with long sticks. But more and more ducks got flushed. There was no sign of the terrorists. It took us more than four hours to search the Nambal marshes with the Dogra troops fanning out in multiple search parties. We emerged empty-handed on the outskirts of another village in the evening. There, vehicles of the 9 Dogra were waiting for us and Khurana dropped me at the 70 Brigade HQ, Saloora, before he made off for his battalion HQ.

Months later, an informer revealed to the Army that the agile terrorist had used bamboo or some kind of hollow pipes that day to breathe while submerged in the marshes. That trick had deceived the Dogra troops. It had turned out to be a wild goose chase for the 9 Dogra troops. (However, the Army officially maintained that the terrorist, Janed, who had escaped into the marshes was wounded and had died later.)

I got back to Srinagar that night after an adventurous series of hitching rides since I had relieved the taxi earlier in the day. As night fell at Saloora, it had started to snow heavily. Colonel Deepak Malhotra, the 70 Brigade's deputy commander, ordered his troops to hail down a civilian vehicle going towards Srinagar. An official vehicle of a Kashmiri judge of the district and sessions judiciary was flagged down, and the judge was directed by the troops to give me a lift to Srinagar. A few kilometres on our way to Srinagar, and as soon as the brigade HQ was well behind us, the judge ordered his driver to stop the vehicle. There was a civilian transport truck behind us. The judge curtly informed me that there was a change in his plans and that he would not be going to Srinagar. His driver stopped the truck, and I was bundled into the driver's cabin! The judge's driver instructed the Kashmiri truck driver to take me to Srinagar.

It was snowing heavily by now, and there were no other vehicles in sight on the Ganderbal-Srinagar road. I kept my fingers crossed. My bearing and look were distinctly non-local and resembling that of an army officer. Had the terrorists intercepted the truck or had the snow prevented further journey, what would have happened? But the driver was a good man, like the many Kashmiris who had come to my help during my deep forays into the killing fields of the countryside. He got me safely to Soura on the outskirts of Srinagar. From Soura, I hired an autorickshaw to my office on Zero Bridge in Srinagar's heart and reached there safe and sound at 9.30 p.m. The snow was falling thick and heavy, shrouding Srinagar in a white blanket.

I did file a report that night, which was published the next morning (25 February 1998) in *J&K Newsline*, the local news supplement of the *Express'* Jammu & Kashmir edition. But it was confined to the Army's competence at having averted an IED threat to the CM's life. I was not allowed the leeway to report on the troops of the 9 Dogra unsuccessfully trawling the Nambal marshes on a wild goose chase and my eye-witness account of a complex and offbeat army operation in a wild duck haven. Had the army shot four or five terrorists in the Nambal marshes, I would have stood a better chance at publishing an account of the live reportage. But that was not to be. It was not the first time I had returned from a hunt with an empty bag.

CHAPTER 11

Ducks Tumbled from Kashmir Skies

It was a surreal spectacle in a zone as militarised and security-proofed as the Kashmir Valley of the late 1990s. The patrols of the BSF marching along the Srinagar-Baramulla national highway would stop and gape at the migratory ducks tumbling from the skies late every afternoon to a barrage of illegal shotgun fire from the fields adjoining the national highway. The BSF jawans would shrug their shoulders and resume their 'security duties' despite having been within yards of the VIP poachers from Srinagar. The boom of the shotguns could be heard for miles. The nearby Parimpora Police Station would, similarly, turn a deaf ear to the daily bouts of firing in the evening. Had any common citizen dared to indulge in a much lesser act under the nose of the troopers, the BSF would have come down on the 'offenders' or 'terrorists' with all the force of law and the arrogance of power at its command.

It was the middle of March 1998. Outside the world-famous Hokersar Wildlife Sanctuary, 20 wealthy houseboat owners from the Dal and Nigeen lakes of Srinagar would take position every evening in a wide arc in the middle of the fallow fields. They were armed with shotguns and cartridge belts and attired in alpine hunting gear and hats. It was a scene straight out of a European duck shoot. The poachers' group had been habituated to taking illegal potshots at flock after flock of migratory waterfowl that rose from the core area of Hokersar in the late afternoon and flew over the fallow fields. The birds would be winging their way to shallow, nocturnal feeding grounds deeper in the Kashmir valley. As long as the birds were within the Hokersar Sanctuary's limits during the day, they were safe and protected. But once out of the boundaries of the sanctuary, they would be ambushed by the poachers while in passage to the feeding grounds. These poachers seemed to enjoy a strange impunity.

The field staff of the Jammu and Kashmir Wildlife and Forests department would cower with fear inside the sanctuary, unable to lift a finger to protect their winged guests that had travelled thousands of miles from Central Asia, Siberia, China, and Europe to winter in Kashmir and use the valley's famed wetlands as a staging ground for their passage to the Indian plains. The field staff had been intimidated severely, to the point of abject surrender, by the very influential houseboat owners—the Wangnoos, Kotroos, and Batkoos. Linked to the ruling politicians of the time and exerting substantial influence over the police, the well-heeled poachers were knocking the ducks clean out of the darkening Kashmir skies. They had gone unchecked in the poaching spree for 15 days. Instead of taking the poachers to task for security breaches, illegal hunting, and brandishing firearms in a sensitive security zone governed by the laws of disturbed areas, the police had filed cases against the wildlife field staff. The demoralised rangers and guards were in no position to resist the powerful poachers. The Wildlife Wing of the Forest Department was anyways an orphaned entity, even more so in the troubled days when the State Government had mightier things to worry about than the fate of its wild birds and animals.

The poachers had been emboldened by a controversial hunt sanctioned by the Jammu & Kashmir Government a few months back in December 1997. Special hunting licences had been granted by the department—under a political directive from the Farooq Abdullah Government—to the late Mansoor Ali Khan Pataudi and his guests, which included members of erstwhile princely families and one hunter from the diplomatic corps at Delhi. Though hunting had been banned in the rest of India, the state enjoyed the power to grant special hunting licences with a bag limit of 20 for each gun under its own separate laws, i.e., the Jammu & Kashmir Wildlife (Protection) Act, 1978, while the rest of the country was governed by the Wildlife (Protection) Act, 1972. During that controversial Pataudi shoot, 150 migratory birds had been downed at Hokersar over two days in December 1997. The VVIPs granted the special licences had shot ducks, coots, and greylag geese inside the Hokersar Sanctuary. Some hunters who were not influential enough to get a license but were influential enough to exercise influence took position on the Hokersar bund and the fallow fields outside and had a free-for-all at the birds disturbed and dispersed by the gunfire of the Pataudi shooting party inside the sanctuary's core area. These influential poachers taking potshots while positioned outside the Hokersar Sanctuary included the same houseboat owners, police officers, and bureaucrats who were habituated and addicted to shikar for decades. This lot of shikaris had not been issued hunting licences since 1990 following the advent of armed militancy in the valley. But the special licences granted to the Pataudi shooting party in 1997 had given them hope, and they were licking their lips at the imminent resumption of the good old shikar days.

In the era before militancy struck Kashmir in the 1990s, the cream of the Indian shikar elite would travel to Kashmir to legally shoot duck, chukor, and black bear and included the diplomatic corps (in particular, the US Embassy), former princes, politicians, and sundry VVIPs. The houseboat owners would arrange the hunts; hence, their influence over the state apparatus in March 1998. It had been garnered over decades of shikar in the paradise of Kashmir.

The Hokersar Sanctuary had been cordoned off in December 1997 by the police for two days to ensure the privacy of the Pataudi party and keep at bay the pesky newshounds from Srinagar. Hokersar was not too far away from Srinagar, and the city was brimming with multiple and varied species of media reporting the Kashmir conflict. The Srinagar media corps was a powerful one and its daily dispatches routinely made international headlines. The Pataudi shoot caught the attention of the Srinagar media because of the VVIPs from outside. It also attracted national criticism from wildlife conservationists. However, the powerful Kashmir lobby that had legally permitted and facilitated the extravagance of this blood sport in a conflict zone was deeply entrenched in the Abdullah Government. It remained quite unfazed by the criticism from the green activists.

It was a low, hesitant voice over the *Express* office landline that tipped me off in March 1998 about the brazen illegal shikar by the lobby of houseboat owners, the studied indifference of the BSF, the complicity of the police, and the abject helplessness of the official protectors of migratory ducks. It was a wildlife officer posted at Srinagar whose conscience would not permit him to turn a blind eye to the massacre of the valley's avian guests at Hokersar. Knowing of my deep interest in wildlife conservation, the officer pleaded with me to do something. He was desperate. The department's top brass was under political pressure, and the police were hand-in-glove with the houseboat owners. I assured him that I would go to Hokersar, verify his tip-off on the ground, and file a report.

The Pataudi shikar extravaganza had attracted the Kashmir media's attention, but that was because of the VVIP involvement and the hunters were from outside. Otherwise, reportage on wildlife protection in Kashmir was not considered a worthwhile pursuit for the media as the state was a conflict zone. To a somewhat lesser extent, investigative journalism that unearthed corruption in development works also attracted a measure of disdain from the officialdom. I was once ticked off by a wily bureaucrat in whose department I had unearthed corruption in development works. He had told me: 'You are reporting on so-called corruption when people are being killed in Kashmir, bombs are bursting in the markets, and we are on the verge of war with Pakistan.' He was implying that as an 'outsider media person' in Kashmir, I did not seem to be sufficiently cognisant of the grim realities! It was a cunning ploy of an entrenched bureaucracy to fob off pesky reporters and ensure zero accountability from those siphoning off massive funds that came in from the Government of India for the welfare of the common Kashmiris.

Anyway, I was not one to be waylaid by cunning *babu* talk or misled by the whispers and intrigue that characterised the Kashmir corridors of powers. There was bureaucratic immunity in Kashmir, similar to what I had witnessed in the dark days of Punjab, and it took shelter under the rhetoric of 'conflict zone priorities'. These so-called priorities were assigned imperiously by the powers that be to the media. I was expected to follow suit.

On a Sunday afternoon, 15 March 1998, after having lunch at Srinagar, I hired a taxi and drove to Hokersar. It was about 3 p.m., and the duck gunners were already taking position. My source had been very accurate in his tip-off a few days earlier. Five of the poachers had set up an arc on the bund fringing Hokersar. They looked completely in command of the situation. I went up to them and sought their credentials. I asked them to show me the special hunting licence issued by the department. It was a must for shooting ducks. They told me very bluntly to mind my own business. They were emboldened by the fact that I was not a local and was alone. On being told that I was a correspondent of a national daily posted at Srinagar, they piped down a bit and the arrogant smirks that crossed their lips vanished. They resorted to the alibi that hunting was not banned in Kashmir and that the state enjoyed a special status with regard to its laws. To this, I agreed. However, hunters needed a special licence issued by the department and it was granted on an annual basis. Did they possess those annual licences? Flabbergasted at my persistence and intricate knowledge of the state's wildlife and game shooting laws, they decided to brazen it out. They stopped responding to my questions and would not budge from their positions on the Hokersar bund. As the ducks flew over them, a couple of them let fly defiantly at the birds with their shotguns; the other three chose discretion as the better part of valour. I had hit a wall very early on in my endeavour.

As luck would have it, in drove Nazir Ahmed, the then SP,[1] Police Control Room, Srinagar, in a two-vehicle convoy. He was, by chance, driving from Baramulla to Srinagar and had stopped at Hokersar for a brief look at the birds. He turned out to be a proverbial angel for the helpless birds. A very gentle, quiet man and a nature lover, he was accompanied by two security guards equipped with assault rifles and a subordinate official. I went up to Ahmed, and seeing that he was fond of birds, explained to him the illegality of the prevalent situation and the adamancy of the influential poachers. Ahmed asked me to take him to the spot where the poachers were positioned on the bund. It was the turn of the poachers to be ambushed. They tried all kinds of tricks to fob off Ahmed, dropping names, vainly seeking refuge in the chicanery that 'hunting was allowed in Kashmir', etc., but Ahmed

1. Superintendent of Police

was having none of it. It was obvious by now that they did not have a special hunting licence. Without it, they were indulging in an illegal act and violating the security laws that prohibited carrying of personal weapons. Ahmed packed them off from the bund. They retreated, eventually, without so much as a whimper. His security guards were brandishing lethal assault rifles, and he was not going to let himself be intimidated or distracted by a bunch of fancy poachers clad in European hats and armed with silvery tongues. I let a restrained smile cross my lips, but it did not remain for long. It was time for Ahmed to depart, and he bid me adieu, leaving me alone again at Hokersar.

Soon enough, the poachers arrived in strength from Srinagar in their luxury vehicles as the late afternoon slipped towards the evening. It was prime time for the waterfowl in Hokersar to rise in flocks and wing their way to feeding grounds outside that comprised shallow waters, paddy fields, water chestnut plantations, and innumerable marshes. The poachers were, by now, 20 in number, including those five sent packing earlier by Ahmed. The five poachers were smirking in unabashed glee; the frustration and desperation exhibited in Ahmed's stern presence earlier was no longer visible on their faces. What could a lone reporter do now in the face of such strength?

The 20 poachers set up a wide arc in the fields lying between Hokersar and the Baramulla-Srinagar highway a few hundred yards away. As the air resounded with the flapping of the heavy greylag geese and the whistling of the smaller ducks, such as common teals, pintails, and pochards, the poachers let fly with their shotguns. I was left gaping at the proceedings. Who could have thought Kashmir was in the grip of an insurgency where the security forces were tasked to pounce on a proverbial pigeon's flutter? I initially decided that discretion was the better part of valour, that I should retreat from Hokersar and devise another way of tackling the poaching in consultation with the wildlife officer back in Srinagar. But something would not let me leave that spot. The sight of those birds being knocked down was ghastly. The sky over Hokersar was full of feathers blown off by barrages of lead pellets. The dislodged feathers trailed the falling ducks, which fell in the fields with a dull thud. Their feathers landed silently a few minutes later. I had never turned my back on terrorist bullets, and the Hokersar poaching again presented a moment of reckoning for me. I gathered my courage and wits. I put up as poker a face as I could to camouflage my thudding heart. I found a youth who was working as a casual labourer with the wildlife department at Hokersar. Unlike his senior and more seasoned colleagues there, he was unwilling to digest the poaching. I had sensed his disquiet, but he, too, was helpless. He was a lad from one of the neighbouring villages. I asked him if he could guide me to the positions the poachers had taken in the fields. He nodded. The two of us then strode across to the poachers. They watched us approach with a sense of disbelief, two lone unarmed men striding purposefully towards the 'enemy lines' belching fire. The same dialogues and exchanges ensued. All of them slowly drifted towards the spot where I had confronted those positioned in the middle of the poaching arc. The 20 poachers surrounded both of us and tried to intimidate us in a typical manner. I repeated my request firmly and politely for them to furnish the special hunting licences. I knew they had none because the department had not issued any after 1990, except for the Pataudi shooting party in December 1997. The poachers were over-clever, so they pulled out a newspaper clipping that stated that hunting was not banned in Kashmir. Sensing that they were up against a national daily with a dogged reporter deployed on the firing line, the poachers finally stopped discharging their guns at the ducks flying over. They haggled with me and, in turn, heckled me. The Parimpora Police arrived, alarmed by reports from locals that a huge controversy was brewing in the Hokersar fields with the media on the spot. The local cops had, by now, got apprehensive that their roles would be called into question in the next morning's newspapers. I explained in detail the illegality of the duck-shoot to the policemen. They had no choice but to ask the 20 poachers to accompany them to the Parimpora Police Station. The fields lapsed into silence, and the ducks continued their flights over us, their wings whistling to the tune of the setting sun. We had won the day! But the night was still to be done with.

I walked back to the hut housing the wildlife staff at Hokersar. They were silent and barely able to grasp the passage of events. I had a cup of tea with them and gave them an encouraging pat on their back. From there, I proceeded to the Parimpora Police Station. I wanted to know whether the police had filed an FIR (First Information Report) against the poachers for the illegal killing of wild birds and the unlawful carriage and use of personal weapons in a high-security zone. Night had fallen as my taxi driver made it to the Parimpora Police Station. The gates were opened for the taxi after I informed the police guard at the entrance of my credentials. He came back after seeking clearance from the SHO,[2] but as soon as the taxi drove in, he shut the gates and locked them from inside. I soon realised I had landed myself virtually in a prison. As I stepped out of the taxi and into the courtyard of the police station, I was surrounded by a mob of 20 poachers and a posse of cops. This time, they had a real go at me. The cops asked the taxi driver to sit in a room away from the scene. Had I blinked even once or lost my nerve, I would have been lynched that night, so murderous was the mood of the frustrated houseboat owners. I could have been shot, my body thrown in the fields, and the security forces would have passed off my death as a militancy-related crime in the daily situation

2. Station House Officer

report. There was a tried and tested impunity enjoyed by those indulging in such acts and operating under the camouflage of the 'troubled security situation' in Kashmir. As I stood by the taxi's front door, the poachers heckled and provoked me, with the cops weighing in with all kinds of ugly mutterings and rabble-rousing in Kashmiri. They waggled their fingers under my chin. They were very experienced men, knowing precisely how to work the levers of power to their advantage and how to pressurise those who resisted. The poachers' mob was led by a squat, clean-shaven houseboat owner armed with a particularly sharp and vile mind. I did not blink even once. I was prepared for any eventuality that may befall me. I firmly told the SHO to give me a list of the names of the 20 poachers and supply me with a copy of the actions he had initiated under the law against them since they did not possess the required hunting licences. After about 45 minutes of this constant heckling and seeing my determined mood, the mob lost its spine. I told them that I would list their names in the newspaper the next morning, come what may. The proverbial tables turned, and the boot suddenly shifted onto the other foot. The mob's leader and his cronies literally fell at my feet that night at Parimpora Police Station. They pleaded that I should not list their names in my story on duck poaching at Hokersar for the national daily. Promising them nothing and having jotted down their names from a rattled Parimpora SHO, I summoned the taxi driver and curtly told the cops to have the gate unlocked. I was given a 'sentimental' see-off, the pleading eyes of the poachers pressed to my taxi window and literally begging for anonymity in the newspaper the next morning. They were all very well known in Srinagar. The mob had lost its spunk, and its feigned righteousness had evaporated into thin air. The cops tamely let me go.

My Hokersar report on the poaching was published in *The Indian Express* the next morning, 16 March 1998. It left embarrassed faces in the state government and the top hierarchy of Srinagar Police District under whose jurisdiction fell Parimpora Police Station. The 20 poachers were not prosecuted by the police—given the traditional influence they exercised in the proverbial corridors of power—but the daily massacre of ducks at Hokersar stopped after that. The birds were left to their unfettered flights into the setting sun, and the humble wildlife staff to their salty, salmon-pink Kashmiri tea. The evening whistle of the wings was not drowned by gunfire. There were no more bundles of broken flesh and feathers tumbling out of the Kashmir skies and landing on the ground with sickening thuds.

The state's separate set of wildlife laws enacted under the J&K Wildlife (Protection) Act, 1978, was finally amended in 2002 on the lines of the National Wildlife (Protection) Act, 1972. Recreational hunting of birds and animals was banned in consistency with the strict laws in vogue in the rest of the country. The last special licences granted in Jammu and Kashmir to shoot wild birds for recreational purposes were those granted to the Pataudi shooting party in December 1997.

CHAPTER 12

She Waited Two Years; He Lay Dead in a Kargil Cave

It took two years for the truth to confront a widow and divest her of an unshakeable belief in her soldier husband's invincibility. The doughty lady had vehemently doubted his death in the Kargil War after he had gone missing in battle. His body had not been found. She had held out stoically against the dying light of hope. If his body had not been found two years after the Kargil War ended, how could the Army be so sure he was no more? He could be alive and, unknown to all, rotting in a Pakistani prison.

Tek Kumari Shrestha believed her hopes and her prayers for her husband's well-being were mightier than the mountains whose peaks pierced the clouds. She refused to accept the hefty compensation awarded to the family after a soldier's death even though she had meagre financial substance. In her husband's absence, she had to look after two small sons, her in-laws and her own parents.

'Show me the body. How do I believe he is dead?' was Tek Kumari's retort when the Army entreated her to accept the compensation for the sake of her family and little children. The doughty lady refused to relinquish her marriage *choodees* (bangles) and the daily practice of applying *sindoor* (vermilion cosmetic powder) along the central parting of her hair.

The truth finally prevailed and lifted, once and for all, the veil of hope that had shrouded it for two long, painful years. A bugle sounded the Last Post outside a lonely cave in the Kargil heights at above 14,000 feet in July 2001, more than two years after Lance Naik Dun Narain Shrestha had gone missing in May 1999 in the Batalik LoC Sector. The bugle blew to honour the soldier whose last remains had been put to fire outside the desolate cave. His ashes were collected. The *matka* containing his ashes covered in red cloth journeyed from there all the way to his home in Nepal. The *matka* was bequeathed to Tek Kumari's trembling hands in an Eastern Nepal village. Finally, there was a closure to the Gurkha soldier's life and to his existence as a son, sibling, husband, and father. The doughty widow had no choice left and she accepted the compensation in all humility.

Shrestha's skeletal remains were found following a tip-off by an old shepherd from a village on the river Indus, which flows south of the Batalik battlefield. The remains of the Nepali Gurkha hailing from the highly decorated 1/11 Gurkha Rifles (Bravest of the Brave, Batalik) were cremated by a pandit from the 1 Bihar and a team of five personnel from his parent unit. The small team of mourners, assisted by local porters, had trekked up to the spot where his body had been lying since the war. It was a desolate cremation at the ad hoc *shamshan ghat* where the flames smouldered and devoured his remains amid huge, gloomy rocks and the utter solemnity of the alpine zone. None of his near and dear ones from Nepal could attend because it was not feasible. Neither could the remains be collected and flown to Nepal for cremation. It had to be done on the spot and outside the cave. Shrestha was the only soldier of the Kargil War who was cremated at those heights. The rest of the spots on the Kargil heights bearing the dead were occupied by Pakistani soldiers of the Northern Light Infantry, who had been disowned by their own army and were buried by the Indian Army.

Parallel to this saga was the plight of numerous bodies of Indian soldiers strewn on the battling heights. Unlike Shrestha's body, which was hidden from view, the bodies of some other soldiers and officers, though they lay exposed, could not be recovered while the war was going on due to enemy fire. Exposure to the sharp glare and ultraviolet rays of the sun in the high and super-high altitudes had led to decomposition and pronounced discolouration of the bodies of these Indian soldiers. The respective battalions of these martyred soldiers recovered their bodies after the war from where they lay in front of the Pakistani bunkers, some with their personal weapons clutched defiantly in their hands. The bodies were embalmed and flown to their homes across India.

Bodies of officers and soldiers of the 1 Bihar, 17 Jat, 8 Sikh, 12 Mahar, 1/11 Gurkha Rifles, 11 Rajputana Rifles, 4 Jat, 10 Para SF, and 12 JAK Light Infantry, among other battalions, were retrieved one by one from positions previously under enemy fire. The relatives of the officers/soldiers had heroically desisted from mounting pressure on the Army to retrieve the bodies quickly. They understood that it would have imperilled the lives of their comrades sent to retrieve bodies under enemy fire. Pakistan Army officers claimed after the war that they had shouted to the Indian soldiers and even conveyed over radio sets to Indian counterparts that the Pakistanis would not fire upon Indian troops if they ventured to retrieve the bodies while the war was on. However, the trust deficit had nixed any such effort.

There were a few Indian bodies that just could not be sent home after retrieval because they were so badly decomposed. One such body was that of Naik Rathod Mukesh Kumar Ramnik Lal of the 12 Mahar. It was retrieved 64 days after he went missing in action in the Mashkoh LoC Sector. He was cremated in the Mashkoh Valley itself by grieving troops of his battalion. Another soldier of the 12 Mahar, Sepoy Baria Bhala Akham Bhai of Charlie Company, had gone missing in the attack on Steeple-Hump on 27 June 1999. His body was found 17 days later, highly decomposed, after the enemy retreated, and was cremated on the battlefield of the Matayin valley.

There is the tragic case of Purushottam, a soldier-driver from the 5231 battalion of the Army Service Corps. His body has never been found. Just after the war, a Court of Inquiry (C of I) was held into his disappearance by Colonel Bijoy Mukherjee, commanding officer of 1 Bihar. The finding of the C of I was that Purushottam and the Army truck he was driving had probably plunged into the Indus River between Biamah and Batalik in May 1999 while ferrying supplies for the war effort. The 'missing' case of Purushottam was then brought to a close. Based upon the findings of the C of I conducted by Mukherjee, the family pension was finally released to Purushottam's next of kin.

However, the case of the missing Shrestha was one of the most tragic episodes of the war as closure was effected after two long years. For the Indian public regaled by the tales of a select few Kargil heroes and battles, the story of the humble Shreshthas went unnoticed all these 25 years. Shrestha had officially been declared 'Missing, Presumed Killed in Action' by his battalion within the first couple of weeks of the War. His body could not be found despite his battalion searching the crags and crevices with a fine comb and a hound's nose just after the war ended in July 1999.

While stories abound as to how relatives fight over the compensation money, with scruples thrown to the winds, here was a woman who dug in her heels and refused big money. 'He must have been taken prisoner by the Pakistani intruders,' she valiantly assumed, 'or else show me proof he is dead.' 'Where is his body?'

Tek Kumari had retorted when entreated by the battalion's officers to accept the compensation.

She chose to assume he was alive and would one day, doubtless, return to their two little sons, Ashok and Sunil, and to the hearth she had kept warm for him.

To the children, who would repeatedly ask when 'papa' would return, she would purse her lips, steady the quiver in her voice, and assure them that the promised time was near at hand and that he would definitely come back. It was her promise to them.

Shrestha had gone missing on 15 May 1999, while attacking a Pakistani bunker on the Kukarthang feature in the Batalik LoC Sector. A scrap of paper submitted to the battalion's officiating CO, Lieutenant Colonel Amul Asthana, just after the battle had blandly reported the incident on the war front. The paper scrap had listed two names with service numbers from Delta Company and their ranks and reported them as missing during the battle. They were Havildar Gambhir Man Rai and Lance Naik Dun Narain Shrestha. Rai was found alive soon after, but Shrestha had disappeared into thin air.

'I refused to accept compensation due to a widow for a soldier's death because my husband's body could not be traced. Why should I have accepted his death in the absence of his body? I believed that since his body could not be found, he must have been taken alive by the Pakistanis as a prisoner back to their side,' Tek Kumari (51) had said when I spoke to her in July 2023. She resides in a village in Nepal's Pokhara region.

That night of May 1999, which was to prove so fateful for the Shresthas, had commenced with a platoon of Delta Company ascending the Kukarthang feature under the command of Subedar Kirpasor Rai, who later retired as an honorary captain in 2010.

'Our target was to reach below the top of the Kukarthang Ridge and secure a lodgement there because the summit was occupied by the enemy in great strength. We could not have captured the top of Kukarthang. When we were climbing, the soldiers were split up due to artillery shelling, incessant sleet, and snow. We were ambushed at about 2 a.m., and the Pakistanis opened machine-gun fire from the top along the very narrow, steep, and scraggy ridgeline. Some of the men moved upwards under fire while a couple went down towards the nullah of Area Boulder. All of us got scattered. Shrestha had moved upwards that night when he was last seen. When I was able to muster my platoon the next morning, I counted the men and found Shrestha missing. Havildar Gambhir Man Rai had also gone missing in a different action, but he was found alive. Shreshta could not be found. We searched for him then, but it was limited by the fact that we were under fire in a war and had to keep under cover. The search for Shrestha had to wait till the war ended. Evidently, as we realised much later, Shrestha had been hit by bullets, taken shelter, and had died in the cave,' recalled Rai.

As the war entered into its final phase, the battalion's officers found an opportune moment to relaunch the search for Shrestha even as other troops, such as those from the 12 JAK LI and 13 JAK Rifles, were burying unclaimed Pakistani soldiers in unmarked graves at heights ranging to 16,000 feet.

The Indian Army adheres passionately to the ethos of 'no man left behind'. Brigadier Amul Asthana (retired), who was in July 1999 serving as the Second-in-Command (2IC) of the 1/11 Gurkha Rifles, recounts: 'On 12 July 1999, we were ordered to fall back at Yaldor. I thought this was a God-sent opportunity to look for our missing braveheart. I ordered the splitting of all available troops into five search parties and gave them each a portion of the northern slopes of the Bharkar feature. I told the troops to use their noses as Shrestha's body must have decomposed and would be giving off a stench. The search was meticulously conducted based on a "grid", but we could not find him. One or two patrols continued to search the Bharkar Ridge area every day till the time came for the battalion's de-induction from the Batalik LoC Sector after handing over the area of responsibility to the 1 Bihar in August 1999.'

Nearly a year after the war, in April 2000, Asthana visited Nepal to look up the Gurkha troops and their families along with the Pension Paying Officer (PPO).

'My wife and I visited Tek Kumari Shrestha, walking the few hours it took to reach her remote village. She was not very well off and had two little kids to look after besides her distraught parents as well as her in-laws. We requested her to accept the ex-gratia compensation for Shrestha's death, which amounted to about ₹60 lakh in Nepali currency. But she refused as her husband's body had not been traced. For her, he was still alive,' Asthana recounted.

The search for his body had reached a virtual dead-end.

'After the 1/11 Gurkha Rifles de-inducted from the Batalik Sector, the area was taken over by 1 Bihar. The focus of 1 Bihar shifted to securing the LoC. The battalion occupied 13 posts on the LoC till Point 5465 Knoll and till the Chorbat La LoC Sector, where 14 Sikh was deployed. After the war was over, the attention waned from the ridgelines of Jubar, Khalubar, Kukarthang etc., which were the battlefields of the Kargil War. These ridgelines were way inside the LoC, and no one really climbed them after the war, as the priority was to set up and maintain posts in the immediate vicinity of the LoC. However, in the year 2000, roadbuilding started in the Batalik LoC Sector, and attention again came to the battlefield sites of Jubar, Kukarthang, etc. It was then that the remains of the body of Shrestha were discovered,' recalled Brigadier OP Yadav (retired), YSM, who commanded the 1 Bihar during the war in the Batalik Sector.

After Yadav was posted out, Colonel Bijoy Mukherjee took over the command of 1 Bihar. During the war, Mukherjee had served as the second-in-command of 1 Bihar under Yadav, who was the then CO. It was during Mukherjee's tenure as the commanding officer of 1 Bihar that Shrestha's body was discovered in 2001.

'As the war was drawing to a close in July 1999, I met Asthana in the Yaldor area. He told me of the body they were searching for in vain. He suspected at that time that Shrestha may have been taken as a POW[1] by the Pakistanis. However, after that, and with the passage of time, the POW angle got ruled out as the Pakistanis would by then have declared that they had Shrestha in their custody. So, it was confirmed as a case of Shrestha having not been taken POW but missing on the battlefield. I was looking for two Indian bodies as my battalion went about the task of securing the LoC and patrolling the Batalik ridges after the war. One body was of Shrestha and the other of a soldier from 10 Para SF (Special Forces) who had gone missing in a crevice under the Shangruti heights. We could not retrieve the body of the 10 Para SF soldier as it was under direct observation of the Pakistanis about 500–800 m away. But we were able to locate Shrestha's body. It was found upwards towards the Kukarthang Ridge from a pine-log bridge that lies in the valley between the Kukarthang and Muntho Dhalo ridges. I was told that it was at this bridge that the Gurkhas had been ambushed that night of May 1999. After my patrols confirmed it was the body of a Gurkha soldier, I informed the then 192 Mountain Brigade Commander for Batalik, Brigadier HS Panag, and I told him that we would leave it there and let the 1/11 Gurkha Rifles decide what to do with it. Shrestha's body was in very bad shape, almost in pieces and eaten by wild animals. I suspect that Shrestha, that night, got separated from the rest and fell into a crevice, breaking his leg. He may even have taken enemy bullets. Alone and wounded, he took shelter in a cave and died there. The location of his body suggested that. We could not confirm the exact cause of death

1. Prisoner of War

as no post-mortem could be carried out on Shrestha's remains,' recalled Colonel Mukherjee.

'In July 2001, the 1 Bihar battalion holding the Batalik area contacted my battalion, the 1/11 Gurkha Rifles. A skeleton had been found by an old shepherd from a nearby village in a tunnel-like cave. We asked them to ascertain the numbers inscribed on the army shoes, carbine, and MMG tripod that Shrestha had been issued at the time of his death. They exactly matched the numbers of what was found on the skeleton. Apparently wounded that night of battle, Shrestha may have tried to reach friendly troops but navigated in the wrong direction. He must have taken shelter in that cave between rocks where he breathed his last,' added Asthana.

A five-member team of 1/11 Gurkha Rifles soldiers under Subedar Kirpasor Rai was dispatched to Batalik in July 2001 from Delhi, where the battalion was stationed. 1 Bihar had retrieved the weapons found on Shrestha's skeleton in the cave and had deposited them in its armoury. But his skeleton, for whose last rites the team from the 1/11 Gurkha Rifles was dispatched from Delhi, remained in the cave.

'The clothes on Shrestha had rotted with the passage of time. 1 Bihar extended all help to us. We took a pandit from 1 Bihar and assembled wood, ghee, oil and other materials required by the *panditjee* for the last rites. We were given porters to lug the wood and other materials required for cremation at the cave. We climbed to that spot from the 1 Bihar's location above Dah on the river Indus. It took us three hours to reach the cave. We collected the remains from the cave and shaped them into a body. It was then shrouded in a white sheet. After that, we conducted Shrestha's final rites with religious rituals and whatever military honours were possible at that very spot outside the cave. His ashes were collected in a *matka* (urn),' Rai said.

It was unfeasible to muster a contingent of troops to deliver a befitting gun salute at the cremation of Shrestha's remains outside the cave. But Rai had taken along a bugle, and 1 Bihar gave him another one to deliver a ceremonial touch to the funeral. The Gurkha team with the two bugles sounded the regimental tune and the Last Post for their fallen comrade outside the cave as the logs smouldered and consumed his remains. The ashes were collected in a *matka* and covered with a red cloth for carriage to Shrestha's village in Pokhara, Nepal. Rai's team took back the weapons found on Shrestha's skeleton from 1 Bihar's armoury and the *matka* containing the ashes to the battalion HQ in Delhi. The weapons were deposited in the battalion's armoury, and Rai was further tasked to leave for Nepal, meet the Shrestha family, and hand over the ashes.

With the help of the Indian Embassy in Nepal and the Pension Paying Officer at Pokhara, Rai was able to locate Shrestha's widow and family. He handed over the *matka* to the family. It was only then that the brave and exemplary spouse finally accepted the 'compensation package'. There was finally a closure, albeit a tragic one, to Tek Kumari's long wait. A battle extraordinaire had been waged by Tek Kumari with silent tears streaming down her cheeks all those years, her suffering far distanced from the glories, commemorations, and recollections of war history. For her, the war had snatched away the father of her children. Unlike other Veer Naris, for two long years, she did not even have the consolation of knowing whether he was alive or dead.

Tek Kumari has made a small temple at her house as a memorial for her husband. Her soldier husband was steeped in religion and had served as the 'replacement *panditjee*' whenever the official *panditjee* of the 1/11 Gurkha Rifles went on leave.

CHAPTER 13

His Memories Will End Only on My Pyre

When wounded mortally, the last words and thoughts of a dying soldier turn to his mother, the family deity, the temples of his Gods, his wife, and his children. The last words of Lance Naik Kripal Singh of the 17 Garhwal Rifles were, however, different from the usual last utterances of dying soldiers.

One eye of Singh's had been blasted out, and the innards of his stomach were spilling. He had been struck by the huge, jagged splinters of a Pakistani artillery shell. Singh was singularly unfortunate; he had been hit at the very fag end of the Kargil War on 24 July 1999, two days before the war was officially brought to an end by the Indian Army.

The blood oozing from Singh's wounds was dripping onto the stretcher party of his comrades as they speedily descended the uneven Batalik slopes to the waiting casualty evacuation helicopter. Singh's wounds were so severe that field dressings and medical aid would not have saved him. Only an evacuation to an advanced medical facility equipped to handle such severe splinter injuries could have averted the impending doom. The stretcher party had covered most of the distance and the trek of six hours to the helipad when Singh sensed that his time had come. He knew with certainty that he would not make it. He requested his comrades to halt. He asked them to open his breast pocket and take out a small pocket diary that listed the debts he owed to fellow soldiers of the battalion. Singh requested the stretcher-bearers to ensure that the debts listed in the diary were duly repaid from the salary due to him at the end of July 1999. He did not want to leave this life with unpaid debts.

'The pocket diary, when examined later, rightly had the details of a few of his fellow soldiers from whom he had borrowed amounts ranging from ₹30 to ₹75, totalling 400-odd rupees,' recounts Lieutenant Colonel Prahlad K Jetley (retired) of the 17 Garhwal Rifles. Jaitley was himself wounded with three bullets through his thighs while assaulting the Kaala Pathar-Saddle feature during the moonlit night of 29 June 1999. On the same night, he was also struck by splinters from bullets that narrowly missed him and instead, hit the rocks behind which he had taken cover. (A dozen tiny splinters remain embedded in his lower body till date as they could not be removed by the surgeons). This was the same assault during the course of which Captain Jintu Gogoi, Jetley's subordinate officer, was awarded a Vir Chakra posthumously. It took Jetley four days to crawl back to the base from Kaala Pathar, after which he was airlifted to Kargil's 2121 Field Ambulance and subsequently to Command Hospital, Chandimandir, for a prolonged convalescence.

Singh, who had been recruited under the army service number 4070666P, had suffered a stroke of sheer bad luck. The Kargil War was drawing to an end on 26 July when an artillery shell burst on the administrative base of the 17 Garhwal Rifles on 24 July, literally shredding the quiet, unassuming Singh. Singh's injury was initially unknown to his family who were residing in the Pajyana village situated in the Chamoli mountains of Uttarakhand and were pining for his safe return. News on TV at that juncture was all about the War coming to an end after a glorious Indian victory. His wife, Vimla Devi, and sons, Amit (3) and Prakash (1), had no idea what a cruel blow fate had inflicted on them. Vimla Devi had married the doughty soldier at 17 and was widowed after seven years of conjugal bliss. The remorseless Pakistani Artillery shell with a heart of iron ensured that Singh would be forever 29.

'He was a simple man from a family of farmers and was scrupulous about his obligations. How can I describe a life without him? Life seems very long without him. I can only say this: memories of him will leave me only when I commence the journey to my pyre,' Vimla Devi says.

Her elder son, Amit, chokes with emotion to voice a life without his dear father. Children of soldiers who are gone feel the pain most acutely when they see other children joyous with their parents at school functions, whereas when they look back into the audience, they only glimpse their widowed mother with silent tears streaming down in loneliness, helpless to get the father back for her kids. No prayers or tears can get him back.

'I have no memories of my father as I was too young. The only memories I have of him are those that mother narrated to both of us brothers after he died,' Amit said years after the Kargil War.

The brothers run the petrol pump granted to families of the Kargil martyrs. Known by his name, the Kargil Shaheed Kripal Singh Rawat Filling Station was incorporated in 2008 and is located at Dadimdali, Gairsain, Chamoli district (Uttarakhand).

Apart from the few popular names of martyrs from the Kargil War, which are repeated ad nauseam every Vijay Divas, the vast majority of soldiers died unsung. Their stories of valour and sacrifice—as also the long battles waged by their families—remain unknown, especially those from the inaccessible Batalik war zone and further east towards Chorbat La, Turtuk, Chalunka, and South Siachen Glacier, where no TV crew could venture to beam the battles and their heroes live into Indian homes. In fact, Singh's story of relieving himself of the 'debt unto death' lay buried and came to light only in 2019 when one of his stretcher-bearers, Rifleman Ram Singh, happened to narrate the incident at a function organised by the Pune-based Lakshya Foundation in Kargil town. Jetley then penned down the last hours of Singh while also underlining the difficulties faced in evacuating the wounded from the far-out Batalik battle zones, which were 1–3 days' march from the nearest road heads on the Indus River.

'After administering first aid to Singh, a stretcher-bearer party was hurriedly dispatched to take the critically injured soldier to the makeshift helipad. It could be reached by a six-hour trek down the mountains. Despite the best efforts of the RMO,[1] Singh's bleeding could not be stopped because of the extent of damage to his abdomen. The sole foot track that existed in that high-altitude, boulder-strewn, barren terrain was difficult to traverse even for a single person, and one can only imagine the plight of the stretcher-bearer party negotiating the arduous journey while delicately carrying a fully-grown injured male with intravenous tubes sticking out from his four limbs. None of the four stretcher-bearers could actually make use of the track. Instead, they had to walk on either side because of protruding rocks and boulders. That made the descent not only very tedious and time-consuming but made it all the more uncomfortable for the wounded soldier due to the numerous jolts,' Jetley said.

'The blood, which had been oozing out of Singh's wounds, slowly drenched the canvas stretcher and subsequently started to drip onto the hands and shoulders of the stretcher-bearers. The numbing effect of morphine administered at the start of the long journey must have started to wear off after five-odd hours

1. Regimental Medical Officer

of this gruelling journey, and despite all the words of comfort and encouragement from the stretcher-bearers, the braveheart had started making low gasping sounds due to excruciating pain. Somewhere just short of reaching the helipad, Singh had asked the stretcher-bearers to halt. Beckoning them to listen to him carefully, Singh, in a very feeble voice, told them that in his breast pocket was a small pocket diary in which he had written the names of all those soldiers from whom he had borrowed money prior to the sudden move of the battalion from the peace location of Pithoragarh to the Kargil front. His comrades, bearing the stretcher valiantly, tried to dissuade him from those pessimistic thoughts, telling Singh that the helicopter was near at hand and the doctors would definitely save him once he reached the hospital. In an effort to inspire confidence in the dying soldier, the bearer party apparently told him to close that "issue of debts" in person once he recovered and returned to the battalion. The last hour of the journey was a race against time, with the helipad clearly visible from high mountain slopes. The Army Aviation Corps' casualty-evacuation Cheetah helicopter was waiting with the engine running. Singh had lost consciousness. He was hastily loaded onto the helicopter, but as soon as the "big bird" took to the sky, so did the spirit of the brave soldier. He was declared dead on landing at the Kargil helipad,' added Jetley.

Jetley penned a poignant epitaph for the brave soldier who had displayed such sterling qualities of character in his last moments: 'Singh set new standards for all to emulate. The qualities he displayed prior to a certain death showed the strength of his character that must have been duly shaped by the positive influence of his parents, his upbringing, his teachers, as well as the overall environment of fair play and justice that pervades the spirit of the Indian Army.'

CHAPTER 14

21 November
The Divinity of Coincidence

On a routine flight of 15 July 1999 from Palam to the Jorhat airport in Assam, passengers found no reason to remark on a calm and composed young lady attired in a white *salwar kameez.* On landing, Anjana Parashar breezed through the airport terminal, bypassing the queue around the baggage conveyor belts. Officials quickly gathered and escorted her out of the departure terminal. At that moment, her co-passengers might have speculated that the unknown lady with a quiet bearing was some VIP. As she stepped out of the airport, she slipped on a pair of dark sunglasses. Her luggage had been fetched for her. The main item was a coffin she had escorted from Palam. In it lay the body of her fiancé, riddled with 20 Pakistani bullets. He had valiantly charged the enemy bunkers at Kaala Pathar (Point 4927, 16,165 feet) in the Batalik LoC Sector during the early morning of 30 June 1999. He was Captain Jintu Gogoi of the 17 Garhwal Rifles to whom she had got formally engaged in a ceremony attended by both families on 2 June 1999 in her Palam, Delhi, home. The families had not fixed a date for marriage at the engagement ceremony but had agreed to take things as they came and settle on an auspicious date whenever it presented itself in the future. Little did Anjana know that just over a month after the joyous engagement, she would enter the home of her would-be husband in Assam for the first time as the undertaker of his coffin.

Two weeks after that ceremony, the bugle blew, and Jintu was called to war as part of the induction of the Army HQ reserve, 6 Mountain Division, into the Kargil theatre for prospective cross-LoC manoeuvres. In his last letter, written on 21 June 1999 to his father from the inaccessible Batalik front devoid of telecommunication links with the civilian world, Jintu had asked him to keep in touch with Anjana. Jintu had ended that letter with the last words: 'Nothing known about my next visit.' Six weeks after the engagement, Anjana was on a flight to her would-be husband's home, his coffin in the hold of the check-in baggage.

As the crowds, relatives, Army officials and functionaries of the civil administration welled around the stoic lady and her guardianship of the coffin carrying the mortal remains of a freshly minted hero of Assam, media persons at Jorhat airport observed the virtually tearless face of Anjana. There were no smudges under her eyes. Her stoic bearing verged on a seemingly icy, dry-eyed composure. Instead of her warrior, Jintu, triumphantly bringing her home one day as his bride bedecked in bright colours, 'sindoor' and sparkle of marriage couture, here she was escorting her dead warrior to a smouldering pyre at his ancestral cremation grounds in Khumtai village of Assam's Golaghat district. The fate of the two young lovers, one whose bullet-torn and decomposing body was bedecked in the Tricolour, the other attired in the funereal aura of a white dress and dark glasses. Only she knew the memories flashing in her inner eye of a 10-year romance with the strapping Jintu, a bodybuilder, boxer and a young lad given to volunteering for 'Mission Impossible'. Jintu had a sensitive side, too, he had dabbled in painting and art since his school days in Ambala. They had met at Kurukshetra University a decade before their engagement while both their warrior fathers were deployed with the Indian Air Force (IAF). After Jintu was commissioned into the Army in 1995, they had met less frequently. Jintu had a very hard tenure on the Keran LoC posts of Naga and Kunjiwala Spur (KW II) from 1996 to 1998. Those were the days when Keran's 268 Infantry Brigade deployed on the Shamsabari ranges faced relentless, war-like artillery duels and countered infiltration without the LoC fence. With his head down in the bunkers of Keran, Jintu would wait for Anjana's sweet voice to reach him amid the fighting. She was a Hindi news presenter with All India Radio, and he would tune his radio set from his bunker to hear her programmes beamed from Delhi.

Soon after Jintu's battalion de-inducted from the Keran LoC in September 1998 and relocated to the peace station of Pithoragarh in Uttarakhand under the command of HQ 69 Mountain Brigade, which was a formation under 6 Mountain Division, a magical moment in their love life presented itself. The doughty and spirited lady that she was, Anjana took a bone-jarring and winding bus ride of 14 hours to Pithoragarh. Jintu was completely unaware of the surprise visit that Anjana had planned with the blessings of his doting brother officers. The stage was set for a dramatic presentation of Anjana. An unwary Jintu was given orders by his senior officer to present himself at the married quarters of Lieutenant Rajesh Bhanot (later Colonel), he being the sole young officer of the unit with a wife. When Jintu arrived at Bhanot's residence, his initial surprise and shock at seeing Anjana standing shyly by the door soon changed into the biggest, happiest smile. It could be argued that no one on earth could have been happier or carried a bigger smile than Jintu on that day of 21 November 1998. It was his birthday, and he had turned 28. His exultant comrades had wrapped Anjana as the most beautiful birthday gift for the warrior who had just returned scarred from the bunker and ambush battles of the LoC proxy war. The Bhanots lent the jeans and shirt-clad Anjana the requisite formal attire from Mrs Bhanot's wardrobe so that she did not infringe the dress code prescribed for a lady's stay at the officers' mess in Pithoragarh.

Who could have thought in those happy and lilting moments of young love blossoming at Pithoragarh in November 1998 that the two were actually star-crossed lovers and they would never spend another 21 November together? Henceforth, from 1999, that date of 21 November would mark the most tragic of birthday anniversaries for Anjana. Yet, just a few years later, in the unexpected turns of life's tragedies and fortunes, the same date turned into a cause of celebration for Anjana. It was 'divinity of coincidence' at play, as believers may have it. But more of that later.

The Assamese crowds had lined the road leading from Jorhat airport as Jintu's body was taken in a cavalcade to Khumtai. The decision of the Army's higher command to send the bodies of officers and soldiers killed in action in the Kargil War to their ancestral cremation grounds brought the war home in unprecedented ways. After the combat was beamed live into living rooms across India from the Kargil battlefields, the bodies travelled the streets of home, followed by public cremations. It brought home to the people the realisation that 'you can never be far away, it is your war, too'. It had not been an easy task to get Jintu's body back home. It could not be recovered from the battlefield due to the challenges of enemy fire and the precipitous terrain of Kaala Pathar (KP). It had taken the personal intervention of Prime Minister AB Vajpayee to return the son to his ancestral cremation ground.

'On 9 July 1999, Vajpayee came to inaugurate the 3 MMTPA Numaligarh Refinery in Golaghat district. I was asked to meet him. The PM asked me as to what he could do for us, the family of martyr Captain Jintu Gogoi. I said we don't want anything, we are self-sufficient, we have our ancestral lands, and we live in a peaceful joint family. The only request I have is to please get my son's body back. The PM said nothing in response but raised three fingers to mean: give me three days' time. True to his word, during the night of 12 July 1999, the Army informed me that my son's body had been located,' recalled Honorary Flying Officer TR Gogoi (retired), who had battled for India in the 1962 War while attached with an IAF helicopter unit at Bomdila, Arunachal Pradesh.

However, after the Garhwali soldiers had located Jintu's body lying in a KP crevice, they realised some of his things were missing. These included an Olympus camera and Jintu's weapon, a 5.56 mm INSAS rifle. The camera had been gifted to him by Anjana and the officer had placed it in his backpack before going in for the assault on KP. The young, brave lad had imagined himself after a victorious battle with the dead Pakistanis at his feet and plenty of war trophies and captured bunkers to capture for posterity with the camera gifted by Anjana. But he never got that chance. After he was shot, it had been looted by the Pakistani soldiers along with the rifle as the spoils of war. Recalling the KP battle, which claimed Jintu and his brave soldiers, his senior officer of the battalion, Colonel P Rajnarayan (retired), said: 'Jintu was an extremely fit officer. He had done a winter warfare course at the High Altitude Warfare School (HAWS) and had come back with an instructor grading. My battalion was ordered to attack KP and Bump on a moonlit night. The hours of darkness were less due to the summer solstice. Both factors ensured that there were not enough hours of darkness for our troops to reach the enemy bunkers undetected. Consequently, our troops got daylighted before they could traverse the long, treacherous climb to the Pakistani bunkers. At about 6.45 a.m. on 30 June, when Jintu was about 300 m from the summit, the Pakistanis surrounded him and his soldiers and told them to surrender, promising they would be spared. But Jintu was not the one to surrender. He fought back and killed two enemy soldiers. For 10 minutes, the battle raged before Jintu laid down his life. He was always fighting a losing battle because of the terrain and the adverse conditions. But in his death and that of the valiant soldiers of the platoon he was leading, the 17 Garhwal Rifles derived great inspiration and resolved to drive out the enemy. The honour of the battalion kept us going after that, and we ultimately succeeded against great odds.'

Naturally, there was a surge of public emotion at the arrival of the hero's body in Assam, following the post-mortem at Leh and a day's stop in Delhi where Jintu's body was kept in state for dignitaries and the public to pay homage. 'At Khumtai for the cremation, there was not a space left to stand. I cannot even estimate the number of people who turned out for Jintu's last rites. Anjana was there with his coffin and stayed with us for a few days after the cremation before returning to Palam. At the cremation spot, we created a memorial for Jintu. It has to be shifted now because a new road is coming up through the area, and the former memorial is in the way,' said Gogoi.

After the cremation, the Gogois ventured on a unique spiritual quest. They handed over a part of Jintu's ashes in a *matka* (urn) bound in a red cloth to the officers of the 17 Garhwal Rifles who had accompanied the young captain's body. They were flying back to Leh and from there to the Batalik battlefield, where the war was still on. 'For us, Jintu never died, his spirit dwelt among the rocks of KP. He belongs there. So, we sent the ashes back to re-establish our connection. We requested the officers of 17 Garhwal Rifles to disperse the ashes at KP where Jintu had laid his life,' said Gogoi, who now manages the gas agency allotted to the family by the Central Government after Jintu's death.

The urn of ashes was dutifully taken back to Batalik. It fell upon another very young person to undertake the tragic mission. Lieutenant Rishi Singh, fresh out of the academy, had been inducted into the 17 Garhwal Rifles in June 1999 amidst the war. Due to the imperative of warfighting, Rishi had not been allowed the breather of a two-week stint at the Garhwal Rifles Regimental Centre before being posted to the battalion. In those few days on the battlefield of Batalik, Rishi had not even glimpsed his senior officer, Jintu, whose ashes his young hands cradled and his youthful energies harnessed to disperse these at the daunting heights. Having to deal with the ashes of a legend of his battalion as the first principal task accomplished for the battalion must have stood Rishi in good stead. Rishi rose to command the 17 Garhwal Rifles in the Nowgam LoC sector of Kashmir and is currently serving on deputation with the National Security Council Secretariat in Delhi.

In earlier chapters, I have narrated poignant stories of burial ceremonies of enemy soldiers and the cremation of a few Indian soldiers on the battlefield itself But here was a unique instance of the ashes of an Indian officer sprinkled on the Kargil heights while the war was on, and all in a matter of weeks: his death in action on 30 June, the body flown to Assam, and ashes flown back from Assam to the battle site of death. 'No stream flowed at the KP heights. There were just boulders, broken rocks and slippery shale. Jintu's battalion was still deployed on the Batalik heights. We tasked young Rishi to bring up the urn to KP, and he merged the ashes with the blood-stained soil and stones where Jintu and the Garhwali soldiers had laid down their lives. One of the very few cameras that troops had during the war was with me, my personal one. I took photos of Rishi sprinkling the ashes at KP,' said Rajnarayan, who, as a Major during the war, commanded Delta Company of 17 Garhwal Rifles. Rajnarayan had been deployed for the entire month of July 1999 on those unforgiving Batalik heights and had shouldered his command responsibilities admirably, fighting bravely while escaping death by a whisker at the hands of an enemy sniper.

After the war, Jintu's father paid a visit to the Batalik sector. There, soldiers pointed out the fourth peak in a series of towering mountain features touching the skies in the far distance. That was KP, where his son had laid down his life. Gogoi yearned to undertake a pilgrimage to the battlefield heights like the fathers of some other officers who had fought to the last. Gogoi wanted to pay homage to his son and feel communion with the soul of the battlefield where his son's spirit dwelt. It would somewhat ease the welling grief in his soul at losing a son so young. However, the Army could not let him climb to KP as the ascent was too daunting, strenuous and inadvisable for a man of his age. In 2023, the Army decided to provide the family some solace for the soul. Soldiers climbed to KP, collected soil from Jintu's battlefield and despatched it to the Gogois in Assam in a petite red urn. The handful of Kargil soil was sacred and symbolic of sacrifice, solace and remembrance. It was as if Jintu had sent something home to his family.

It could never have been imagined before the War that a pinch of soil from the forsaken Kargil heights would one day come to mean so much in faraway Khumtai. The peaks of Kargil had not even been mapped properly or occupied by the Army before the war, and it was only when hostilities commenced that the Army quickly coined handy names for the anonymous mountain features (Bumps, Rhino Horn, India Gate, Helmet, etc.) to lend a ready reference to the troops tasked to retrieve the lost alpine collection. 'We had sent the ashes to Jintu's battlefield just after the cremation. That gesture served to re-establish our connection with our son. Last year, the Army sent us soil from KP. It was as if Jintu had sent us something in return to reaffirm our eternal bonds. I have reserved a part of the KP soil received from the Army, and will sprinkle it at Jintu's new memorial coming up at Khumtai. The rest of the soil we have kept in our prayer room in our Khumtai home,' said Gogoi.

With Jintu's death, his romance with Anjana took a haunting, tragic turn. She refused to marry anyone else and would not heed her parents' pleas. In the mirror of her heart, only one reflection dwelt. In the sieve that life had given her to gaze at the full moon, it was only the outlines of Jintu's beaming face that she discerned. The plot of the 1990 Hollywood blockbuster *Ghost* seemed to visit her haunted love. Beneath that stoic bearing and tearless eyes, glimpsed when entrusted with the guardianship of her warrior's coffin, there lay a tender heart, one that was faithful to the point of absolute and self-defeating pain. Her parents, who had settled in Panchkula, Haryana, upon her father's retirement from the IAF, had all but given up in the face of her heart's adamancy. After all, as poets and lilting love songs fading into the forbidding night have since time immemorial and across cultures declared: who can remonstrate with the ways of the heart? *Dil to pagal hai.*

It was then that the noble, progressive and visionary role played by Jintu's parents came into play and they helped this brave and pure-hearted young lady to start life afresh. 'My wife, Duluprabha, and I were very keen that Anjana should move on in life. She was very young and had a long life ahead of her. We did not wish that she would spend the rest of her life pining for our son, who was gone. A few years after Jintu died, both of us visited her parents in Panchkula. We learnt from them that Anjana was not heeding their counsel and had thwarted their efforts at match making. So, we drove to Delhi after that and visited her residence in Palam. Having been forewarned of her inflexible stand, we had gone to Palam prepared with a plan. On meeting us, Anjana was vehement—she would remain faithful to Jintu's memory. So, both of us went on a hunger strike there and then and threatened to cancel our air tickets to Assam unless she promised she would be open to marriage. Our planned threat worked! She relented upon our insistence and finally bent to the wishes of her anxious parents. Anjana went on to marry a software engineer and has two children. Look at the ways of the divine: her daughter was born on 21 November, which is Jintu's birthday,' Gogoi said.

CHAPTER 15

Moral Courage under Fire

Soldiers of the highest pedigree confront a dilemma that lies at the core of warfare. In the heat and fast-paced action of battle, do they opt for the path shown by moral courage, i.e., in doing the right thing for the men under their command? Or, do they obey flawed orders and surge forward in acts of foolhardy bravado to lead their men into needless death?

The futility and avoidable carnage of battle, as brought by the Tennyson poem *The Charge of the Light Brigade* played out numerous times in the first three weeks of the Kargil War. Troops were pushed up daunting spur lines and ice walls by panicky Kargil generals who had not cared enough to provide them with the wherewithal for conventional operations of an offensive orientation in such high altitudes. Before being sent up, troops were briefed with misleading assessments of the strength, profile and intention of the enemy entrenched on the top. The odds were stacked against the Indian troops and body bags tumbled down the slopes without the infantry soldiers having achieved their given aims during the opening month of battle in May 1999.

Protests by the officers on the ground, who were in direct contact with entrenched enemy forces, fell on deaf ears. Such officers were accused by the Kargil generals of 'cowardice', 'going slow' and drumming up excuses to avoid going into battle.

One such encounter was exceptional. It was a rare scenario of command hierarchy being overturned. A brigade commander took responsibility and called off the sacrosanct orders issued by the corps and division commanders. The brigade commander went by the assessment of battle from the ground troops. The voice of the men facing the heat was heard, and it overruled the orders issued by a remote, insensitive, panicky and obdurate higher command. The incident involved none other than Captain Manoj Pandey, an officer commissioned into the celebrated 1/11 Gurkha Rifles, who was later awarded the PVC posthumously.

His saga of valour extended virtually through the entire duration of the war—from Yaldor to Kukarthang to Jubar to Point 5203 and, finally, his most glorious hour on the Khalubar Ridge where he busted three bunkers on 'Bunker Area' the night of 2 and 3 July 1999, before succumbing to a burst of machine-gun fire that struck him square on his forehead.

As dawn broke over the battlefield location of Ganasok in the Batalik LoC Sector on 3 July, a stream of sleeping bags containing bodies of brave soldiers was trickling down for helilifts to their loved ones. The bodies waited for a final ascent to pyres at their ancestral *shamshan ghats*. Among them was the body of Captain Manoj Pandey, his iconic, infectious grin frozen forever.

The young officer had paid heavily to defy his mother, Mohini's advice to him just as the war had commenced in May 1999:

'Manoj, do not venture too forward into battle as you are an officer. Send the jawans ahead.'

Pandey, had retorted: 'Mummy, if you and I are going somewhere and there is trouble, will you, as a mother, put your child in front or will you remain in front and keep me behind? In the same way, the Gurkha jawans are like my children. I will stay ahead when the firing starts and keep my jawans behind me.'

A very plucky and level-headed Pandey had stuck to his guns in the heat of battle. He had put his foot down on the fateful night of 17–18 May 1999, when orders to assault the enemy entrenched o n an ice wall of 800 m had weighed heavily on his youthful shoulders. It would virtually take 25 years for Pandey's heroic stand in favour of his men to come to public light. The entire nation knows of Pandey's final heroics in July 1999, but what happened at the beginning of the war in May 1999 is unknown to most, save a bunch of veteran officers privy to the exchanges over radio sets.

What is not known and blithely touched upon in war histories is that critical moment of reckoning when combat leadership is put to a severe test of a different kind.

Pandey and his officiating CO, Lieutenant Colonel Amul Asthana, had risked dire consequences and a court martial by challenging the wisdom of going in for a suicidal assault on the Kukarthang feature with zero chance of success. The orders for the assault had come from the highest level, i.e., HQ 15 Corps, in Srinagar.

All hell had broken loose in the Army's higher echelons on 17 May when the officers and soldiers of the 1/11 Gurkha Rifles, who were in fire contact with a well-entrenched enemy on Kukarthang, conveyed to then 70 Infantry Brigade Commander, Brigadier Devinder Singh, VSM[1] that the battalion had insufficient resources and no artillery fire support to launch the assault successfully around midnight of 17–18 May. The intermediary in the radio exchanges and conveyance of messages between the higher command and 1/11 Gurkha Rifles officers on the ground was Brigade Major M Indrabalan, who was positioned well forward

1. Vishisht Seva Medal

into the Batalik battlefield at the brigade's TAC HQ in the Yaldor Nullah. The Kukarthang incident had led Asthana to later write a Forces Inland Letter directly to the then Army Chief General VP Malik, bringing out the fact that his battalion required machine guns, rocket launchers, radio sets, and ammunition to launch conventional attacks (which Malik had ensured in due course by over-ruling his own senior officers at Army HQ and Northern Command/15 Corps who had claimed the troops on the ground were well equipped with the required weaponry and equipment).

What the officers of the 1/11 Gurkha Rifles faced was the classic soldier's dilemma of having to choose moral courage over bravado in battle.

'Prior to the planned attack, 15 Corps Commander (late) Lieutenant General Krishan Pal came on line and dismissively told me there were only a bunch of militants on the heights and that Batalik must be "cleared" up to the LoC in three days. The Northern Army Commander, Lieutenant General HM Khanna, had also spoken to me over the radio set and asked me to maintain the glorious tradition of the Gurkha's valour. I had been left literally stammering when Khanna (who had also served in the Gurkha Rifles) had spoken to me as he was so senior to me, and I had never before interacted with an Army Commander. I could not convey to Khanna the difficulties we were facing before the Kukarthang attack,' recalled Asthana, who retired as a Brigadier.

'My assessment on the ground was that the enemy was in great strength and numbered 400–500 in the area that we had so far encountered between Ganasok, Khalubar, and Kukarthang ridges. Unlike the enemy's heavy artillery bombardment, we did not have artillery support for the attack that particular night; there were only three mortar shells with us and no machine guns or rocket launchers. From the direction of Point 4821, Pandey had said that his column could not scale an ice cliff of 70–80 degrees incline as the enemy was sitting right on top with machine-gun nests, and we would suffer extremely heavy casualties with no chance of success. An attack at that juncture, with barely 90 men, zero artillery, no mortars, and no supporting weapons like MMG, AGL, and RL, I was convinced that it was prudent to launch the attack the next day, by which time artillery fire would be available, and we could have more strength and maybe mortar ammunition, too. However, Pal threatened me with a court martial if I did not go in for the assault that very night, but our saviour was Brigadier Devinder Singh. He was on the ground and knew that our assessment of the enemy's true strength was correct. Singh took responsibility and ordered that the assault be called off and planned for a later juncture when the forces were better prepared. But Singh faced the flak for his decision and paid a heavy price for that order as senior officers came down heavily on him later,' said Asthana.

The incident got a lot of play in the higher echelons of the army because the then Vice Chief of the Army Staff (VCOAS) and acting COAS, Lieutenant General Chandrashekhar, was also an officer from the Gurkha Rifles. The prestige and valour of the Gurkhas was put at stake, and in weeks subsequent to the Kukarthang incident, a section of senior officers mouthed unsavoury remarks directed at the 1/11 Gurkha Rifles. The hapless battalion was rumoured as 'one fit only for sand model assaults', 'refusing to attack', and 'having frozen in its tracks'. The battalion, however, performed gloriously in the fierce battles for the Khalubar Ridge in July 1999, for which Pandey was awarded the Param Vir Chakra posthumously.

The flawed assessment of enemy strength and enemy intention by the higher command, and its reluctance to shed its preconceived notions and accept the considered assessment of officers and troops on the ground was in evidence through the chaotic weeks of May 1999 and across the battle zones of Drass, Mashkoh, and Batalik. It led to avoidable casualties suffered by the troops rushed up to tackle an alleged 'bunch of terrorists/jihadis'. The operational style dictated to the attack troops by the higher command, including by some of the brigade commanders, was the CI Ops and CASOs[2] mode. This operational mode was successful in Kashmir to snare the irregulars/jihadis. But, here in Kargil, conventional Pakistan Army troops were entrenched in strength on the heights in a series of well-coordinated defences. The intruders had built up in strength over the winter of 1998–1999 and had ample time to consolidate their hold over the Kargil heights. The Kargil generals approached the war with a standard CI-Ops mindset and, till the arrival of General VP Malik on the scene, were hell-bent on pushing up the troops without a proper build-up for the attacks. The motive of the generals was to somehow, and very quickly, sweep the national embarrassment of the Kargil invasion under the carpet.

'What Pandey and Asthana displayed at that critical juncture was "moral courage". I backed them because I realised they were speaking the truth. I got through directly to Pandey that night on the radio, and he told me, "Sir, it is not that I will not attack. It is just that the time is not right. We need to attack when we are better prepared to evict a well-entrenched enemy." Pandey's assessment was that there was a 0.5 per cent chance of success for the attack while Asthana gave it one per cent chance. I, too, was convinced that there would be no positive results from the attack. Artillery support for the assaulting infantry troops had not built up in the Batalik Sector at that juncture. The troops were faced with a moonlit night that would expose them as they climbed an 800-m ice face. It would take them more than an hour to navigate that ice face. By the time they were halfway up, the enemy would have caused 30–50 casualties out of the strength of 90, and the

2. cordon and search operations

attack would have to be called off. I spoke three to four times daily to my superior officer, GOC, 3 Infantry Division, Major General VS Budhwar. I relayed the evolving situation to him on the radio set that night. Since the Northern Army Commander had directly spoken to Asthana on the "Gurkha net", I asked Asthana if he had relayed the challenges he faced for the Kukarthang attack to the Northern Army Commander. However, Asthana told me that it was the first time he had ever spoken to a superior officer as high-ranking as the Army Commander, and he could not communicate much to him as the line had been cut. So, that avenue of conveying to the higher HQ the difficulties on the ground while launching the Kukarthang attack was also lost,' recalled Brigadier Devinder Singh.

'It was a very sensitive situation because the orders for the assault on Kukarthang had come from the Corps HQ. Budhwar was himself not willing to take responsibility for aborting the attack as he was apprehending action against him for the Kargil intrusions. He did not enjoy good personal relations with the 15 Corps Commander Lieutenant General Krishan Pal either. Fortunately, I was not in the line of fire as far as the issue of fixing responsibility for the Kargil intrusions was concerned. I was not commanding a holding formation on the LoC when the intrusions had taken place. I had been inducted into the Batalik Sector only after the intrusions were detected. I repeatedly conveyed to Budhwar that night my assessment that in the given circumstances, the attack on Kukarthang was meaningless. Ultimately, I took the responsibility onto myself. I issued orders around midnight to my brigade major to send a log message to the Division HQ that the attack had been called off on my orders. The next day, there was a furore in the higher command over a brigade commander calling off the orders of the corps and divisional HQs. Pandey was debriefed by Brigade Major M Indrabalan at Yaldor, and we put him up before Budhwar so that the ground situation could be conveyed directly to the GOC. On 19 May 1999, Pandey was summoned to the 70 Infantry Brigade HQ at Dah on the Indus River, and Budhwar flew down there to question the battalion's refusal to attack at that juncture. But Pandey was unfazed by the threat of disciplinary action. Following a grilling, Pandey was able to convince the higher officers of the lack of resources, the absence of artillery support, and the resultant futility of such assaults. He was exonerated and was immediately pressed further into operations by launching his company to stop the Pakistani advance on the formidable Jubar Ridge before 1 Bihar got there,' added Singh.

Immediately after the incident, Asthana wrote a handwritten letter directly to General VP Malik in violation of laid-down channels of command and communication. The letter managed to find its way to Malik by the end of May 1999, and it set him thinking because the feedback that he was getting from his principal staff officer at Army HQ, Northern Command HQ, and 15 Corps HQ was that the troops on the ground had been provided with the requisite wherewithal for the Kargil battle. In his book *Kargil: From Surprise to Victory*, Malik vindicated the stand taken by Asthana before the Kukarthang assault. The COAS had realised that Asthana was speaking the truth from the ground. The state of equipment and weaponry available with the troops of the 3 Infantry Division (with the exception of the 102 Infantry Brigade for Siachen) was inadequate as compared to the 8 Mountain Division, which was inducted into the Drass-Mashkoh Sector from the Kashmir Valley in May–June 1999 to fight the war. The state of equipment and weaponry available to the troops in the neglected Ladakh sector was 'hollowed out', while the fact was that they were facing a conventional force at commanding heights with entrenched defences, artillery support, adequate supplies, and even weapons such as Stingers, howitzers, and anti-aircraft guns deployed in the ground-fire mode.

In his book, Malik makes the sorrowful situation of Ladakh evident while referring to Asthana's emergency missive to him from the heart of the battlefield. It dovetails into the famous remark Malik made during the war: 'We will fight with whatever we have.'

In his book, Malik wrote: 'This (Asthana) letter pointed out the deficiencies in the machine guns, mortars, and communication equipment in his unit. (His unit had handed over most of the equipment in its custody to the relieving battalion in Siachen.) Apparently, the unit was in no state to fight with such major deficiencies. That letter set me thinking and I spent a whole day in Headquarters 15 Corps, making enquiries in the concerned branches. I instructed Army Headquarters to carry out rationalisation of medium machine-guns, mortars, and other such small arms and radio equipment on an all-India basis. We had to withdraw some material from other commands, and from some battalions of Rashtriya Rifles, which had been raised without receiving the government sanction for equipping these battalions till then. The reserve stocks of such weapons and equipment held in the ordnance depots for war had been used up to equip these Rashtriya Rifles battalions. On my orders, Headquarters 15 Corps met the requirements of 1/11 Gorkha Rifles immediately. I also made sure that no one in the chain of command took any action against Lieutenant Colonel Asthana for violating the channel of correspondence!'

What Pandey, Asthana, and Singh displayed was practising the IMA[3] motto in real-life situations where you stand by your men through fire, flawed orders, and intimidation and bullying by the higher command. The higher a soldier or officer rises in rank, the greater the demand imposed on him to display moral courage or

---

3. Indian Military Academy

fearlessly voice a truthful and rightful assessment of the warfare scenario that may run contrary to that of his superior officers and possibly jeopardise future career prospects. What possibly the Kargil higher command displayed was contrary to Field Marshal Sam Manekshaw's stand in 1971 when he demanded six months of preparation time before going in for the offensive.

The aborted Kukarthang attack saved the Army from needless casualties, including possibly that of Pandey himself, a very young officer. Pandey went on to deliver the great victory of Khalubar seven weeks later and earn a posthumous PVC. It redeemed his name and that of his battalion that had been blighted by the aborted Kukarthang attack.

Pandey was the only soldier who was awarded a PVC for battles east of the Drass-Mashkoh Sector and waged in the vast Batalik-Chorbat La-Turtuk-Chalunka-South Siachen Glacier characterised by very challenging terrain, towering heights and extended supply lines. The battles of the Drass-Mashkoh Sector, attended by TV crews and media contingents from national and international outlets, hogged the lion's share of three of the four PVCs awarded for the Kargil War.

CHAPTER 16

Humble Donkeys Saved the Day

The popular lore that spilt over from the Kargil War confined itself to heroic infantry charges, booming Bofors and strafing fighter jets. But the soldier on the ground swore by the unsung lore of a vital part of the war effort—an effort shouldered silently and humbly by the fighting porters of Ladakh/Kargil and their super-acclimated native donkeys (Bongboos). The donkeys withstood shelling and treacherous cliffs to carry critical weapons, ammunition and food with a soldiering zeal that the army's own trained, regulation mules struggled to match.

During World War I, war donkeys had lugged wounded soldiers from trenches and ferried battle resources. One famous WWI donkey, Jimmy, was wounded thrice and bestowed a sergeant's rank by the British Army. A monument was erected in his honour and is currently a military museum exhibit! Doubtless, if the Indian war narratives were to explore and document the role played by the native donkeys of Eastern Ladakh during Kargil, many shining Jimmys would emerge from anonymity.

Compared to the army's war mules of the Animal Transport Company, the Ladakhi donkeys showed better nerves under shelling. In some battle scenarios of Kargil, army mules would go berserk with fear under shelling and plunge off the cliffs or fall off the mountainsides while navigating the treacherous high-altitude stretches. But the native donkeys knew exactly how to press against the mountain walls and avoid shelling. Native donkeys could be loaded with uneven weights on each of their sides and made to carry awkward loads like infantry battalion support weapon systems (mortars, rocket launchers etc.). The native donkeys worked without rest and would, if there was no choice, suffice with mountain vegetation, unlike the army mules that had to carry their own specialised fodder plus war loads.

Here are two sterling, unique instances that serve to showcase the role that the domesticated animal played in the furtherance of the Kargil War effort. So startling, that they deserve glory's recall from the abyss of anonymity where most of the humble, silent folk of the Kargil war effort lie in silence.

PVC's debt to two donkeys

As the Kargil War entered its final phase, troops of the 1/11 Gurkha Rifles assembled at Yaldor, Batalik LoC Sector, on 13 July 1999. Yaldor was the battalion's under-fire battlefield HQ and a 12-hour march from the nearest road head at Dah on the Indus River. It was time to etch the deeds of the battalion's valiant lads in eternal remembrance. Citations for gallantry awards had to be meticulously drafted because they would be vetted up the entire chain of command till Army HQ, Delhi, and engage all the way in strenuous competition with other worthy battalions of the war. When blood, bone, and life are shed copiously, the battle for awards is naturally very competitive between the battalions.

The Second-in-Command (2IC) of 1/11 Gurka Rifles, Lieutenant Colonel Amul Asthana was entrusted with the formidable task of drafting citations.

Here is when the dauntless donkeys won the battle honours! Now, what could the 'fabled donkey' have to do with writing citations in the midst of war in Kargil?

'At Yaldor, in the second week of July, another battle was on: the battle of citations! HQ 3 Infantry Division ordered that these were required in a computer printout, a soft copy in a floppy in WordStar IV and a data part in dBase III Plus. For us soldiers, mauled by the operational vagaries of previous months, this was a reality shock, a perplexing but understandably essential requirement. It entailed the move of computers from Nurla (our rear base 100 km midway to Leh) to Yaldor (Batalik), plus the induction of a generator/diesel to run the computer! And, construction of a water-proof shelter in the Yaldor battlefield to house the "Computer God!",' recalled Asthana.

So, a surreal exercise was initiated to establish computers at Yaldor and get the software and the citation format from HQ 3 Division 150 km away at Kargil. A desktop computer was transported from Nurla (the battalion's rear base) to Dah and, from there, hastily loaded on donkeys (one donkey with a computer monitor and the other carrying a CPU plus generator and diesel drum). From Dah, guided by an able Ladakhi war porter, the donkeys marched 12 hours up the nullahs to Yaldor. Asthana himself went to Kargil and procured the software and citation format from the Division HQ after a tedious and mentally exhausting battle with the staff officers there.

Anyways, things had to be done; the stakes were too high. Citations delivered late up the chain of command or in an incorrect format could have invited a summary rejection, and another competing battalion would have been the lucky gainer.

'It was, for me, the sight of a lifetime as this train of donkeys emerged from the boulders at Yaldor after a 12-hour march guided by a brave local Ladakhi porter. The "high end of technology" was being carried by lowly donkeys! The tedious exercise to get the required citation format from HQ 3 Division was completed only by 24 July after which we wrote citations on the Yaldor computer, including the posthumous PVC one for Captain Manoj Pandey,' added Asthana.

All in all, the battalion was awarded one PVC, three Vir Chakras and two Sena Medals. In 2005, the battalion was awarded the Battle Honour Batalik and Theatre Honour Kargil.

It's well-accepted that an army marches and fights on its stomach.

Delving on the role played by donkeys in the overall war effort and logistics chain to far-flung Batalik battlefields, Asthana recollected: 'In the initial phase of Kargil, troops were operating in fluid actions far away from the logistics base at Dah. The criticality was food, ammunition, weapons, warm clothing and building-up logistics at Dah. With almost every soldier and even clerk, tradesman and driver pressed into the contact battle, it became very difficult to even move a few bags of *pooris* from Dah to Yaldor. Onwards, troops in close contact with the enemy on peaks/ridgelines was another 12 hours. Building up a *langar* at Yaldor was a top priority, but it required at least ten porters. In came the god-sent civilian porters with the humble donkeys. And, within a day, we had food and set up a cook house.

'The honest donkey could carry large loads with ease and even moved without a human "donkey driver". The donkeys could follow steep and narrow paths and cross nullahs full of water and rickety log bridges on their own. They would continue to move nonchalantly despite very close enemy artillery fire and magically reach destinations—without maps—day and night! My regard for this quiet, self-effacing "workhorse" caught the imagination of my young officers. On my birthday, 3 August, young officers gifted me a hand-sketched card featuring a cartoon of smiling/laughing donkeys and me amidst them with the caption: "Battle friends of 21C!"' he quipped.

'I humbly salute the physically strong, truly patriotic, and brave volunteer citizens (which included bank managers, teachers, and businesspersons) of Ladakh and their invaluable donkeys. I would like to place on record the incomparable effort put in by Major Vinay Dutta (Army Ordnance Corps) in organising hundreds of porters from Ladakh in just a few days to galvanise the war effort in Batalik and other warzone sectors of 3 Infantry Division,' added Asthana.

I asked Asthana if he had a photograph of donkeys in action during the war. He did not, but very kindly agreed to create a sketch by drawing upon his vivid memories. The sketch depicting the donkeys lugging the computer and its associated requirements for citation drafting to Yaldor is included in this book.

Where eagles, angels, and donkeys dare

The 70 Infantry Brigade's Brigade Major, M Indrabalan, was frozen with fear. He pressed his body against a virtually perpendicular cliff sheathed in ice. He dared not glance at his feet below for fear of losing balance. His toes squirmed as they fought for every inch of toehold afforded by the thinnest of cliff ledges that would invite the respect of the legendary Himalayan ibex. Indrabalan's olive green tunic was warm. He was sweating profusely, though he was hanging on to an ice cliff and perched precariously over a cold, yawning crevice deep in the mountains of Kaala Pathar, Batalik. The Kargil War was heading for its decisive and most brutal climax in June 1999.

The officer said his prayers, virtually bid his goodbye to life, but pressed forward like a diehard to navigate that 50 m of cliff. He was under orders to proceed and reach his objective, the firm base of the 17 Garhwal Rifles. And, then, a unique moment of 'leadership under fire' came war history's way; moments when soldiers marooned and without reinforcements at hand only have the option of a proverbial miracle to save them. A native donkey of Turtuk accompanying the officer as a battle-proven and sure-footed load carrier stepped in calmly and trotted across the narrow ledge to safety on the other side.

Indrabalan had been tasked by his brigade commander, Brigadier Devinder Singh, VSM, to take a 48-hour trek of 15 km from Batalik to the firm base of the 17 Garhwal Rifles at Three Pimples, Kaala Pathar. The battalion was to launch an assault during the night of 29 June, and the BM was to position himself there, monitor the battle, and coordinate with his commander over the radio set.

'I took three men, my radio operator, map reader, and a local Ladakhi handling the two donkeys lugging our loads. I was determined to reach my position as ordered, but that cliff stretch not only put a big question mark over fulfilment of the orders but also as to whether I would live to tell the tale,' recalled Indrabalan.

What Indrabalan faced that day was a routine peril, a nightmare that soldiers and officers confront in the line of duty while operating on the LoC, AGPL[1] on the Siachen-Saltoro Ridge, or during war at heights ranging to 20,000 feet. Some have just plunged off cliff faces, and their bodies recovered with no bone left intact. No gallantry awards have sung the deeds of those soldiers whose lives were claimed by the daunting cliffs. Major Ritesh Sharma of 17 Jat survived Kargil's Mashkoh battle with a war wound but died unsung after he plunged 200 metres off the cliff in the Machhil LoC Sector in Kashmir a few months after the war on 25 September 1999, while leading an ambush team to nail infiltrating terrorists. Sharma was the company commander

1. Actual Ground Position Line

of Captain Anuj Nayyar, who was awarded the MVC (Maha Vir Chakra) (Posthumous) for the same Mashkoh battle.

Similarly, Major Manoj Talwar (3 Mahar) had volunteered before the war for an attachment with the 9 Mahar so that he could serve in the Siachen Glacier. Amidst shelling, Talwar plunged off an ice cliff at a height of nearly 19,000 feet while leading a forward domination patrol to secure Point 5765 on the Turtuk LOC during the night of 13/14 June 1999.

It was the third time in the war that Indrablan was left staring at death, in circumstances that were very different. 'One of the two donkeys accompanying me took to the ledge and trotted across in a very sure-footed manner. The creature's calmness while negotiating the ledge stabilised my nerves. That inspired me, that it could be done, and my morale rose. Clinging to the cliff wall and making use of every little cleft, nook, and cranny to dig in with my hands, I made the passage across in agonising time, a step at a time. If I lost my nerve for even one moment, I would have plunged off thousands of feet into the crevice below. I am a soldier trained for negotiating the high mountains, but that passage is etched forever in my mind as I had one leg thrust into death's door. But the donkeys had again proved their mettle in war,' recalled Indrabalan, who retired as a major general in 2023 but went unrecognised for his versatile and courageous performance as the most forward of the eight brigade majors (BMs) of the Kargil War.

'The role of native donkeys and the volunteer corps of Ladakhis, who came to us as porters, was crucial. This was because, unlike the Drass Sector, where the national highway ran right through, and the occupied peaks could be viewed like a sand model from the roads, the battles in Batalik were fought deep within the toughest terrain where no TV crew ever reached. For example, it took a two-day march to get soldiers and war supplies to the base of the feature to be assaulted, such as Point 5203, as the nearest road head was far away at Dah on the Indus,' recalled Brigadier Devinder Singh.

To insert a small team of combat soldiers onto a towering feature for bunker busting, many times their number, by way of support services and carriage animals, are required to work in the shadows of war's limelight. Whenever a grateful nation recalls the deeds and sacrifices of Pandey and his brave band of men, we must also gratefully remember the donkeys, mules, porters, and all the other unsung heroes who shouldered the successful war effort.

CHAPTER 17

After the War, Rommel's Scar

Captain Rommel Akram (retired) bears an unmissable scar on his left cheek, which he describes as the 'most beautiful part of his body'. Slightly less visible is another scar on the lobe of the left ear. What is unseen is the permanently impaired left eye and ear of the veteran of the Pakistan Army's 6 NLI (SIKKIS-Saifullah). The scar is a Kargil tattoo. It was etched across his face by a sniper round fired accurately by an Indian marksman in the thick of battle. To date, 'Captain Scarface' sports the brutal 'badge of honour', which is earned only by devouring the bullets of war. Time will not wipe off the tattoo and Rommel will take it to his grave.

The officer fought a pitched battle with Indian troops on the iconic battlefield of Gun Hill (Point 5140 Complex, 16,864 feet) during the latter half of June 1999. In that fateful battle, Akram received two heavy sniper rounds fired by an Indian marksman even as most of the troops under his command lay around him dead or wounded. The first sniper round missed his head and splintered the rocks. A mix of lead and rock splinters ricocheted onto his forehead causing severe bleeding. The second sniper round got him square on, cleaving through bone and tissue after entering through the left cheek, under the left eye, slicing the left optic nerve, and exiting from the left ear. To put it mildly, the impact of the round left Rommel shell-shocked.

The stitching of the bullet wound left a long, curving, jagged bullet trace on Rommel's cheek. The scar's contours echo the rugged terrain of the Kargil conflict. Its form mirrors the army's maps of the high-altitude battleground, resembling either a jagged ridgeline with elongated spurs or a snowmelt nullah with steep tributaries. The Kargil battle earned Akram the gallantry award of a Sitara-e-Jurat (the equivalent of India's Vir Chakra), and he is the only living SJ awardee of *Operation Koh-e-Paima* from the 6 NLI. Akram takes his unusual first name from the legendary German Field Marshal, Erwin Rommel, also known as the 'Desert Fox'. Akram's grandfather had fought World War II in North Africa with the British Indian Army against Rommel's Afrika Korps. The Indian troops were enamoured by the German genius of warfare, and Akram's grandfather insisted upon naming his grandson, Rommel, upon his birth decades after World War II.

The scar left on Rommel's cheek relinks him to his German legacy. In the ninteenth and twentieth centuries, upper-class German and Austrian students would passionately indulge in fencing with naked blades. The Prussian Junkers (landed nobility) also indulged in this blood sport. The fencing left duelling scars, known variously as 'Mensur scars' and the 'bragging scars'. Taking a bloody cut on the face that left long, jagged, irregular scars was taken as a sign of courage. Men who sported such fencing scars were perceived as 'good husband material' and also preferred by some ladies looking for a short, sharp, exciting fling! German officers brought their fencing scars to both the world wars. Colonel Otto Skorzeny, the Waffen SS officer and World War II war criminal associated with the Gran Sasso raid to rescue the Italian dictator Benito Mussolini, was one such officer with Mensur scars. Most of the Mensur scars were inflicted on the left side of the opponent's face as the majority of the fencers were trained in the right-handed style. Some fencers would prefer to have their wounds stuffed with horsehair before these were stitched up without anaesthetics. This led to the formation of thick, hard scar tissue and rendered the 'badge of honour' all the more 'scary and sexy'. The horse hairs were pulled out after the scar set in deeply. Archival European news reports from the nineteenth century note the case of a 'duelist who died in 1877, who had fought no less than 13 duels and had 137 scars on the head, face and neck.'

Rommel's scar on his left cheek is the ultimate badge of honour. In comparison, the Mensur scars are superficial and can be perceived as symbols of Prussian vanity and indulgence in a macho blood sport. After his grievous injury in Kargil, where he literally clambered out from a deep grave dug for him by the Indian sniper, Akram underwent plastic surgery in the UK for more than five months to ease the sniper scars. He left the Pakistan Army and was recruited into the Police Service of Pakistan, where he currently serves in a senior position at the National Counter Terrorism Authority (NACTA).

In his interviews recalling the battles at the 6 NLI's Tashfeen Post, Rommel assessed that three Indian Infantry battalion companies had laid siege to his bunkers. The Pakistani intrusions had been subjected to a 36-hour bombardment by the Indian Artillery to soften the bunkers for the infantry assaults. It was at the very same Point 5140 Complex that the late Captain Vikram Batra of 13 JAK Rifles earned the first of his two citations for the posthumous award of the PVC. Batra had waged the battle during the night of 19 and 20 June 1999. The battle for the Point 5140 Complex was immortalised in popular consciousness by Batra's *'Yeh dil maange more'* victory signal. The Point 5140 Complex was many years after the War—on 30 July 2022—officially renamed 'Gun Hill' in honour of the battle-winning role played by the Regiment of Artillery in *Operation Vijay*. To date, the Point 5140 Complex is strewn with the rusting remains of the bombardment in the form of 81-mm, 120-mm, and 160-mm mortar fins and shell splinters from the discharge of 105-mm, 130-mm, and the 155-mm Bofors howitzers. These remains, lying among blooming little alpine flowers and ruined rocks at the Point 5140 Complex, constitute a poignant memorial to the firepower and destruction wrought by Indian Artillery guns firing en masse during that fateful summer of 1999.

Rommel was commanding the Tashfeen Post with a strength of 22 soldiers in June 1999. It was the last of his deployments in the Kargil War after a series of movements undertaken by him up and down the intruded LOC in response to the evolving battle scenario. He was moved from one intrusion post to another due to the high degree of faith his senior officers reposed in his capabilities, courage, expertise in map reading, and leadership on the ground. In his final battle at Tashfeen post, Rommel was joined by the 6 NLI's CO Lieutenant Colonel Saleem Mahmud Khan. The CO had staged well forward and reached the Point 5140 Complex to reinforce and bolster the morale of his troops. The 6 NLI was reeling under the pressure of having lost the Tololing Complex during the night of 12/13 June 1999, after three weeks of fierce battle. Six Pakistani soldiers at Tashfeen took a direct hit from an ATGM[1] fired by the 13 JAK Rifles CO, Lieutenant Colonel YK Joshi, Vir Chakra, and were killed. More were wounded in the fire by Indian troops and the artillery bombardment.

'My automatic weapons at the post were not functional as the continuous Indian bombardment and fire had given us no time to clean and maintain the machine guns. My wounded armourer,

1. Anti-Tank Guided Missile

whose task was to maintain weapons, was firing a G3 rifle at the approaching Indians. I was left with an RPG-7 launcher, which only I had the expertise to fire. I left my bunker, took position behind rocks and fired the rockets wherever the Indian troops had concentrated. The splinters from the rockets hit the Indian troops and halted their climb to our post. It was then that the first sniper bullet hit the rock in front of me and went over my head. The piece of rock splintered and flew to hit my forehead causing heavy bleeding. I took shelter in the bunker and, after 15 minutes, went again to the position in the rocks to fire the rockets at the advancing infantry,' Rommel recalled.

It was then that the second sniper bullet precisely picked the cheek's softness with the devastating jab of a Mensur fencer. 'The bullet hit me in the face. The shock and impact were devastating, to say the least. The impact of the bullet was as if a bus had suddenly slammed into my car from behind at top speed. I lay there for a minute, thinking that death was now close at hand. I was ready to embrace *shahadat*. However, I got up and went to the bunker, where I applied field dressings to my wound. The bleeding from the cheek wound was very heavy and the dressings were able to staunch the flow for a mere 15 minutes. However, it could not contain the bleeding after that. My CO was present there and had staged forward to reinforce the post. I vaguely recall his voice urging me not to venture out again after the bullet went through my cheek. I also recollect the shock on his face when he saw my face completely drenched in blood. After the war, my CO told me that had there been a looking glass available at Tashfeen Post, I would have simply died of shock seeing the mangled, ghoul-like condition of my face,' said Rommel.

Despite his courage and determination to fight on, Rommel collapsed soon after. By now, the blood was pouring from his nose and ear like gushing snow melts. What Rommel remembers of those hours is that he felt as if he had entered a vacuum and it was as if devoid of gravitational stability, he was floating freely in space like an astronaut. He was evacuated across the LoC as part of the 6 NLI's retreat from the Point 5140 Complex. It took him eight hours to reach the medical facility across the LoC after the bullet struck his face. In that evacuation on foot from Tashfeen, Rommel, with one eye functional, faced the (ineffective) plunging fire from Indian machine guns while he was traversing the cliff face on the way back to his rear lines. There was not so much pain that he encountered in the hours after the bullet struck home but more numbness and weakness due to severe blood loss and low blood pressure The Pakistan Army medics back across the LoC gave him up for the dead, saying he had bled too heavily and that the wound was far too grievous. But true to his warrior legacy, Rommel walked back from the dead. His iron will prevailed over the odds stacked against him.

Doctors and surgeons found that the sniper bullet had broken Rommel's zygomatic bone (the prominent part of the cheek and the outer side of the eye socket) into 13 pieces. His jawbone was broken, too, while the left eye's retina had got twisted on impact and the eye had been pushed back. The left eardrum had been virtually blasted out before the bullet had exited from the ear lobe. The bullet had caused severe damage to his facial and optic nerves. That accurate shot from the Indian sniper has left Rommel with a permanent impairment to the powers of his left eye and ear.

The Point 5140 Complex was held by the 6 NLI in a tactical posture of three posts codenamed after the officers who had set them up: Tashfeen, Jamal, and Iftikhar OP, the last being critical for directing of Pakistani artillery fire on Indian troops, artillery guns, and the Drass national highway. The Point 5140 Complex was connected to the southern Tololing Complex, which had been wrested from the 6 NLI during the night of 12/13 June. Tololing had fallen after three weeks of intense battles by the 18 Grenadiers and 2 Rajputana Rifles, whose assaults were bolstered by an unprecedented barrage of 120 Indian artillery guns in direct-fire mode. Keeping in mind the indefensibility of the Tololing Complex and to avoid further loss of the lives of his men, the 6 NLI's CO, Lieutenant Colonel Tariq Ahmed Mansoor, ordered the withdrawal of his troops without seeking the approval of the higher HQ FCNA.[2] It led to Mansoor's removal from command of the 6 NLI soon after the fall of Tololing and his replacement by Lieutenant Colonel Saleem Khan on 17 June. The FCNA was a divisional-sized formation ranged against India's 3 Infantry Division in Ladakh and was commanded by Major General Javed Hassan.

Tariq had, at the outset of the Kargil invasion, expressed his misgivings over the planned conduct of *Operation Koh-e-Paima* in front of the Commanders, FCNA, and 80 Brigade. When his battalion was ordered to conduct reconnaissance of the Indian side of the LoC and establish posts, Tariq and the young officers of 6 NLI had pointed out the unviability of intruding so deep and in a huge bulge of forward troops till Tololing. The young officers of 6 NLI had, with the passage of time, developed an in-depth understanding of the terrain, weather and the likely administrative issues that would crop up in case of a deep incursion. They advised against an overly ambitious intrusion. The 6 NLI officers had assessed that the terrain around Tololing offered a smooth climb to the attacking infantry due to its relatively gentle inclines. The attacking infantry could utilise the cover on the Tololing inclines and charge the 6 NLI bunkers successfully with the support of massive artillery fire. Tololing was located eight kilometres deep on the Indian side of LoC. Due to the dissenting views of its officers, the 6 NLI was not in the good books of the command echelons of the FCNA. The fall of Tololing and the removal from command of Tariq, an officer respected and loved by his men as he always stood by them, come what may, demoralised the

2. Force Command Northern Areas

battalion's rank and file. The higher command found in the 6 NLI a convenient scapegoat for the loss of Tololing and heaped blame on its men deeply scarred by months of deployment in adverse weather, glaciated terrain and finally the weeks of bloody battle.

However, the Indian Army's officers who fought the 6 NLI did not hold such a dim view of their worthy opponent. None other than Lieutenant Colonel MB Ravindranath, Vir Chakra, the CO of 2 Rajputana Rifles, paid a rich tribute to the 6 NLI during his media briefing at Drass on 21 June 1999, where he provided details of the Tololing victory. For this public tribute to the enemy's fighting prowess, Ravindranath later got a rocket from his own higher command in the guise of an infuriated Brigadier (General Staff) at 15 Corps HQ, Brigadier Arun K Chopra! In his book, *Kargil War: The Turning Point*, Ravindranath wrote: 'Questions followed (at the media briefing) of which one was how tough was the opposition. I replied that the enemy was well-trained, motivated and fought bravely, but we were better than him and had carried the day.... After the press conference, the Brigadier (Chopra) was livid and hauled me over the coals...how could I speak so highly of the enemy....(I) tried to reason with him regarding the rationale behind my praise for the enemy. How could I have told the press the enemy was incompetent, cowardly, and ill-prepared without giving rise to the question, I reasoned, why it took so long to remove such an incompetent enemy?'

Interestingly, Ravindranath's troops recovered the tracksuit of a Pakistani officer of the 6 NLI with 'Saifullah' and 'SIKKIS' inscribed on it following the battle of Black Rock Complex waged during the night of 28/29 June. Ravindrath later wore the 6 NLI tracksuit as a war trophy before consigning it to the museum of the 2 Rajputana Rifles. The fact is that the 6 NLI had heavily intruded on the eastern flank of Tiger Hill and fought some of the hardest battles of the War at Tololing, Point 5140, Point 4700, and Black Rock Complex. Five of the 11 MVCs for Kargil, including four as posthumous awards, had been earned in blood by Indian officers and other ranks in the battles waged against the 6 NLI in the Drass sector. Though Ravindranath unknowingly attributed 'Saifullah' to the name of the Pakistani officer to whom the tracksuit had belonged, the fact is that the 6 NLI is officially known as the 'Saifullah Battalion'. Saifullah means 'The Sword of Allah'. 'SIKKIS' stands for the Balti pronunciation of 'six' or the peculiar way in which the troops from the Northern Areas give voice to this numerical. The troops of the 6 NLI are recruited from Pakistan-occupied Jammu & Kashmir (POJK) regions of Gilgit, Baltistan, Chitral, and Kashmir. They are drawn from the Shia, Sunni, Ismaili, and Noorbakshi sects.

The role played by a group of young, motivated, and brave officers of the 6 NLI in the Kargil War was of an extended duration and had depth to it. Prior to the initiation of *Operation Koh-e-Paima*, the 6 NLI had its battalion HQ at Gultari, with one company at Buniyal at its disposal, while two other companies were located at Marpola and Shaqma. The 6 NLI was earmarked as a reserve for the 80 Brigade. It was tasked for the surreptitious reconnaissance of unheld Indian territories, which could be exploited for capture during the winter of 1998–1999 and then further used for observation, domination, and interdiction of NH-1A when Zojila Pass opened to traffic in the summer of 1999.

Months before the first shots were exchanged in the summer of 1999, officers of the 6 NLI frequently intruded into the Indian side of the Drass sector in October 1998 leading small teams and observing strict radio silence. This was about the time that the FCNA had initiated the invasion plan for the coming winter. The Pakistan Army's higher command sought pinpoint information and tactical perspective with regard to the dominating features in the Drass heights and the ones that could be captured for the impending invasion, codenamed *Operation Koh-e-Paima*. The high command sought an assessment from the intruding reconnaissance teams with regard to the defensibility of the critical features. Contrary to the impression doing the rounds in certain circles that the officers commanding the Kargil intrusions belonged to the Special Services Group, the leaders were, in fact, handpicked from the regular infantry battalions. These regular infantry officers could navigate and scale the toughest of routes to intrude beyond the snowbound LoC. The selection criteria not only required mental and physical strength, but the officers were proficient map readers of unknown and treacherous mountain terrain of the high and super-high altitudes. The 6 NLI officers carried out a meticulous, undetected reconnaissance of the Drass sector in October 1998 by pinpointing potential tactical positions on the map and taking photographs of the critical heights on the Indian side of the LoC.

In fact, just prior to the 6 NLI's movement from Gultari to Buniyal, a small self-contained team of the 6 NLI reached Tiger Hill in July 1998 without encountering Indian troops of the 121 (Independent) Infantry Brigade Group. It was not the first secretive patrol the FCNA had tasked to cross the LoC for reconnaissance and testing of the Indian Army's responses. The FCNA had been sending out patrols across the LoC since the 1980s while at the same time keeping the Kargil sector seemingly dormant so as not to alarm the Indians. For example, in 1988, troops of the 6 NLI, under the command of Lieutenant Colonel Mehboob Janjua, intruded across the Shaqma Sector, i.e., the Kaksar-Kargil LoC, and withdrew undetected. In August 1997, a Pakistan Army patrol was detected by the famous shepherd and field source of the 121 Infantry Brigade Intelligence Team, Tashi Namgial, several kilometres deep into the Yaldor Nullah of the Batalik sector. However, that tip-off by Namgial did not lead to any enduring response from the Indian Army. In the winter of 1998–1999, the Pakistanis, emboldened by a consistent lack of response from the Indian Army to their probes across the LoC, went ahead with a full-blown invasion of Kargil that encompassed the sectors of Mashkoh, Drass, Kaksar, Batalik, Chorbatla, Turtuk, and till the South Siachen Glacier. Measured up and down the peaks of the LoC, the width of the intrusions was more than 200 km, and at certain points, they ran 11–13 km deep. It again fell to Namgial's lot to report the invasion of the Batalik heights on 3 May 1999, to the holding battalion, 3 Punjab.

The series of reconnaissance patrols undertaken by the small teams of 6 NLI across the Drass LoC was not challenged at any stage by Indian troops during July–October 1998. The entire area was empty. The same would repeat itself a few months later in winter when the 6 NLI commenced the intrusions across the LoC in full strength. There were no Indian patrols to maintain the sanctity of the LoC. The Indian helicopter surveillance sorties of the LoC in winter were scarce and not effective. The green signal for *Operation Koh-e-Paima* was given by the Pakistan Army's higher command when it became dead sure that the Indians 'had given up on patrolling in the LoC areas'. The lack of Indian troops in the massive gaps between the LoC posts was so stark that Captain Rommel Akram of the 6 NLI assured his CO: 'If you permit me, sir, I can carry out a reconnaissance till the Amarnath cave and get back undetected.'

A similar reconnaissance into the Mashkoh Sector, which adjoins the Drass Sector to the west, was conducted by the 12 NLI's Captain Nadeem and Captain Ali along with Havildar Lalak Jan. The 12 NLI's patrol crossed the LoC on 18 December 1998, carrying small arms, rations, and a high-altitude tent. The patrol returned across the LoC to the 12 NLI base in Pakistan-Occupied Jammu & Kashmir (POJK) on 21 December. They reported to the command echelons of the FCNA that the Mashkoh area was empty and devoid of vegetation as well as the enemy.[3]

3. *Witness to Blunder: Kargil Story Unfolds*, by Colonel Ashfaq Hussain (retired), 2013.

A critical aspect of the reconnaissance patrols carried out by the 6 NLI in the Drass Sector in October 1998 by Captain Sharif, Captain Iqbal and Captain Rommel pertained to the Point 5353 feature that fell on the Indian side of the LoC. The reconnaissance teams drove home the tactical value of Point 5353. This feature, which is visible from Drass town and is shaped naturally at the top as a Bactrian camel's double hump, constituted an excellent vantage point of the Drass-Kargil NH-1A without any feature in between to hinder the observation. Lamochen Top, where the Kargil Vijay Divas celebrations are held every year and are attended by serving and veteran Army officers, is also visible from Point 5353. This feature, at a height of 17,562 feet, held the tactical advantage that it was nearer to the LoC and its steep slopes were very difficult to negotiate for attacking infantry troops. The 6 NLI patrols found that the Indian Army patrols would come to Point 5353 seasonally for a temporary period and stay there in field shelters improvised from rocks and sheets.

Captain Rommel brought back photographs of the ascent to the Point 5353 summit along with images of other high-altitude features unheld by the Indian Army. Upon assessing the Point 5353 feature as a critical one and unheld, the 6 NLI was given orders to occupy it in the winter of 1998–1999. The task fell upon Captain Waseem. Despite suffering from an acute stress fracture to his shin bone, Captain Waseem scaled the ice wall of 1,300 feet and occupied Point 5353 that winter. The Point 5353 feature was named Waseem Post in the Pakistan Army war maps for *Operation Koh-e-Paima*.

Having secured Point 5353 successfully, the assessment of the 6 NLI officers on the ground was that the feature would serve the operational requirements of observation and interdiction of NH-1A and that there was no need to intrude till the Tololing Complex further ahead. However, the ground view did not find approval from the higher command and orders were given to 6

NLI to move deeper and ahead of Point 5353 and set up posts till the Tololing Complex.

Following the defeat of the Pakistan Army during the summer of 1999, Point 5353 was initially vacated by the newly-deployed 11 NLI as part of the withdrawal orders issued by higher HQ in July 1999. The 11 NLI, by that time, had replaced the 6 NLI in the Drass battle zone. But Point 5353 was re-occupied soon after a hue and cry was raised by officers of the 6 NLI, who understood the significance of this feature owing to the observation it afforded of a 23 km stretch of the strategic Drass-Kargil road. The 11 NLI, being new to the Drass zone, was unaware of the significance of Point 5353. But the 6 NLI officers were vehemently opposed to its vacation, lest the victorious Indian Army got to it and succeeded in undoing the heroic efforts displayed by Captain Waseem. The Point 5353 feature turned into a major controversy after the War as it came to light that the Pakistanis were still holding on to it and it even figured in the proceedings of the Parliament. A quarter of a century after the war, the Point 5353 controversy is yet to die down. Its 'ambiguous' status was referred to in national media reports filed from Drass in July 2024 to mark the silver anniversary celebrations.

A parallel development during the July 1999 withdrawal phase took place in the Kaksar LoC sector situated to the east of Point 5353. Captain Ifthikar Awan of the 6 NLI had discovered the famous Bajrang Post (South-West Spur Point 5299) on the Kaksar LoC in March 1999, and it was held by the 4 Jat. The discovery of Bajrang Post during the reconnaissance patrols of the 6 NLI came as a surprise to the higher HQ as it was not marked on any Pakistani operational or intelligence map. Once the FCNA HQ realised the importance of the Bajrang Post upon its detection by the 6 NLI, orders were issued to capture it. Bajrang was captured by a detachment of the 13 NLI (Shingos) under the command of Captain ZA Changezi, Sitara-e-Jurat, once the unwary CO of

4 Jat, Colonel MS Kukshal, vacated it on 2 March 1999, citing 'climatic and logistic considerations'. Upon observing for three days no sign of movement or life at Bajrang following its vacation by 4 Jat, the 13 NLI had climbed an ice cliff and captured Bajrang. The post was a well-fortified one of concrete and afforded critical observation on both sides of the LoC. It was an area domination post and afforded a view of the Pakistani road between Shaqma and Buniyal. The 6 NLI advised the FCNA HQ against vacating Bajrang during the withdrawal of July 1999 but the significance of this dominant feature of the Kaksar LoC was lost on the new NLI battalion that had been inducted to replace the 6 and 13 NLI. Bajrang was then reoccupied by the Indian Army following the permanent withdrawal by the Pakistanis.

About the Author

Vikram Jit Singh is one of India's finest and bravest war correspondents who was working for *The Indian Express* in Srinagar since October 1997 when the Kargil War broke out. Having worked extensively with the Indian Army while reporting from their innermost cordons about Counter-insurgency Operations, he was given the unique opportunity of covering the Kargil War from the high-altitude frontlines with the troops under fire. Singh again took a reporting assignment to Kashmir in 2004 for *India TV* and was stationed in Srinagar.

Singh entered the profession of Journalism in 1992.

In addition to being a war correspondent, Singh is a nature lover and wildlife expert and writes columns regularly for *The Times of India* and *Hindustan Times* in Chandigarh.

Singh has featured in several podcasts and national and regional TV interviews relating to defence, security, geopolitics, Kashmir conflict and the Kargil War.

More from Fauji Days

General's Jottings

Lt Gen KJ Singh

ISBN: 978-93-92210-91-4

₹TBD

General's Jottings is your guide to National Security and the 'Strategic' domain. No longer a domain reserved for soldiers, National Security now entails a 'whole of nation' approach—it includes you and affects you. Everyone has to be 'Nagrik Yodha' (Citizen Warrior) in the mode of a vigilant or 'Jagruk' Hindustani.

These jottings were first written as newspaper columns and articles. This book weaves them thematically, highlights important issues, updates latest developments, and flags key takeaway points.

The book's approach is geo-centric, which is used as the prefix, making it geo-political and geo-economic within the ambit of geo-strategic. It will be an invaluable companion for the professional and amateur alike.

Black Horse Down & Other Stories

ISBN: 978-93-92210-75-4
₹ 395

The Crossover Girl and Other Stories

ISBN: 978-93-92210-22-8
₹395

Continuing in the spirit of his first volume of military tales, The Crossover Girl and Other Stories, military man Ashok Ahlawat gathers some even more remarkable stories in his second collection.

Featuring cavalry tales like Match Fixing and the titular Black Horse Down, anecdotes drawn from India's most revered Field Marshal's life, tales of daredevilry powered by 'Old Monk', poignant heroism on the battlefield (Give Me Your Black Scarf and Till My Eyes Can See), to the hilarious I Think I Am Having a Heart Attack, the author proves to be a raconteur par excellence. Turning these pages, don't be surprised to find yourself transported to a leisurely evening in an Army Mess, listening to him, drink in hand, as he regales you with story after story till the evening has long been subsumed into the night.

With an authenticity that springs from having 'been there, done that' meshed with an eye that misses nothing and words that spare no humbug, Ahlawat's book brings alive the true and humane military spirit in your hearts and minds.